KEVIN RUSHBY studied psychology and philosophy before setting out on a life of travelling and writing. After periods living in Sudan and Yemen he worked as a journalist in Asia. He now lives in York and is a literary reviewer for the *Guardian* as well as a regular contributor to other publications, television and radio.

Praise for Kevin Rushby

'Rushby has a deft wit and... a deep understanding of his territory.'

Independent

'Rushby is always a pleasure to read'

Charles Allen, *Spectator*

'Kevin Rushby could write about any place with distinction, wit and humanity.'

Asian Affairs

'Rushby is... "a camera with its shutter open"; the pictures he's taken with his camera eye are undeniably fascinating.'

Washington Post

Other titles by Kevin Rushby

Hunting Pirate Heaven
Children of Kali
Eating the Flowers of Paradise
Chasing the Mountain of Light

PARADISE

A HISTORY OF THE IDEA THAT RULES THE WORLD

KEVIN RUSHBY

ROBINSON
London

Constable & Robinson Ltd
3 The Lanchesters
162 Fulham Palace Road
London W6 9ER
www.constablerobinson.com

First published in the UK by Constable,
an imprint of Constable & Robinson Ltd, 2006

This paperback edition published by Robinson,
an imprint of Constable & Robinson Ltd, 2007

ISBN: 978–1–84529–484–7 (pbk)
ISBN: 978–1–84529–001–6 (hbk)

Printed and bound in the EU

1 3 5 7 9 10 8 6 4 2

For my children: Caitlin, Con, Niall and Maddie

Contents

Acknowledgements

It has been a fascinating experience exploring the intellectual hinterland of paradise, and I have had a lot of help along the way. My mother, Averyl Rushby, was ever helpful with family background. Dr Geoffrey Maycock and Albert Ford provided useful insights and references on religious matters and Don Beadman let me use his thesis on the origins of the Christadelphians. Bruce Wannell was generous with his profound knowledge of the Islamic world, and was my knowledgeable guide in Iran. Carol O'Brien, my editor, was a staunch friend and supporter at all times. Dr Peter Finch shared many discussions and offered many insights as well as substantial improvements to the text. Lisa Chaeney, Tim Mackintosh Smith and Helen Armitage also made perceptive comments and helped me shape the final manuscript. Other assistance in particular subjects and places came from Jack Carr, Nicola Tipton, Ahmed Siam, Professor Jane Moody, Sarah Davies and Professor Greg Kucich. Throughout the process my publisher Nick Robinson gave valuable insights and guidance. Most of all I would like to thank Sophie Carr who spent hours discussing the content and helping sift through the vast mountain of material that the idea of paradise has helped create over the past 3,000 years.

Introduction

A friend once told me how his ancestors came from the very centre of what is now the Democratic Republic of Congo, an area untouched by the outside world until the 1930s. So remote and inaccessible was their homeland that even slave-traders had passed them by. Intrigued by this, I asked if the tribe had had any notion of paradise, the perfect life in a perfect place for perfect people – a working definition that was advantageously vague, unlike, for example, 'eating *pâté de fois gras* to the sound of trumpets', the view of the Reverend Sydney Smith in the nineteenth century.

The Congolese friend thought about the question for a long time before answering. There was, he said, no parallel concept for them. They had possessed no notion of an afterlife and consequently no heaven. Then what about paradise on earth? Admittedly Dante had called his heaven, *Paradaiso*, but for me paradise has an earthly aspect too. The friend shook his head. 'We had no idea of wonderful gardens or of perfect places, not at least until the missionaries arrived. There was only the belief that the forest would always provide.'

The beauty of his answer was that it clearly shows what most of us suspect: that all talk of paradise only starts when something has been lost. Perhaps that is how the whole myth began: way back in prehistoric times when a growing population finally managed to do what mankind has been doing ever since – namely destroy its own environment – then talk of paradise could begin. Perhaps now, as we finally mess up on a far grander scale than previously, that is why the myth seems peculiarly relevant.

Long before Genesis was written down in around 900 BC,[1] there were myths about lost paradises. The Sumerians who flourished in Mesopotamia from about 4000 BC believed in Dilmun, a fabulous land in the east where no sickness was found and animals lived in harmony.[2] Around 2000 BC the Babylonians first wrote down their Epic of Gilgamesh, in which Enkidu, a wild man who lives happily with the gazelles, is enticed by a harlot to make love on her cloak by a waterhole. In the wonderfully direct words of the epic: 'His lust groaned over her for six days and seven nights ...'[3] On the seventh day Enkidu discovers she has taken his energy but given back knowledge. His loss is that he can no longer be at one with the wild animals, his gain is human society and civilization.

The Roman poet Virgil saw the lost paradise as a Greek pastoral idyll, Arcadia, but the Greeks themselves had long before felt the same nostalgia. The Cynic philosophers identified civilization as the problem: what was required was a return to a natural state. Diogenes[4] famously did this by living in a barrel, going about naked, preaching self-reliance and requesting Alexander the Great to move out of his light. The status and position of kings, even emperors, meant nothing to the philosopher. In India some followers of Shiva, the Aghoris, live in a similar way to this day, even eating human flesh and faeces in order to destroy psychological constraints and so restore the mental perfection that mankind once possessed.

These traditions open up new avenues of exploration in a history of paradise: the idyllic place clearly requires worthy inhabitants who are perfect, but in trying to develop themselves, the seekers may create paradise inside their own skulls. The road to bliss is littered with stories of such self-perfected beings, and the way forwards begins to look more complex. Some might say an eighteenth-century English country house with a Capability Brown park is paradise, and mean it quite literally; for others it is only a metaphor, and for yet more a damp cave on a hilltop in Gujarat (where I once found some Aghoris) is just as good because the perfection is all internal anyway. Lesser mortals want the mental transformation to come with good plumbing and a comfortable bed.

Whatever one's own paradise might be, however, there is always a border to that place, a separation from normality, enforced by physical walls, culture, language, psychology or any other kind of barrier. The early Puritans who went to America clearly thought 3,000 miles of Atlantic Ocean was a good start. This need for separation is one reason why the Genesis story of Eden is such an effective myth: Adam and Eve are expelled because of their own failings and the gates are firmly closed behind them, never to be re-opened until those failings are recognized and conquered. The gates can be seen as literal or symbolic, or perhaps both.

The idea of a Fall is common to the three main monotheistic religions, Judaism, Christianity and Islam. Interestingly, Islam identifies the forbidden fruit as wheat, thus linking the Fall with civilization, whereas Christianity does not identify the fruit, focusing instead on the importance of sexual knowledge as the catalyst.

Once fallen from perfection, our lives become a struggle to regain that blessed state and all three faiths offer two routes. We can follow the religious precepts sufficiently well to please God and be granted admission to heaven, or we can follow the same precepts until a Messiah comes and establishes heaven on earth. Often the two are interlinked: good behaviour by the righteous will encourage the Messiah to return; alternatively, certain prophecies about his arrival might be helped along perhaps by teasing out dates from holy books or even by instigating Armageddon. This return to paradise by the righteous group – the Chosen People – is very different to the individual path of the Cynics or the Aghoris.

In his last book, *Apocalypse*, D.H. Lawrence said that seekers after paradise fall into two categories: the individuals taking a personal route to salvation via love, and the groups heading that way by hate and destruction – for them the elevation of the good people always came with the eradication of the bad. The message of Jesus, Lawrence thought, had been of the former type, but had been hijacked by the latter with their End of Time apocalypse and Day of Judgement. Writing in 1929 Lawrence could see how the modern world was still holding on to religious myths when he believed a return to pre-Fall pagan thinking was needed: 'I wish you would always look at the great heavens and damn the candlesticks,' he wrote to a friend.[5]

A decade later the political scientist Eric Voegelin, chased out of his Austrian professorship by the Nazis, began a deeper, if less poetic, analysis. In his view post-Enlightenment secularism and its beloved notion of progress were rotten right through: the human need for a religious salvation myth, now unconnected to faith in a deity, had produced the monsters of Nazism and Communism. It was as if Karl Marx, having vociferously denounced religion as opium, had been caught red-handed dealing in heroin.

The belief that paradise was up ahead, always just out of reach, had never wavered during the relentless rise of European secularism since the sixteenth century. From then until now, the tenacious grip of the symbolism of the paradise myth on human minds has remained tight, outlasting even that of God for many. Paradise has become the unacknowledged faith of our times, the driving myth of progress and consumer capitalism. We see aspects of the old perfection myth born again everywhere: in arcadian dreams of country living, in environmentalist hopes for a return to a Golden Age of global harmony, and even in the supermarkets' ambition to make a Perpetual Spring in the fruit and vegetable department.

And yet this myth comes to us after many centuries in the temples of the Abrahamic religions, it carries baggage – Armageddon, apocalypse, distorted sexuality, original sin and terrorist martyrdom. Our notions of paradise, often hidden beneath the surface of modern life, bear the triumphs and the scars of old faiths. Sometimes, despite a common ancestry, the various visions of perfection and paradise have appeared to be in conflict, denouncing each other as evil and perverted. But it is my belief that the same underlying myth still drives us, believers and unbelievers alike.

In Iraq in 2003 I saw the spot that locals call the Garden of Eden, a flat area of dried mud haunted by a single dead tree. A month before that I had been to Kabul where the Mughal Emperor Babur built an idyllic garden in the early sixteenth century. I found the wreck of it on the outskirts of town, its groves still mined, its symmetries destroyed by modern additions, including a Soviet-era swimming pool. (As for Babur, he was in his grave at the top of the hill, no doubt spinning.) In a sense, both of those assignments had been caused by modern paradise-seekers, the men who hijacked planes and flew them into buildings. Post-September 11 I wanted to know more about this curious blissful place that could encompass vastly different dreams. I wanted to know where my own ideals came from, and those of supposedly-martyred killers, and where, if at all, they connected.

This book is a chronological account of how, over the centuries, paradise was shaped first by religion, then by secularism. It includes all types of seekers and much about the search for human perfection, but it certainly does not claim to be exhaustive – that would need several volumes – and despite being a history, it includes a few personal experiences couched as prefaces to each of the five parts. But then paradise-seeking is an intensely personal affair and this is an attempt to explain why so many people, myself included, are still looking for that elusive place, even without a god to guide us.

PART I

Origins:
800 BC–AD 1000

Albrecht Dürer, *Adam and Eve*, 1504

The stone cottage was set on a hillside above a wooded valley that ran to the sea a mile away. The rushing stream below was hidden by many kinds of trees: white mulberries with their large soft green leaves, Oriental planes with huge greenish trunks, apples, walnuts, avocados and pears. Farther away the hillsides rose in ridges, all bathed in golden afternoon sun, the terraced vineyards and olive groves punctuated with tall dark cypress trees. Higher still these terraces gave way to pine forests and bare crags where only the goatherds and honey-collectors went. It was that moment of the day in a hot country when you slowly wake from a midday slumber and know that the heat is over and it is time to rise.

Yannis, a Greek hotelier, stood on the cobbled steps next to the white-washed tins filled with geraniums and looked up at the cottage. 'I think it is a good place for you. Fruits and vegetables grow easily here. You make wine. You make olive oil,' he grinned. 'You make babies. You try to make a little paradise for yourselves.'

He had come to the island of Samos from Athens in the mid-1980s, dreaming of a new life away from the pollution and concrete. When he discovered an abandoned village in the woods along the northern coast, he saw a chance to make a living. As each house was restored, he either rented or sold it, then moved on to another. Now there was a collection of stone cottages delightfully strung together with steep flower-lined paths. Along the tops of walls the vines stretched themselves out in the sun and small fawn-coloured rats strolled past, unmolested by the heat-wilted cats that lay panting in pools of shade. I thought of Isaiah: 'The wolf also shall dwell with the lamb.'

Although several of the buildings had been restored, others were still picturesquely ruined in among the olive trees and mulberries. It was one of these that we were examining. I let my mind drift, transforming the reality into what I wanted to see. The crumbling terrace wall which was too close to the front door – or rather the empty space where once had been a door – became a tidy patio shaded by vines where a rough-hewn table held a stone jar of wine. The terraced area to the left flourished with fat tomatoes and zucchini flowers, rather than yellow grasses and burrs. On the other side the pile of stones that once had been an outhouse was transformed into an enclosed garden where a spring came gushing from the mouth of a stone dryad. Beyond, in the kitchen garden, various types of thyme made tapestries of the paths, and there were stone seats overgrown with camomile.

It seemed that I had come here for this moment. The vision of a garden sanctuary in the warm sun was intensely pleasurable. I could be happy here.

'There are four hectares of land behind that house,' Yannis said and I seamlessly incorporated this bonus with terraced olive groves laden with fruit. 'You can bulldoze a road through.'

I smiled. As if I would allow that to happen.

'That makes things cheaper – there's a lot of concrete involved in renovating these places.'

Concrete.

'You need it with the new European Union earthquake regulations. You put in four steel pillars with mesh across. Concrete posts and floors.'

I nodded. 'We only want a simple house. No electricity. Lamps at night. Water from the jar.'

Yannis smiled indulgently and I wondered if every single guest who came through this hotel had a similar conversation with him.

'Then this is not for you – not this renovation work.'

I liked Yannis. He heard what you said.

'There is another place – up towards Manolates. Perfect for you. It's secluded, with water – a real paradise. I'll try and contact the owner.' He left me there contemplating this possible leap towards the perfect life in the perfect place.

My idea of that tantalizing hope has always been quite straight-forward: a country house and garden, health and sunshine, a good love, lots of wine and no hangovers. Judging by the numbers of British people who are moving either to the countryside or to sunnier overseas locations, it's not an unusual dream – neither is it a new one. The Golden Age of the Greeks, or Virgil's Arcadia, touched the same human aspirations, and in modern terms those aspirations can look very like things possessed by the original paradise inhabitants, Adam and Eve: perfect bodies, perfect relationship with nature, perfect diet. So much of what we do is tilted at gaining those things.

I was given a head start in paradise-seeking by my parents. During my childhood they had been members of the Christadelphians, a Protestant sect who believed that paradise would come when Jesus returned and the righteous were bodily resurrected on earth. It was a faith born, I later discovered, on the American frontier in the early nineteenth century where pioneer qualities of self-reliance and inde-pendence were prized. My father built our house in Cumberland himself and avoided contact with the world of officialdom and bureau-cracy. Our furniture and clothes were home-made, our food was home-grown.

There was, however, a paradox buried somewhere inside that retreat to peaceful simplicity: the Christadelphians, like many Protestant sects, are millenarian,[1] and their quiet road to redemption also involves a cataclysmic Armageddon. In the 1960s of my childhood, it was not difficult to pick up the message: Vietnam, Biafra, riots, assassinations and the inexorable rise of the Rolling Stones – Judgement Day was coming soon. D.H. Lawrence may have been right about the two extremes of paradise-seeking, but he omitted to mention that the two are usually mixed up together. All that peaceful simplicity and rural harmony of my childhood felt like the right path to perfection, but somehow the final salvation could only come with faith and violent transformation.

Even without the faith, we can all understand that need for winter frost before spring revival. Most of those people courageous enough to start anew understand it: they change career, they change friends, they change location, and they often do it extremely abruptly as if they were determined to bring on their own personal apocalypse in order to be purified and rise from the ashes.

Dig back in human history to find the origins of the two perfectionist extremes – the quietly evolving harmony and the noisy revolutionary cataclysm – and you come, eventually, to Samos. In the south-west corner of the island is a cave that local guides have optimistically designated Pythagoras's Cave. The tale is that the philosopher (a word Pythagoras was said to have invented) came here to meditate, musing no doubt on the topics that would occupy his entire life: harmony, perfection and universality. Pythagoras blazed the trail for many subsequent paradise-seekers, blending mathematics and mysticism, a man who tried to understand the cosmos (another word of his) and how an individual could reach bliss within it.

Curiously, the mountain top above the cave gives good views of Patmos, an island 20 miles away, and a very different environment to green and fertile Samos. Patmos is dry and barren, and though it may provide some people with holiday idylls now, in the first century AD it was a rocky and inhospitable place of exile for John the Divine. There is an historic cave there too, identified by tourist guides as the spot where John received his visions of the last cataclysmic battle between good and evil. At the rear of the cave are three narrow slits, symbolic of the Holy Trinity, and through one of them came the Holy Spirit, wrenching John's mind towards the Last Days when terrible destruction and death would precede the reborn paradise of the Chosen People in their New Jerusalem.

Two caves then, within signalling distance, but nothing could be further from the elegant geometries of Pythagorean thought than John's visceral and tortured outpourings. While Pythagoras's reputation is for the clean mathematical lines supporting the universe, John's Revelation, the last book in the Bible, gives us a coded explanation of time's violent end. This pair of visionaries are the alpha and omega of paradise-seeking, as different from each other as their neighbouring islands, and yet, as we shall see, this pair of extremes are always somehow together – the Doctor Jekyll and Mister Hyde in humanity's dreams. And between these two all subsequent forays into perfection are squeezed, from the timeless eighteenth-century arcadias of the English aristocracy, to the dark and horrible madness of suicidal terrorists slaughtering themselves and others.

I was not going to get my own apocalypse on Samos, however, not yet at least. On the third day after Yannis had promised to contact the landowner at Manolates, I went to find him, searching the rambling stone paths and cool houses – no locks here. There was only a friend, sent to deputize. 'Yannis had to go to Athens,' he told me. 'Family crisis. He should be back in a week.' But before his return I had to leave and, once again, paradise was postponed.

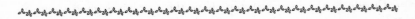

1

Pythagoras and Harmony

Pythagoras was born in about 580 BC, the son of a corn merchant from Tyre who had been granted citizenship on Samos after saving the island from famine. The father's trade gave the boy plenty of opportunities for travel and they sailed together to ports all across the Mediterranean. There are tales that the boy's remarkable intellect was first stimulated by experiences on these journeys – he was certainly well-educated and could recite Homer and play the lyre. Little is known of his early life, but in 535 BC he travelled to Egypt, a land that had close ties with Samos as they faced a common enemy, the Achaemenid empire founded by the Persian, Cyrus the Great.

Pythagoras probably went to study in the temples, an obvious place to seek further knowledge at that time. With his mathematical interests and mystical nature, he no doubt immersed himself in Egyptian numerology which regarded the numbers 3, 5 and 8 as divine (they are part of an important mathematical progression called the Fibonacci Series, familiar to readers of *The Da Vinci Code*). Among the priests he also picked up a few customs, including a regard for purity and, it is said, a dislike of beans.[1]

After six years, Pythagoras's sojourn was brought to a sudden and dramatic end when the Achaemenids invaded. Polycrates, ruler of Samos, had unexpectedly changed sides, presumably after a handsome bribe was paid, and with his ships the Persians managed to seize power. If we are to believe records from 700 years later, Pythagoras was taken prisoner and transported to Babylon.

Under Cyrus and his descendants the city had become capital to an empire that stretched from the western shores of Turkey to the borders of India. All kinds of Middle Eastern and Mediterranean peoples crowded through its handsome streets, as well as exotic groups from distant places in Africa, central Asia and India. The pagan Cyrus was famously tolerant of all their peculiarities. Members of one Indian sect were said to practise necrophagy – eating the corpse of their father. Ktesias, a Greek physician who served at the Persian court from 405 to 397 BC, wrote of birds brought from India that could talk, of unicorns (the first known reference) and magical water that could make men speak the truth. His reputation for tall tales exceeds even that of Herodotus, but the image of a city filled with wonders and marvels is a fair one. The wealthy empire sucked in all kinds of fabulous treasures from all over the known world. Its citizens looked and smelled good too: according to Herodotus, the fashion was for a dashing combination of long hair, capes and plenty of perfume. The streets were straight and beautiful, the main thorough-fares running down to the vital ship quays on the banks of the Euphrates. Most spectacular were the 82-feet-high terraces of the Hanging Gardens built by Nebuchadnezzar to remind his wife of her native Kurdistan.[2]

The religious melting pot of Babylon must have fascinated a man of Pythagoras's interests. Zoroastrianism was particularly influential and its astronomers, the magi, had a strong mathematical tradition, including the trademark law that would eventually bear Pythagoras's name. Ironically, for all the man's ingenuity and creativity, this theorem for which he is best remembered was not his – it actually dates back to much earlier times. A stone tablet from about 1600 BC records:

4 is the length and 5 the diagonal. What is the breadth?
Its size is not known.
4 times 4 is 16.

5 times 5 is 25.

You take 16 from 25 and there remains 9.

What times what shall I take in order to get 9?

3 times 3 is 9.

3 is the breadth.

The Babylonians had devised a number system to the base 60 and it has survived to modern times for use in time and angular measurement. As 60 is divisible by 1, 2, 3, 4, 5, 6, 10, 12, 15 and 20, the system made mathematical calculation simple, especially with fractions and angles, a big advantage when it came to their preoccupation with astronomy. (They were the first to divide the night sky into the 12 signs of the zodiac.)

For Pythagoras the mathematical proofs were essential to understanding a cosmos in which number was the moving spirit, but there was much else in the diversity of Persia to stimulate his interest. He was fascinated by the idea of an immortal soul and believed in reincarnation. This notion that the soul was indestructible, reiterated by Plato in the *Phaedo*, would be as important in posterity as Pythagorean mathematics.

After five years in Babylon, Pythagoras returned to Samos but seems to have been unable to settle happily. It was then that his paradise-seeking nature came to the fore.[3] He moved to Croton in southern Italy where he established a community whose objective was the divine perfection of the soul. For all his mathematical genius, it is this that makes Pythagoras vital in the story of paradise on earth: the first recorded establishing of a community with perfectionist goals, the sort of place we still see in utopian settlements across America or in Indian ashrams. Pythagoras's ambitious objective was to be achieved by contemplation and study of the mathematical harmony and order of the universe, the Pythagorean term cosmos, implying beauty and order in the universe.

It is not known how this process was carried out, though we do know that initiates would start with five years of silence: 'to learn to think and unlearn to prate', according to one classical source, Apuleis, followed by the same period on mathematics, astronomy, geometry and music. This core knowledge, arranged in four subjects, reflected the importance of the number four – in elements, seasons, humours, ages of man and so on.

Pythagoras's systematic investigations began with music. He discovered that musical harmonies were related to the length of the plucked strings: a string half the length of another, if at the same tension, will be an octave higher in pitch; a relation of 2:3 gives a harmony known as the musical fifth, the diapente; that of 3:4 makes a fourth, the diatessaron. These relationships of number, dimension and pitch were seen by Pythagoras as fundamental to the harmony of the universe. Observing that the number of notes in the musical scale corresponded to the number of celestial bodies, he concluded that the planets in their orbits produced certain notes according to their distance from the earth (which was at the centre). Inaudible to mortals, this was the Music of the Spheres and it governed all the cycles of nature and the seasons. Philosophers of the mystical kind ever since have been straining to hear it.

Music was central to Pythagorean theory. The human body, like the universe, was tuned to the harmonies and so diseases were essentially disharmony – he even claimed to be able to cure drunkenness with a melody in the Hypophrygian mode in spondaic rhythm.[4] The community did not restrict the numerical proportions of musical harmony to medicine, they could be equally applied to art, architecture, gardens, government – everything in fact, as the universe was built on these principles. Most crucially of all, Pythagoras was interested in the Golden Section or Mean: approximately 1:1.618034 (or 1:0.618034, depending on which way you look at it) or:

$$\frac{\sqrt{5}+1}{2}$$

Pythagoras, however, knew it as a geometrical expression. Take a compass, draw a circle, divide the circumference into five equal sections, join those points to make a star.

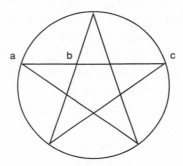

The ratio of the distance ab to bc now equals the Golden Mean and this ratio, or phi ϕ, was believed by Pythagoras and his followers to be vital for universal harmony, one of the essential mathematical constants.

Since mathematics and geometry dealt in perfect numbers and figures, theirs was a higher truth than any other. Through study of such matters, Pythagoras believed, came self-knowledge which was the key to wisdom. The philosopher would build a framework of harmonious mathematics and with understanding would come re-unification with nature and the divine. Eventually the reward would be release from the encumbrance of the body. This objective was no different to those later seekers, the Sufis, the yogis and the Christian hermits: indeed both Christianity and Islam would borrow a great deal from Pythagoras and apply his fascination with numbers to spiritual matters.

To what extent this ambitious goal required the presence of a perfect community we do not know. They do seem to have had many practices that later paradise-seeking groups would share – vegetarianism, secrecy and strong fraternal bonds, for example. They also rejected private property. All this would have helped in building that essential barrier between themselves and the normal world outside, necessary for the transformation they wanted.

Pythagoras, or at least some later disciples, seem to have brought to their quest the first inklings of rationality. He was probably the first to suggest that the earth was spherical, and consequently that the Morning Star, Venus, was identical to the Evening Star. Twentieth-century science, also seeking harmony and unity in the cosmos, would certainly find Pythagorean interest in the Golden Mean justified. The series of numbers made by adding the last two integers together, the Fibonacci Series, beginning 1, 1, 2, 3, 5, 8, 13, 21... has been found to appear in nature with astonishing frequency and if you divide any two consecutive numbers of the series together, you get a figure that approaches that of the Golden Mean as the size of the two numbers increases. The number of petals on most flowers is a number from the series; the angles at which leaves sprout from branches relates to the Golden Mean; examine the head of a sunflower and the spirals of seeds are separated by an angle related to the Mean. This harmony has been picked up in the twenty-first century by plastic surgeons, some of whom now use the Golden Mean to calculate the best dimensions for facial features. They have discovered that what is beautiful in the eye of the beholder is both symmetry and harmony – and that harmony is most effective when based on the Golden Mean.[5]

It seems entirely appropriate that such a modern concern about achieving beauty, and hence the good life, should link back through twenty-five centuries to Pythagoras, the man who had set up what was probably the first paradise-seeking community, a place dedicated to restoring humanity's lost perfection.

Unfortunately, back in 500 BC, there were those outside the group who were not sympathetic. It is recorded that one violent and difficult nobleman, Cylon, asked to be admitted and was refused. Enraged by this rejection, he organized an attack and destroyed the settlement. Pythagoras, by then an old man, fled into exile where he died, perhaps by suicide. Another, happier, version of events is that he lived to be a hundred and died at Croton. His followers certainly flourished and Pythagoreanism spread to many Greek cities, but there does appear to have been resentment surrounding the original headquarters: in about 460 BC a mob broke in, cornered a group of 50 or 60 Pythagoreans and murdered them.

2

Apocalypse and Eden

If Pythagoras's gentle search for harmony marks a beginning for one extreme of the paradise-seeking tradition, then the other end of the spectrum – linked through John of Patmos – has its origins in a series of events further back in time. The first happened in Jerusalem in about 701 BC when the inhabitants of what was then an insignificant Judean hill town woke to find their settlement surrounded by the largest and most powerful army in the world, the Assyrians. It must have been a terrifying sight, all the grandeur and might of the world superpower spread around the walls, with battering rams, chariots and tens of thousands of warriors brandishing sharp weaponry and even sharper hair-styles – judging from the stone reliefs that have survived.

The king of Judea, Hezekiah, hurried to the temple on the north-east corner of his small town[1] and there tore his clothes, covered his head with sackcloth and called for the prophet Isaiah. In the biblical story it is a spectacular moment of high drama and the chroniclers have Isaiah playing his part boldly. 'Thus saith the Lord,' he told the king. 'Be not afraid of the words which thou hast heard, with which the servants of the king of Assyria have blasphemed me. Behold, I will send a blast upon him … and I will cause him to fall by the sword in his own land.'[2]

What happened next would assure Isaiah's one true God of his premier position in Jewish life. Next morning the vast army woke to find 185,000 of its number dead. The remainder soon retreated to Nineveh where their leader, Sennacherib, was murdered. The most plausible explanation for this far-fetched event is that plague struck, but the result for the Jews was that worship of a single God was vindicated.

At this point the Jews had one God whose perfect heaven was entirely separate from an imperfect earth, but a century or so later a disaster overtook the people that would blur the clear blue space between the two. This time the threat was from the Babylonian empire of Nebuchadnezzar, and this time God abandoned Jerusalem. The Babylonians destroyed the city and its temple, despatching about 15,000 inhabitants into exile. There was no doubt in the minds of the Jewish prophets why this calamity had occurred: the Jews had strayed from the true path and God was punishing them. [3]

One aristocratic priest who had been taken to Babylon with the other exiles responded with an incredible apocalyptic vision. Ezekiel saw a burning whirlwind bearing down on the Israelites, an amber-coloured firestorm carrying four human figures each with four faces and four wings, all riding on dreadful wheels covered in eyes. Falling on his face, Ezekiel then heard the Lord command him to stand and listen. He was told that the Israelites were being punished for whoring them-selves with other deities. God offered only more desolation before any restoration.

In Babylon the Jews found themselves in a city that both offended and inspired them. Like Herodotus they were repelled by the practice whereby every woman, at least once in her life, had to sit in the 'precinct of Venus' and wait for a complete stranger to proposition her with the words, 'The Goddess Mylitta prosper thee.' This was a dance at which no woman could refuse the first offer, and for the beautiful among them, quickly led away, the ordeal was at least soon over. But not all had their cards marked so easily. 'Some have waited three or four years,' observed Herodotus.

Such practices were the 'abominations' and 'whoredoms' so hated by the Jewish prophets – the Book of Baruch, dropped from the Bible by Jerome in AD 386, mentions this example. Babylon's name would forever after be linked to the idea of a debauched city, just as Jerusalem would become a byword for the holy and pure. Ezekiel thundered against the Israelites for being tempted by such filth, but at the same time the Babylonian experience was quietly influencing Jewish culture in other ways.

One borrowing from Persian was the word paradise – *pardes* in Hebrew. The Persian meaning of the word can be seen carved into the stone reliefs at Taq-i-Bustan in Kermanshah, western Iran.[4] One relief shows a hunting scene where the king is busily pouring arrows into swarms of wild boar. A rectangular enclosure ensures there is no escape. Outside the fence servants hack the dead animals into bite-size chunks, while others lug them away. It's an image of plenty, endless bacon, provided by the deity-chosen monarch, and all within the safety of the enclosure, the *paradeiza*, the paradise.

The Jews borrowed the image of abundance, and the word, as did the Greeks who discovered it through the writer Xenophon a couple of centuries later.[5]

The haloed king in the Taq-i-Bustan relief was a Zoroastrian and this religion proved to be a particularly fertile source for the Jews. The Zoroastrian traditions of a Messiah, resurrection and an end-game of violent confrontation between good and evil leading to a Last Judgement, were all greatly appealing to oppressed Jews thirsty for justice and revenge. Ezekiel was just the prophet for such hard times: he stalked the streets trembling uncontrollably and eating excrement, his prose scorched with promises of cataclysmic destruction. But his uncompromising message had a final reward: 'Behold, O my people, I will open your graves, and cause you to come up out of your graves, and bring you into the land of Israel' (Ezekiel 37:12). The book of Isaiah, parts of which were written down during the exile, further developed the ideas, promising a time of Judgement and a Messiah, then the paradise: 'The wolf and the lamb shall feed together, and the lion shall eat straw like the bullock: and dust shall be the serpent's meat. They shall not hurt nor destroy in all my holy mountain, saith the Lord' (Isaiah 66:25).

Heaven had until then been a remote and inaccessible place for the Jews, only open to very special individuals, like the prophet Elijah, reportedly swept up by a chariot, or Enoch, who simply vanished skywards, escapes from death that would earn these two a privileged role in apocalyptic narratives to come. Most dead souls had to make do with *sheol*, a valley of gloomy shades and a much less luxurious prospect. Now the apocalyptic prophets drew down to earth that distant celestial paradise and linked it to the lost homeland of Canaan. The result was a heaven on earth, a place of milk and honey, a Promised Land to be reached by religious observances. It was an idea of extraordinary, and enduring, power.

This new Judaism had not only gathered itself a paradise, it had given to history a narrative that had a beginning, a middle and an end: Eden is lost and the people wander in the wilderness; destruction and chaos announce the coming of a saviour; then finally Eden is regained. It kicked the paradise myth into action, gave it the flavour of a quest, plus the figure of a Messiah and a geographical objective.

The Jews kept this tradition alive through the centuries that followed, right up to its last great exponent, John of Patmos. The teachings and life of Jesus added some important nuances to the idea of what constituted the perfect life, notably on poverty, but it was John who made the greatest contribution to the subject of paradise in the New Testament.

The Apocalypse, or Revelation, was almost certainly written after the Roman emperor Domitian (AD 81–96) exiled John to Patmos. In a cave on the island, now inside the Monastery of Apokálypsis, John heard the words of the Holy Spirit coming from a slit in the rock. This message would prove to be vitally important in the development of the paradise idea.

The Apocalypse begins conventionally by New Testament standards, with greetings to the seven churches that had been established at that time.[6] But quickly it moves to a formula reminiscent of the great days of Judaic prophecy: a vision of Christ holding seven stars in his right hand and in his mouth a two-edged sword. Clearly this is a work rich in meaning: seven trumpets announce the End and a terrible battle between good and evil ensues. Satan, the great serpent, is bound with a chain for a thousand years, the millennium, during which Christ reigns with the Christian martyrs and the righteous. Following this first resurrection, Satan is let out once again and a Final Battle occurs between his minions and God's followers. The result is conclusive. Satan dies in the fiery pit, then the sea gives up its dead and all mankind is judged. Those whose names are found in the Book of Life are saved, the rest – murderers, whoremongers, sorcerers, idolators, liars and, of course, unbelievers – are exterminated. Finally the New Jerusalem is founded and God wipes away all tears and pain.

The influence of Revelation is understandable: the suffering of this life may not have to be endured for long, it tells us, a Second Coming with attendant paradise is imminent. It is a message of hope for the oppressed and unrepresented, coupled with the pleasure of knowing that the wicked – those who flout the rules – will receive some extremely painful justice. This is a vengeful Old Testament God, a pre-Christ Judaic deity, destroying the world together with most of its inhabitants.[7] This is not a God of Love, and if Christ is in it, he is certainly not the humane and loving soul who suffered the little children, more like some cosmic life force.

Revelation's numerology draws heavily on Pythagorean ideas: four symbolizes earth (four horsemen corresponding to four winds and quarters, also four Gospels), three is divine (the Holy Trinity), and seven, consequently, represents completeness (the seven days of creation).[8] By harnessing this mystical numerology to the Doomsday justice narrative, Revelation creates a hugely powerful text, a book that captures the reader, even the unbeliever, and sweeps them forward towards the New Jerusalem, a place in which the qualities of Eden are reproduced within something like civilization – 'And the building of the wall of it was of jasper: and the city was pure gold, like unto clear glass.'[9]

The book gives wonderful opportunities to apply Platonic deductive reasoning, working out the logical meaning of every bloody scythe and braying trumpet, not to mention all the calculations regarding the date of Doomsday. It gave Christians a new earthly paradise to aim towards and shifted the role of Chosen People on to them, leaving the Jews in an ambivalent position as far as Christ's followers were concerned, both murderers of the Messiah but also special in the Father's eyes. And yet this powerful text was not immediately adopted by all Christians: a significant number of elders in the early Church denounced it as a transparent fake.

The Eastern Syrian Church rejected Revelation (early Syriac Bibles have been discovered right across Asia from Lebanon to China), the main Syrian Church rejected it (their Bible, the Peshitta, also excluded 2 Peter, 2 and 3 John and Jude – all parts of the King James Version), theologians from Merv and Mesopotamia did not allow it a place. The third-century theologian Dionysius of Alexandria reported that some thought the book the work of a heretic named Cerinthus: 'For this was the doctrine which he taught, that the kingdom of Christ would be on earth; and he dreamed that it would consist in those things which formed the object of his own desires (for he was a lover of the body and altogether carnal), in the full satisfaction of the belly and lower lusts.'[10] It is also missing in an Arabic Bible from the ninth century found in the Monastery of St Catherine in Sinai. A seventh-century Bible from Edessa (modern Şanliurfa in eastern Turkey) does not have it. Armenia, the first kingdom to convert, in the second century, did not accept it until the twelfth century. The Georgians had an alphabet created in order to write the Bible down, but once again there was no place for Revelation, not until the tenth century. One of Christianity's most important early figures, Origen (c.185–253), painfully aware of all the disputes, declared that only the four Gospels were indisputable.[11]

But this suspicion of Revelation, more deeply felt in the East, was not universal. Theologians in Rome had always tended to include, or defend its inclusion.[12] Then in 367 the influential Alexandrian scholar, Athanasius, issued a definitive list, the 27 books of the New Testament that we know today, including Revelation in its current position at the very end. Twenty years later one of the greatest scholars of the day, Jerome, was asked by Pope Damasus to settle finally any questions of authenticity. After extensive travelling and collecting of manuscripts, Jerome settled in Bethlehem and began to sort out the false, the forged and the downright heretical, as well as all the simple errors caused by manual transcription. He taught himself Hebrew – he was probably a native speaker of Greek from what is now north-east Italy – and started on the mammoth editing task. The 50-year-old holy man proved to be a demon with the scissors. Out went the Jewish books of Judith, Tobit, Wisdom, Ecclesiasticus, Maccabees I, Maccabees II and Baruch (with its Babylonian abominations). Out too went parts of Esther and Daniel. By the time he got to the New Testament, however, the scissors were tiring: grave doubts about John II, John III and Hebrews were waved aside. Revelation too was included.

And there, finally, it stayed. Jerome's gargantuan scholarly effort resulted in the Vulgate Bible that became the standard Christian text. Some of the excluded material would eventually creep back in, but for much of Christendom the 27 books of the New Testament were now set in stone. With Revelation and Genesis, plus a few passages from other books, the Western world had got the texts that would help define ideas of paradise for the next thousand years.

The doubts, however, did not wholly disappear. Perhaps the problem was that Revelation invited a literal reading: instead of a mystical internal search for perfection, a well-established Eastern tradition, it appeared to encourage more external and earthly answers to human problems. Origen attempted to promote the idea that John had written an allegory: the entire violent story was actually about the internal struggle that all men should pass through to achieve paradise, but the Christian rank-and-file were unconvinced. In Phrygia, now central western Turkey, there had already been a serious outbreak of millenarian belief in 156, when the priest Montanus declared the New Jerusalem was about to be built there.

Following its official adoption other leading churchmen continued to treat the book with caution. The 'saintly but insufferable'[13] John Chrysostom, supposedly the first person to use the term Bible, never once referred to Revelation while Patriarch of Constantinople between 398 and 404, despite the many opportunities for doom-laden warnings presented to him by the lascivious empress, Eudoxia. In that same period Augustine, Bishop of Hippo Regius in North Africa from 396, also tried to suppress interest in the deductive possibilities of the book. Predicting Christ's return, for example, was impossible, he declared, and any attempt to hasten the Kingdom of Heaven was futile, possibly even blasphemous. Augustine's views on the importance of celibacy had already pushed paradise beyond the reach of most mortals and with his insistence that the Kingdom of Heaven could never be hastened, he further removed paradise on earth from the realms of possibility.

Writing after the sack of Rome in 410, he warned that predictions were hopeless, all we could know was that the world would decay and the Kingdom would come. Nothing more. No setting of dates and no hastening of events. 'The world is passing away,' he wrote. 'The world is losing its grip, the world is short of breath. Do not fear, Thy youth shall be renewed as an eagle.' The New Jerusalem would be gained when God deemed the people were sufficiently pious and the time was right. And yet the book was there in the Bible and when the time came, its promise of an earthly paradise would prove highly significant.

One important aspect of paradise on which Revelation offered no guidance was that of human perfection, particularly in an area which obsessed Augustine: sexual relationships. All down the ages Christendom has wrangled and worried the issue – in the seventeenth century it even came to a heated debate on the sex life of date palms. There were, it was discovered, both male and female trees who

mingled their roots below ground, foreplay presumably. The males —
monsters of leafy lust — were discovered enticing the females by
'enclining towards them, and wagging their boughs', according to a
shocked John Jonstone in his *An History of the Wonderful Things in Nature*
published in 1657. Theologians adroitly dodged the problem by
deciding that palms were an exception created by God to prove the
rule that most plants were sexless and therefore allowed to reside in
paradise. The interdependence of male and female trees, they
surmised, was symbolic of Christ and the Virgin. When male palms
were found to grow faster than female, the case was proven: it
symbolized Christ's ascent to heaven before the Virgin Mary died.

When it came to questions of sex and relationships, the Bible's main
source on what constituted perfection was the Genesis story of Adam
and Eve in the Garden of Eden. With some minor variations the tale
also appears in the Torah and the Qur'an. It is very familiar and consequently we often overlook the fact that this is undoubtedly the most
beautifully concise description of perfection ever written. In the
biblical version, it takes just 25 verses to establish Adam and Eve in
their paradise, 24 more to describe how they lose it. Neither is this a
case of over-zealous editing. Within those verses comes a succinct idea
of what all human beings would wish for, particularly if retreating to a
sunny olive grove in the Mediterranean: impressive bodily health,
physique and longevity; an abundance of good food that requires no
work; exclusive rights to a large and fertile stretch of land, plus, of
course, an attractive and perfectly matched partner.

Those basic qualities are enshrined in the language of the myth
itself. Eden in Hebrew meant 'delight' and the word lives on in
modern language. In the Hasidic community in Brooklyn, for
example, you can hear the derivation in *madana*, a delicatessen. The
name Adam is predictably ancient, recorded in both ancient
Babylonian and Akkadian.[14] In ancient Akkadian *adamu* was blood,
almost identical to the modern Arabic *damm*. The name Eve is a
Hebrew derivation of *hayyah*, meaning life.

With the kind of deductive logic the Greeks pioneered, the basics supplied by Genesis were later adorned by theologians. Some of these elaborations were informed by other lost perfection myths, notably the Greek stories of, for example, the Golden Age and Arcadia. Frequently the questions raised seem absurd: another debate, for example, was on whether Adam and Eve could have possessed belly buttons, neither having been born of woman (the perfectly logical answer was no). Yet in some of these arguments emerge hopes and fears that are timeless. The relationship between longevity and diet for example.

Fruit was the original and perfect diet, said John Milton, and this explained Adam's impressive 930 years. After the Fall, however, this fruitarian diet was augmented by herbs and cereals which reduced Adam's children to lesser spans. Following the Flood, the situation deteriorated further when mankind got a taste for steak. With meat, Milton argued, decay itself became part of the diet with inevitable effects on longevity, though the back-breaking work of farming was also blamed. Eventually we were reduced to our measly three-score-years-and-ten, trapped in the bodies of relative midgets, imperfect imitations of that first man.

While the notion of physically more impressive and vastly longer-lived humans somewhere in our past might seem fanciful, it would be difficult to deny that these are common objectives for many people. The myth of ancestral archetypes puts those objectives within our reach, if not our grasp. Whoever the author, or authors, of Genesis may have been, they managed to distil, with marvellous economy, most of the immortal obsessions of humanity.

The central dramatic moment of the Genesis story is the Fall from grace. This was, claimed Augustine, due to sexual lust. With the act of copulation, he reasoned, the original couple had sinned and the stain of that sin was passed down the generations with every single act of procreation. No one was innocent. Unbaptized infants would be consigned to hell and eternal damnation for their sin.

As one might expect this doctrine came out of Augustine's own guilt and shame. He had kept a mistress from the age of 17 and yet had also been drawn to the idea of celibacy by the followers of the Persian prophet Mani who had been crucified in AD 276 by his Zoroastrian enemies. Manichaean teaching was that the earth was a satanic creation and the human body a demonic vehicle containing a tiny spark of goodness, the soul. The only way to cultivate this spark was through extreme asceticism and celibacy.

After his conversion to Christianity in 385, Augustine spent the next years sorting out his deep hostility to sex in a systematic manner. The adoption of his views as an ideal, in fact the ideal state of a human being, removed sexual pleasure from any Christian concept of paradise or perfection, even making it shameful within marriage; and secondly it downgraded women to dangerous provocateurs of sin. For Augustine the perfect person worthy of life in paradise could only be a celibate man.[15]

Augustine's ideals did not find a positive response with everyone. In Britain a monk called Pelagius, probably of Welsh origins, began to preach a very different message. Human beings, said Pelagius, were basically good. Infants were born, like Adam, as mortals and without sin. The path to perfection and paradise was open to all and could be achieved in a lifetime – in fact, said this optimistic radical, it was mandatory to try. If his message had become dominant in the church, one wonders what might have become of the Dark Ages ahead. That it did not was largely due to Augustine.

Arriving in Rome in about 390, Pelagius preached that sex, marriage and children were good and that a sexual life could be integrated with a simple love of God and nature. This brought a concerted campaign of vilification from Augustine, who after years of attacks ensured that Pelagius was finally excommunicated and forced to flee Rome. He is thought to have ended his life wandering in the East, though another tradition claims he returned to Wales. Pelagian optimism, however, would make a significant comeback in seventeenth-century Protestant England. Pelagius's tormentor, of course, was made a saint.

Augustine's brand of Christianity, bereft of sexual pleasure and any hope of paradise in this life, made huge demands on faith. There was no Perpetual Spring in such a faith, only perpetual guilt and shame. In the East it proved far less appealing than the West, and in the Arabian Peninsula – a popular escape hole for celibate hermits – it held no attraction for the population. The opportunity to become the perfect Christian man, that emasculated, impoverished and saintly inhabitant of paradise, was about to be decisively rejected by a very different ideal, yet one that sprang from the same Judaic soil.

3

Muhammad and the Perfect Man

The prophet Muhammad grew up in an Arabia where there was plenty of appetite for unity with God and for paradisical harmony, but little consensus about where to find it. Christianity and Judaism were competing with old pagan gods – idols whose grip was proving tenacious. At Mecca, for example, the Ka'ba had been worshipped for centuries – some believed its usage dated all the way back to Adam who had made it his altar in Eden. This symbol of the four corners of the earth stood, and still does, next to a holy spring, *zamzam*, and pilgrims would come and run around it seven times, as they still do, before drinking from the spring.

Monotheism had made some inroads among the Arabian tribes, but Christianity had certainly not managed to find the right note for the resolutely traditional tribes. When it came, Islam would have no time for Christian practices like celibacy and eremiticism. This would be a pragmatic faith – hardly surprising since Muhammad spent the best part of three decades on trade caravans, constantly tussling with the inescapable logic of animal transport and the necessities of mutual dependence. Would the people be hardy enough? Would they argue with each other? A good merchant balanced all the elements. Harmony on the journey meant survival; disharmony could spell death.

Muhammad was a success at his profession, known for his honesty and integrity, but he remained unsatisfied, occasionally wandering off into the mountains. When his visions began in AD 610, they were in a

Judaic tradition that Ezekiel would have recognized, the angel Gabriel visiting him in a cave above the city and commanding him, 'Recite!'[1] The process of the revelation went on for 23 years and many visions were evidently brought about by corresponding crises in Muhammad's life. When his wife A'isha was accidentally left behind by a caravan, then rescued by a young man, there were rumours of infidelity. A month later came the chapter, Light (sura 24), with its stringent laws on proving adultery.

The climax of this visionary life came with a mystical transport to another realm. In 619, nine years after his first vision, when the Meccan elite were almost all against him and his first wife Khadija had died, as had his beloved uncle, Abu Talib, Muhammad wandered alone through the streets of Mecca and fell asleep in a shelter near the Ka'ba. During the night he was rudely woken, with three kicks from the angel Gabriel who then led him outside the city. There they mounted a mystical creature, the *buraq*, a beast which, in later Islamic tradition, became something like the fabulous winged creatures that guard the palace of Xerxes in Persepolis. It took him north over Mount Sinai to Jerusalem to the site of Temple Mount and that legendary rock in its centre, at that time a place bare to the heavens.[2]

In the cave beneath the rock, Muhammad was offered three drinks: water, milk and wine. He rejected both the austere water and the inebriating wine, choosing the milky middle path – a symbolic rejection of Christianity and Judaism. Now the *buraq* was transformed into a chariot of fire and they climbed the ladder through the seven heavens to the tree at the end of everything where he glimpsed the Creator. This was the Night Journey, the *Isra*, followed by Ascension, *Mi'raj*.

It was a crucial moment in the birth of Islam: a giant electrical jolt of mysticism had just been delivered. A shamanic journey to the godhead, a quest for the divine, an ecstatic experience of God – the Night Journey gave Islam a vitality and power, plus a pattern for the mystical type of paradise-seeker. Yet Muhammad was also the man who chose the milk, not the ascetic water or the hedonistic wine. It's possible to see quite clearly the type of Perfect Man (if not woman) that this faith would aspire to. The Prophet was married many times and loved the company of women. The strangled celibacy beloved of some Christians repelled him. The Perfect Man in Islam would become something very different, a more rounded figure, both family man and warrior, both mystic and pragmatist.

As for the place where such a being should live, Muhammad's visions contained plenty of detail about paradise. While the Bible gives guidance on how to reach it, there is almost no description at all of what to expect. The Qur'an on the other hand offers a rich and colourful picture of a paradise well suited to desert-dwellers, an oasis-like garden where trees are laden with fruit – dates and pomegranates are mentioned – and all watered by a central fountain and pure rivers. The inhabitants recline on carpets and couches where they are waited on by beautiful youths and by *hur,* a word usually translated as virgins of paradise but more precisely conveying the essential idea of purity and beauty. (The notion that there will be 72 of these damsels for each man comes not in the Qur'an but a saying first recorded in the fifteenth century.)

The question of the nymphs, the *huris,* of paradise is one that the West finds fascinating. Given the heritage that Augustine imparted, it's not hard to see why. Christoph Luxenberg, a pseudonym of a Lebanese Christian scholar, has argued that many accepted meanings of the Qur'an are changed if it is read with a knowledge of Old Syriac, a source for the emerging Arabic language of Muhammad's era. *Hur,* for example, becomes white raisins, sweeping away, no doubt to horrified male Muslim groans, the idea of paradise as a sexual idyll. Luxenberg's thesis has been dismissed by some scholars, but what is undeniable is that the prurient fascination of the West with Islamic paradise continues.

All this becomes irrelevant if one reads for symbolic meaning – *hur* has the essence of freshness and purity – but when it comes to paradise the human weakness is always to want literal truth. Robert Graves said of the *huris* that they 'are creatures of light and offer no analogy to any human being and should be given no physical attributes, as in vulgar fables'.[3]

Muhammad himself made it clear that every truth in the Qur'an had several aspects and he often demonstrated the power of allegory. When his wives asked which of them would die first, he is said to have replied, 'The one with the longest arm.' This brought on a frenzy of measuring, until one understood that he meant the person who extended their arm most often in charitable acts. One suspects that violent extremists, bin Ladin's children, would still be there with the tape measure.

Following the death of the prophet Muhammad in 632 and a period of uncertainty, a campaign of conquest had quickly expanded the Muslim lands out of the Arabian Peninsula, pushing back Byzantium and sweeping away the Persians, then expanding along the North African coast and into Spain. In the east Balkh fell in 705; the rest of what is now Afghanistan soon followed.

If Christendom needed a reminder of how its great rival was forging ahead, a hint came at the end of the eighth century when precious gifts, including an elephant and a marvellous clock, arrived at the court of Charlemagne. The sender was Harun al-Rashid, Caliph of Islam, and a man destined to be remembered for his fanciful exploits in the *Arabian Nights*, dressing up as a beggar and wandering the streets of Baghdad looking for adventure and entertainment. More credibly, Harun had ordered the translation from Greek of various astronomical and medical works. His son, Ma'mun, who succeeded him in 813 took the process a step further, ordering the collection of human knowledge in a House of Wisdom, the Bayt al-Hikma.

Their city was a marvel in itself, built on an ambitious circular plan with the palace, a walled paradise of gardens more than a mile in diameter, at the centre. In 917 ambassadors from Byzantium got to see this hub of the universe (of which almost no trace remains) and described walking in on an endless spread of carpets – 22,000 of them – then through gardens in which a tree made of gold and silver held artificial birds that sang in the breeze.[4]

It was not only in finery and royal palaces that the Islamic world was doing well. Driven by the desire to perfect themselves and Islamic society, knowledge and learning had swept forwards. In mathematics Muhammad ibn Musa al-Khwarizmi made huge advances in algebra.[5] While the hunt for perfection was part of this progress, the Islamic approach always maintained a certain pragmatic flavour. In the case of Khwarizmi it was the hunt for a perfect means of settling inheritance laws and the calculation of the best dimensions for canals that stimulated the discoveries of algebra.

The philosophy of the Greeks, notably Pythagoras, Plato and Aristotle, had crept eastwards over the centuries preceding Islam. Now with Ma'mun's support and encouragement, further works were brought into Arabic, particularly those of Aristotle. The Greek philosopher had stressed man's social and political nature, suggesting that solitary quests for perfect happiness were doomed to fail. Such insights stimulated one of the Baghdad intelligentsia, Abu Nasr al-Farabi (c. 878–950). His book, *Opinions of the Inhabitants of the Virtuous City*, was a utopian tract on Islamic lines written six centuries before Thomas More reinvented the genre for the West. Al-Farabi had started life, appropriately for someone interested in human perfection and paradise, as a gardener. He was said to have studied by night in a Damascus vineyard and survived on a frugal diet of sweet basil and lambs' hearts. His conclusions about the perfect life read as startlingly modern: happiness, he declared, was the ultimate goal of life and it was best achieved in the society of a small city-state. There were no supernatural phenomena, and mystical union with God was 'old women's talk'. Everything was ascertainable by reason. However, many people were incapable of finding happiness through reason and needed symbols – images and ideas communicated by prophets through revelations.

This tradition in Islamic thought reached its peak a generation later with a native of northern Persia, Ibn Sina, a man known in the West as Avicenna. Ibn Sina was fascinated by questions of human perfectibility and the nature of true happiness – as well as just about everything else. He wrote copiously on physics, metaphysics, medicine, astronomy and psychology as well as finding time for an autobiography. There was, he argued, a route to perfection whereby the soul could rise through a series of levels to be reunited with God. Then it would become 'an intelligible world of its own', a kind of microcosmos. Here he had reached a conclusion similar to the Pythagoreans: the keys to paradise were inside each human being.

Not everyone in Islam agreed – perhaps why Ibn Sina now finds himself buried on a traffic island in the Iranian city of Hamedan – but some seekers took the message to heart, among them the mystics known as Sufis. Their primary inspiration came from the prophet Muhammad's own spiritual journey to God on that night he had flown with the *buraq* to Jerusalem. Over the centuries the Sufis refined their mystical experience into programmes of spiritual training and self-development. The first stage in their quest for perfection was *fana'*, or annihilation, the journey into darkness where all ego and consciousness disappear. The seeker finds that loss of self in love of God. With release, progress towards perfection becomes possible. Ritualized practices such as breathing methods, music, dance or even drugs can all help in this spiritual quest. Coffee and qat both first entered culture as chemical prayer-assistants in the ceremonies of Yemeni and Ethiopian Sufis. Al-Junayd, a mystic who had grown up in the rationalist atmosphere of ninth-century Abbasid Baghdad, taught that this reborn perfect human would be in a state identical to that of Adam on the first day of his creation. It was, in a sense, a personal route through the apocalypse to paradise – the very route that Pelagius, Augustine's foe, had unsuccessfully proposed.

Jalal al-Din Rumi was perhaps the most eloquent Sufi master in describing this route to perfection. 'How can I reintegrate you again,' he taught, 'unless you are first disintegrated?' This second stage was the restoration or rebirth, followed by a return to society. The Sufi may retreat to a cave for a while, but the life of the hermit is not the answer: completion only comes with the return to society bathed in love. The spark that lights the way for the seeker could even be the sight of a beautiful woman. For Ibn 'Arabi, an Andalusian mystic, that sufistic moment of annihilation and rebirth would come while circling the Ka'ba in Mecca in 1201.[6] In the crowd was a beautiful young girl, Nizam, in whom the mystic suddenly saw intimations of Sophia, the divine wisdom. He proposed that in each generation there were avatars like her, people who somehow express aspects of God and so create love in our hearts. 'The sight of God in a woman is the most perfect of all,' he wrote.

It was this contemplation of female beauty that provided a ladder to reach to God, and climbing could be blissfully intoxicating. Sufism had further developed the understanding of God in Islam. Grasping the limitations of reason when it came to proving God's existence, they discarded any idea that he might be a facile father-figure. Such a being was all too easily destroyed by rational and intelligent argument. God was pure light, and God was beyond literal explanation. Talking of him was only possible in figurative terms.[7] Figurative language gave them the tool to train their minds: the ego was destroyed, then rebuilt with love. The apocalyptic, applied within the seeker's own cranium, had given them a way forwards to paradise on this earth – a way without violence or cataclysmic destruction. The Oriental mystical traditions, always stronger than in the West, constantly emphasized this idea that growth towards perfection was an internal phenomenon. And if their God had become esoteric, so had their paradise. Ironically for a religion whose holy book gives such clear and detailed visualizations of the blissful place, the Sufis had moved far beyond any literal interpretation, unlike Christianity, where lack of information seems to have stimulated more literal, and literary, speculations – think of the copious utopian literature of the seventeenth century alone.

These later figures – men like Rumi and Ibn 'Arabi – came at the end of a long period, around four centuries, in which the thirst for paradise and perfection among Muslim intellectuals had been prominent. Among those scholars, Pythagorean notions of divine harmony leading to unity with God struck a deep and satisfying chord. This was the bright side of paradise-seeking, blazing forwards in a Golden Age of creative and intellectual energy. Turbaned renaissance men popped up everywhere, from the Hindu Kush to the courtyards of Al-Andalus, all combining talents as mystics, poets, mathematicians, travellers and administrators. These were consciously universal men, aiming at the kind of perfection suggested by the Qur'an and by the life of Muhammad himself.

The notion of the Perfect Man was a powerful force in Islam and while Ibn Sina and the philosophers might theorize about the development of the soul and how one might attain eventual freedom from the body, for most of the population it centred on the very corporeal figure of the leader, the imam or caliph. The Abbasids had emphasized this link between Perfect Man and their own caliphate by claiming divine authority as members of the Prophet's family, and by conduct based on the *sunna* – records of the Prophet's behaviour (hence the Sunni branch of Islam). As in any aristocracy, the genealogy was crucial to establishing a link with a past perfection, and in Islam disputes over those links would be the cause of almost every division. As the Golden Age of the philosophers faded, those divisions grew and in the uncertain times some people turned to the hope of an earthly paradise soon. The return of that Perfect Man as Messiah became more and more eagerly awaited. Islam was about to suffer its first serious bout of apocalyptic millenarianism as paradise-seekers decided to grab their bliss and see the rest destroyed. And at the same time Christendom was preparing its own strike for glory.

The era of the Crusades had begun and Augustine's embargo on searching for paradise on earth was about to be decisively, and irrevocably, blown apart.

PART II

Hastening the Apocalypse: 1000–1500

William Blake, *Death on a Pale Horse*, c.1800

The Afghani farmer leaned on his hoe and with a naked foot casually flicked a clod of earth aside. Water flooded down the runnel and into the crop – a tall and sturdy acre of opium poppies, their deep pink flowers flecked with white. Behind him rose the vast walls of Balkh, a magnificent crumbling pie crust of dried mud, speckled with shards of pottery. I had been walking along the top, admiring the jagged peaks of the Hindu Kush on my left, the green oasis of the city on the right. Beyond the houses, heading north, a flat plain of dusty brown eased itself into an early morning haze, hiding any possible view of the Amu Darya, the Oxus river of legend and also the border of Afghanistan and Uzbekistan. Then I had spotted this farmer, tending his dangerous but very pretty crops, his wife sitting within shouting distance, draped in the voluminous folds of a pale blue *burqa*. I waited for my translator, Ali, a youth from Mazar-i-Sharif, to catch up.

The opium, the farmer said, was not as healthy as it looked, it wouldn't make the finest grade. Did he smoke it? No. People said Iranians liked it, but he personally had never tried the stuff. How did it make them feel? He shrugged. Like they were in *al-jenna*, the Garden of Paradise. No, he couldn't sell me a few kilos, because it was already spoken for. He wouldn't say who by.

'Did you visit the mosque of Haji Piyada?' he asked, changing the subject rather expertly to promote the oldest known mosque in Afghanistan which lay a mile outside the walls.

I nodded. 'It was excellent.'

'The romantic shrine of Rabi'a Balkhi?'

(Romantic = Doomed lover writes last poem in blood from slashed wrists.) I nodded. 'Superb.'

The woman in the *burqa* yelled a suggestion across the heavenly flowers. 'Tell him about Adam's son.'

'Ah yes!' said her husband. 'He was 15 metres tall and lived to be 300 years old. They buried him over there, near the Bala Hisar.'

He pointed north, across town.

In that crooked logic that myths employ, Eden was supposed to have bred huge and immortal inhabitants – all two of them. After the Fall, the lingering aroma of perfection followed Adam and Eve, and traces were passed to their children. But as time and distance from the Garden increased, we humans sank further and further into our current predicament, a kind of de-evolution to being short-lived and stunted.

We like this giant ancestor and his wife. In Hatfield House in Hertfordshire there is a family tree made for Elizabeth I that traces her roots back to Adam and Eve. I've seen similar trees done for the sultans of the Comoros Islands. In India things are slightly different: I once met a former ruler of a princely state in Gujarat who matter-of-factly told me, 'My family tree goes back to the Sun.' Even geneticists cannot escape the lure of single ancestry, hence the 'African Eve' recently discovered as our first mother.

The Afghan farmer was certainly quite attracted by the idea of being 15 metres tall. 'He could walk very far,' he explained. 'Even from Mecca it would take only a week.'

His wife had drifted over and I glanced at the mesh that covered her eyes, but there was no indication of the person behind.[1]

Did she always wear it? They laughed.

'She tried not to once,' the husband explained. 'During the Russian time.'

'It is our custom,' said the disembodied voice. 'Without the *burqa*, women feel...' She paused. Ali translated and waited. The word 'naked' hung in the air unspoken. There was a moment of tension, then the husband cut in. 'They feel something is not right.'

The couple's directions to the grave took us out into the old city, another great circle of pie crust, this time empty. Alexander conquered Balkh in 329 BC and made it his base for two years, but the city was already ancient in those days. Almost every religion known to man has passed through, some leaving no trace. This was why I had come, to see this once great crossroad of faiths. But of the orgiastic pagan rites in honour of Anahita, the water goddess, there is nothing. Of Buddhism there is no more than a strange steep-sided mound where a monastery once held the Buddha's holy tooth and his jewel-encrusted broom. Of the Nestorian Christians who passed en route to Kyrgyzstan and China there is nothing, none of those haunting grave-stones decorated with crosses entwined with lotus flowers and dated from the death of Alexander the Great. No mention of that period of Greek rule under Alexander's successors, or the famous son of this area, a man who would have an enormous influence on subsequent religion: the priest Zoroaster.

We do not know with any precision when Zoroaster lived – experts who have analysed the Avesta holy book have 'pin-pointed' it to between 1400 BC and 1000 BC. Certainly he was a priest and king-maker born in the Balkh region, a prophet who founded a religion that survives to this day. His first vision, we know, came on a riverbank – a favoured location for spiritual flight with its obvious connotations of journeys, change and also ritual bathing and cleanliness.

The faith is dualistic with two evenly matched gods who are locked in combat on earth – Ahura Mazda who is good, and Ahriman, who is not. After death the soul rises towards a Bridge to Paradise and is either met by a beautiful maiden who escorts it across, or by a hideous old hag who grabs tight and plunges over the parapet into hell.

Back on earth, eventually, and with the intercession of a saviour, Ahura Mazda wins the battle of good and evil. Then there will be a Last Judgement before earth is restored to a paradise, *frašegird* (literally, making wonderful), ready for the resurrected souls and bodies of the righteous to inhabit. For the unworthy there is only total annihilation.

Zoroastrianism spread far from its origins, becoming the state religion of the Persian empire and consequently enormously influential. It survives in Iran, but in Balkh, in the hollow bowl where once a great city had been, we found nothing but dust devils. When Genghis Khan arrived in 1220, he erased everything, total destruction. A century or so later, when Ibn Battuta passed through, it was still a ruin.

The shrine to Adam's son was in an area of marshland, a short distance outside the wall. On a low hillock, inside a walled enclosure, was a barrow of earth, 10 metres long, not 15, the grave of the 300-year-old man (though the Bible suggests Adam's sons lived somewhat longer, to around 900 years). A few ragged pennants of green and red flapped in the breeze. There was nothing much to see here. The opium-addled caretaker couldn't recall which one of Adam's sons it was, but as Islamic tradition gives the first father 40,000 sons, even he might have struggled. Balkh was a place of ghosts, a place where meetings and minglings of faith had happened then moved on, heading west – like the opium – to Persia.

Outside the enclosure a band of musicians were lounging in the shade of a mulberry tree smoking hashish. I lingered for a while, watching any hope of an impromptu concert disappear in smoke.

A youth with a pock-marked face and a *rubab*, a small elegant lute, tuned up indolently and spoke to me in English. 'Thank God we can play now – those Taliban! What devils!'

I smiled encouragingly. 'Yes, do play.'

He ignored the hint. 'You know they did bad things here.'

'To you?'

'One day they caught my mother in the street without a male relative. Actually she was standing outside the door of our house. They took her to the stadium in Mazar – you know it?'

I nodded. I had been there the day before, only to be told there was nothing on until next week's camel-wrestling competition.

'They whipped her.'

'For not being dressed correctly?'

'No, she was wearing a *burqa*. It was that she was unaccompanied. They were crazy those Taliban who came here. They killed many people.'

'Why?'

He shrugged. 'The Talibs were not from here.'

'But why do such things – weren't they religious men, always praying and quoting the Qur'an?'

'Yes, they claimed to be religious, but they were crazy. They were not from here, I tell you, they were from Pakistan.'

The other musicians were laughing and he started chatting to them, but I refused to let the question go. 'I don't understand – why do you think they did those bad things?'

He sighed. 'I already told you: they were crazy – you understand? They wanted everything to be pure, but they made life hell.' He might have added, but did not, that the Taliban were modern apocalypticists, attempting to drive humanity through the violent transformation into perfection. They had also got rid of hashish and opium.

Back in the shady square of the town centre, I sat with some students who had come here to escape fighting in their home village.

'Do you know of Rumi?' one asked. 'He was born here.'

The great Sufi master had gone as a boy, fleeing before the oncoming armies of Genghis Khan's Mongols, just as these boys were running from the modern-day warlords. Rumi had ended up in Konya, now in Turkey, where his deliberations into paradise produced his famous poetry collection the Mathnawi. One of the students quoted him.

> Through love the hard stone becomes as soft as butter,
> Through love grief is a joy.
> Through love ghouls turn into angels,
> Through love stings are as honey.
> Through love lions are harmless as mice.[2]

The juxtaposition of Rumi and the Taliban was apposite. Islam has had its own struggles between the two extremes of paradise-seeking: sometimes the ascendancy has been with the lovers of internalized harmony and sometimes it has gone to those who want a violent transformation.

4

Martyrs, Messiahs and Assassins

On the night of Friday, 16 October 1092 a glittering cavalcade was making its way along the road between Isfahan and Baghdad. It carried with it one of the most powerful men in the Islamic empire: Nizam al-Mulk was vizier or prime minister to Sultan Malik Shah, and a ruthless political animal who had risen high in what was essentially a military dictatorship. The heady days of free-thinking philosophers were almost over; instead a climate of suspicion and intrigue prevailed, a time when intellectuals watched their words more carefully. In 1055 the Abbasid caliphate of Baghdad had been overrun by the Saljuq Turks, who kept the caliph on as a puppet.[1] As for the cultured and knowledge-loving regime of his predecessors, it had withered away. 'The Turks as an alien race seeking to rule over an Islamic empire found their greatest source of power in religion,' wrote Iranian historian Ali Dashti. The Sunni orthodoxy was fiercely upheld and smaller sects found themselves victimized and oppressed, setting off waves of resentment. Nizam al-Mulk in particular was hated for his part in this repression.

The caravan had stopped for the night and the vizier, having listened to various petitions, was being carried in his litter towards the comforts of his harem tent. At that moment a man named Bu Tahir Arrani stepped forward from the shadows. He was dressed in the simple garb of a Sufi which must have allayed suspicion, long enough, at least, for him to get within reach of his target. Then from under his woollen robes he produced a knife and, with a single blow to the chest, killed the vizier. The bodyguards, belatedly cutting down the assailant, noted that he made no attempt to escape. In fact he welcomed their blows: they were sending him, he believed, to paradise.

Arrani was a member of a sect known as the Isma'ilis and in Arabic he was termed a *fida'i*, a devotee. (The word finds current use in Iraq for resistance fighters against the Coalition. The standard Wehr-Cowan dictionary gives its meaning as 'one who sacrifices himself'.) In the West he and others like him would come to be known as the Assassins, a fanatical group of suicidal killers who murdered selected targets at the behest of their master, Hasan Sabbah, the Old Man of the Mountains. On hearing of the success of this first mission, Sabbah reputedly declared: 'The killing of this devil is the beginning of bliss.'[2]

In Isfahan at that time, the poet and mathematician Omar Khayyam was someone who might have known the identity of the Old Man. If legend is to be believed, he and Hasan Sabbah had been schoolmates many years before, along with the unfortunate Nizam al-Mulk. Probably an invention of the fifteenth century, the story has a neat poetic validity if nothing else. Nizam is the worldly success, the man who wastes no time on esoteric nonsense, preferring to destroy heretics and get the political house in order; Khayyam is the lover who makes his paradise gently through quatrains of verse and quadratic equations; finally Hasan Sabbah is the apocalypticist, the one who is climbing up to heaven on the corpses of the unworthy.[3]

Sabbah had been born into a Shi'ite family in Persia, but later converted to Isma'ilism and set off for Egypt where the sect were in power. There he began to plot and scheme, eventually returning to his homeland as an undercover missionary before finding a base at Alamut in the inaccessible Elburz mountains that ring the southern shore of the Caspian Sea. This was an area perfectly suited to his task, with mountains rising to over 18,000 feet and steep footpaths known only to locals, the higher slopes home to leopards and eagles. The sole human presence would be semi-nomadic shepherds who bring their flocks up in summer to take advantage of the transient patches of grass strewn with wild crocuses. Alamut is a tiny ruin on a remote rocky crag but when I visited in October 2004 it was being energetically turned into a site of national pride with new road, archaeological digs and accompanying tourist brochures.

Sabbah strengthened the walls at Alamut, planted orchards in the valley below and trained his men. He was ready now, determined to orchestrate a violent campaign of terror against the Saljuq state. His heaven on earth, like that of the ancient Israelites, involved death, revenge and the myth of a Chosen People, the elect, who would be saved. The assassinations were only the beginning, the means of hastening Judgement Day. With Sabbah, Islam had discovered its Judaic heritage of paradise through Armageddon.

Omar Khayyam's life had followed a very different trajectory to that of his old schoolmate, the Assassin leader. This polymath was a man in the Pythagorean mould, preferring to study mathematics and philosophy, often at night, 'when time is asleep'. He produced books on arithmetic and music before he was 25, then moved to Samarkand, over 200 years before Timurlane made it his capital, and there wrote a major work on algebra.

In 1073 Nizam ul-Mulk had come back into Khayyam's life. The vizier was energetically promoting great public works and invited Khayyam to come to the new city of Isfahan to work on an astronomical observatory. He accepted and took up the post that would occupy the next 18 years, calculating, among other things, the exact length of the year to 365.24219858156 days, a figure of astonishing accuracy for the time.

In the Friday Mosque in Isfahan is a marvellous dome whose design he influenced, its interior inscribed with a complex of huge pentagons and its proportions based on the Golden Mean. Like

Pythagoras and the Arab mystical mathematicians before him, Khayyam was searching for that elusive harmony. When algebra could not express it, he turned to poetry, producing elegant verses on the subject of love and longing. He was a seeker, searching within his own heart for paradise and, as a result, finding dividends in literary and creative output.

And yet the life in Isfahan among Nizam ul-Mulk's coterie was not quite as comfortable as it could have been. A climate of growing religious intolerance and a preference for straightforward literal interpretation of the Qur'an forced thinkers to be cautious. With the vizier's assassination, rapidly followed by the death of Sultan Malik Shah, Khayyam had lost his patrons and his comfortable life began to fall apart. In the intensified climate of fear and repression, his liberal views brought criticism from hardliners. He wrote:

> Indeed, the Idols I have loved so long
> Have done my Credit in Men's Eyes much Wrong:
> Have drowned my Honour in a shallow cup,
> And sold my reputation for a Song.

He continued to produce mathematical ideas, some far in advance of his times — one complex theorem on cubic equations would be proved correct 750 years later. But these were not times conducive to lover-poets and mystical mathematicians.

In Europe, at the same time as Sabbah's bloody campaign began, the First Crusade was gathering itself, ready to liberate the Holy Land, fortuitously at a moment when Islam was disunited.[4] It would be the European crusaders, millenarian dreamers themselves, who would assure Hasan Sabbah of his reputation in history as the ultimate evil genius, a maverick who inspired suicidal devotion, supposedly by using drugs. (The Arabic for dope fiends, *hashishīn*, is the most likely source of the word assassin.) Marco Polo would later recount the rumours of how Sabbah had gathered a band of devotees and trained them in political assassination. In order to convince these youths of their reward for martyrdom, Sabbah was said to have built an enclosed and beautiful garden in the castle at Alamut. Running through it were four rivers filled with milk, wine, water and honey, but most alluring of all were the inhabitants, 'damsels, the loveliest in all the world'.

When the agents were ready, they would be drugged, later waking in the idyllic garden with these gorgeous creatures on hand, 'ministering to all their desires'. After a few hours of such sensual delight, the youths would be drugged again and removed. Sabbah would then tell them that this was a glimpse of paradise – if they would only do as he commanded, they could return, and the damsels would be theirs to keep forever. To this day there are groves of cherry and apricots in the valley, but there's barely room for a postage stamp-sized lawn in the ruined fort. It seems likely to me that the entire garden/damsel story was a fabrication based on hearsay about the Qur'anic paradise.

The powerful strain of millenarian belief among the Assassins was not ruled out by the Qur'an, but Islamic theologians agree that Muhammad did not wish to encourage apocalyptic millenarianism, believing that salvation would be achieved by following the tenets of Islam and not scheming to hasten heaven's arrival on earth. Nevertheless, given the right conditions of political repression and hopelessness, it would emerge. Then the ideology of the Perfect Man who will save the faithful would show a darker side: that of Imperfect Men who stand in the way and should be removed, hence Hasan Sabbah's 'bliss' on hearing of Nizam al-Mulk's demise.

The Old Man's sect, now known as Nizaris after another dynastic split in the Isma'ilis, had set up a formidable network. His agents would spend long periods worming their way into positions of trust before the order came to strike. In the households of men who spoke out against the Isma'ilis, servants and bodyguards could suddenly turn on their masters. No one was safe, or trusted. When Sabbah died of

natural causes at Alamut in May 1123, around 50 assassinations had
been recorded in the roll of honour there. After a successor was
appointed, the murders continued.

Meanwhile the last member of the schooldays trio, Omar Khayyam
had moved to Merv, in modern Turkmenistan, and died in obscurity, a
man whose ideals of harmony and bliss were sadly out of step with those
of his age.[5]

Forty years after Hasan Sabbah's death, the guardian of Alamut, also
named Hasan, called an urgent meeting during Ramadan. Emissaries
hurried in from the various strongholds in the Elburz and further afield
to find the castle decorated with flags and Hasan II dressed all in white.
In a solemn ceremony he informed them that the Day of Judgement
had arrived. He himself was the long-awaited resurrected hidden
Imam.[6] All laws were finished. Paradise on Earth was officially
installed. All true believers loyal to the Imam were now in paradise
while all others, the unbelievers, were consigned to eternal damnation
and hellfire.

The celebrations were boisterous. The law was made redundant by
the arrival of perfection: people feasted and played music, wine was
drunk and pork eaten. The rule of praying to Mecca five times a day
was abolished, the requirement to pray at all went with it – everyone
had God inside them all the time so there was no need. In Syria, where
there was another Nizari community, the end of the law was greeted
enthusiastically, if the horrified reports of Sunni historians are to be
credited: 'the people of Jabal al-Summaq gave way to iniquity and
debauchery, and called themselves The Pure,' wrote one observer.
'Men and women mingled in drinking sessions, no man abstained from
his sister or daughter...' Even worse was to come: some of the
women, presumably taking advantage of their menfolk being
otherwise engaged, 'wore men's clothes'.[7]

Allowing for exaggeration, it still seems likely that such an upheaval
did occur. Back in Alamut, most believers accepted the arrival of
heaven, but there were significant abstainers. After 18 months of what

the chronicler Juvayni calls 'shameful errors', Hasan II was fatally stabbed. Eventually the outbreak of licentiousness was brought under control and ended. A new leader wrote to colleagues in Syria demanding they refrain, amongst other things, from drugs. Perhaps it was the secondhand gossip of such events that Marco Polo seized on. He and his ghostwriter picked out the colourful, sensual and exotic components of several stories, ignored any political context and any possibility of metaphor in the language, then created a new fairytale monster: the Assassins. It was a peculiarly 'Eastern' phenomenon — dangerous, possibly depraved and sensual, certainly given to extreme cruelty and fanaticism.

Polo's account was a case of romanticized demonization, and though that may have been due to simple-minded Western prejudice, he was also reproducing Sunni Muslim propaganda. They detested and feared the Assassins, and for good reason. By the 1170s the new force of Saladin, a Kurdish general, had united Sunni Islam and was pushing the crusader kingdoms back out of the Holy Land. His success was as disliked by the Assassins as by the Christians. In early 1175 an Assassin almost made it to the door of Saladin's tent before a guard spotted him. Following this incident Saladin started to wear chain-mail under his clothes.

On the night of 22 May 1176, a second *fida'i* burst into the leader's quarters and stabbed him in the head. The blow hit the chain-mail under Saladin's fez and bounced back. The Assassin lunged at the throat, but once again the blow was foiled by a high collar of mail. Now the leader's shouts roused the guards who rushed in and killed the man. Two further attackers appeared and were killed. Saladin took further precautions, sleeping in a tent surrounded by blazing torches and guards. Ashes were scattered all around to reveal any footprints.

The crusaders were suffering attacks too. In 1152 a gang of Assassins had murdered Raymond II of Tripoli, thus unleashing a massacre of Nizaris by Frankish crusaders, then an invasion of their mountain fortresses by the Knights Templar. Into this maelstrom of seekers after power and paradise, there now came an Englishman seeking both.

5

Crusaders and Last Days

It is of course grossly unfair to call Richard Coeur de Lion, king of England, an Englishman. It's unlikely he spoke the language, he had a French mother, and spent as little time as possible on the island. He did, however, deserve his soubriquet Lionheart. Not only was he courageous in battle, he also had the confidence to believe himself a catalyst in the great game of hastening heaven down on earth.

Having been crowned on 3 September 1189, Richard immediately began scouring the land for crusading funds and, appropriately for an anti-Islamic war, buying up thousands of pigs to feed his men. He even claimed he would sell London if it were possible. After just three months on the throne, he set off on the Third Crusade, pausing to gather his forces at Messina in Sicily.

The campaign had gone reasonably well up to that point, at least by Richard's bullish standards. He had seized the town of a Christian monarch, snubbed the king of France, and almost been killed by Calabrian villagers when he stole a falcon from them. But now he faced the real challenge: the recapture of the Holy City.

This was a major undertaking, a giant step on the road to heaven on earth. Retaking the city was widely seen as an essential prerequisite of the Messiah's return; the other conditions being the conversion of the Jews and defeat of Islam. As the Muslims, under Saladin, had been in control of the city for about three years, Richard's hope was to fulfil two of the three conditions in one decisive action. God ought to be smiling on such a mission, success should be a foregone conclusion.

But there were those who advised caution. Taking their cue from Augustine, they said that mankind could do nothing to speed Christ's return — any attempt to pre-empt divine will was folly. But the Crusades had set aside Augustine's embargo on millenarian impatience — one that had held for over 600 years — and Richard was a man of action. Not for him the dull wait for paradise to be bestowed when he could snatch it for himself.

In Messina word came to Richard of a renowned monk in the Calabrian mountains across the Straits, a man with a great reputation for untangling the intricacies of destiny and the precise moment when paradise on earth might be expected.

The port at that time was filled with rumour and fear. The Apocalypse of St John was a favourite text: the 'Beast who would come from the Sea', once thought to signify Rome, was now widely believed to be the Saracens. Messina was an obvious target of attack. Fuelling the anxieties and speculation were reports that this Calabrian monk, Joachim, had identified the brood of Satan, the names of the seven heads on the ten-horned sea beast that John had seen in his vision on the island of Patmos. Hoping for a prophecy concerning the great venture he had started, Richard arranged to meet the monk.

Joachim was born around 1135 in Calabria and served at the Norman court in Sicily, then went on the pilgrimage to Jerusalem. The Holy Land was in Christian hands, but these were volatile and difficult times for both major monotheisms. Heresy crawled from the cracks in both Christian and Islamic theology: Cathars in France announced that the world was a devil-made pit, while the Isma'ilis in Persia and Syria were declaring paradise arrived. On his return home, Joachim became a hermit, dedicating himself to intensive study of the book of Revelation.

In 1184, his reputation growing, he was commissioned by Pope Lucius III to write down his commentaries on John's vision. He tried to make a start in Fiore, but disciples kept arriving and disturbing him. Eventually he did what all paradise-seekers do: he withdrew to a remote and natural place, for him a Calabrian mountain. He was now totally absorbed in the esoteric significance of numbers within Revelation. Ironically, a few miles away was Croton where Pythagoras had settled and studied numbers, not that his methods or conclusions bore much resemblance to those of Joachim.

When understanding came for the hermit, it was sudden and awesome. He woke on an Easter morning and the scales had fallen away: the hidden meaning of Revelation and all its implications for humanity were laid bare. Calling for scribes, Joachim began to dictate. He saw history as divided into three eras: the time of the Father, the Son and the Holy Spirit. The first era was that of the Old Testament with the tribes of Israel with their 12 patriarchs, it lasted 42 generations and was the germination period of human history.[1] The second era, also 42 generations long, related to the New Testament and the 12 apostles, and was fructification. The third would be associated with 12 great abbots of monasteries, leaders for the era of contemplation when perfection would be finally achieved.

Joachim saw things in pictorial and geometrical terms. He drew diagrams to expound his visions and the numbers and harmonies grew. The three divisions were, Joachim explained, like winter, spring and summer; nettles, roses and lilies; fear, faith and love. The vision grew more complex: add to the initial three the two testaments and you have five – the number of the physical senses, the outer world. Add a further two for the covenants with God and you have seven, the number of prophetic gifts brought by the Holy Spirit, the inner world. Seven is the number of days in Creation, each corresponding to an age on earth. The final third era of history will come only when we reach the end of the sixth age and before that can happen the Beast with Seven Heads must die.

Back in Messina, all this came pouring out for Richard who found it most encouraging. The monk may have shown him one of those diagrams, a parchment on which the seven-headed dragon was vividly enscribed in scarlet. The first head was Herod, the second Nero, the third Muhammad. After that came two figures familiar to Richard, if not so well-known now: Constantius Arianus, son of Constantine and a heretic, then Mesemothus, probably the Berber king Almohad Mahdi Ibn Tumart (d.1130) whose descendants were shortly to halt the Christian advances in Iberia at the battle of Alarcos (1195). Richard was more interested in the sixth monstrous head of Satan: it was his enemy Saladin. If he could just remove that despot's head, Joachim explained, there would only be one more Antichrist to go before paradise. These were indeed the Last Days: with the seven heads destroyed, a millennium of perfection would be inaugurated, then, with a final swipe of its tail, Gog the Beast would be gone and Christ could reign in eternity.

It was thrilling stuff, a vast drama sprawling across a universal stage. Joachim's ambitious assassination plans – just two men between us and paradise – were strangely congruent with Assassin policies. However, since both religions were rooted in apocalyptic Messiah myths, it was, perhaps, not so surprising that revered holy men on both sides should come up with the idea of murdering a way to paradise.

Joachim had shaken history apart and reconstructed it in the light of Revelation. Over a thousand years after John's feverish vision in the lonely cave on Patmos, it had become the lens through which time itself was to be seen. Human history now had three eras, it had shape and form, it had purpose and direction. That trinity of beginning, middle and end was going to dominate ideas of progress, perfection and paradise. Scholars claim to see his influence in the familiar division of time into ancient, medieval and modern. Little wonder that Professor Bernard McGinn of Chicago says: 'Joachim of Fiore is the most important apocalyptic thinker of the whole medieval period, and maybe after the prophet John, the most important apocalyptic thinker in the history of Christianity.' More than that, Joachim had completed the task started by the ancient Israelite prophets, bringing heaven down to earth and making paradise-seeking an earthly pursuit. 'Modern history began with the revolutionary desire to bring in the Kingdom of God,' said Friederich Schlegel, looking back from the 1820s. Robespierre, Karl Marx and Adolf Hitler were all going to owe Joachim a debt one day, but so were the Pilgrim Fathers, the Mormons and many others. What he had done was to finish what John the Divine had begun, placing paradise very firmly at the end of time and in a context that would allow believers forever after to convince themselves that they were part of the Last Days.

As for Richard, he realized that reaching paradise by killing the Muslim Antichrist might take time, but in the meantime an assassination policy could usefully be applied to an unwanted ally. On 28 April 1192 his co-crusader, Conrad of Montferrat, was murdered by assassins, then two days later Conrad's young widow married Richard's friend, Henry of Champagne. Richard's dislike of Conrad had been well-known and rumours spread that he had done a deal with the Old Man of the Mountains, rumours that were reinforced when Henry went to visit the Assassin leader.[2] If such tales are to be believed, it would appear that the Assassins had suffered the same fate as many a violent revolutionary hardcore, drifting from fanatical zealotry into organized crime.

The capture of Jerusalem, however, was not achieved by the English king. Although he had won a great victory, trouncing Saladin at Arsaf, ten miles north of modern Tel Aviv, the advantage was never pressed. With news of trouble back in England, Richard decided to return, setting off in October 1192 on the long journey home. Saladin remained in Cairo, an eminently civilized ruler who kept good relations with other religions: his court physician was Maimonides, the greatest Jewish thinker of the medieval period. According to the Muslim chronicler al-Umari, this courtly monarch had sent his enemy, Richard, peaches, pears and mountain snow when he was sick with fever. And, in a marked contrast to the crusaders who had slaughtered Muslim and Jewish residents when they took Jerusalem in 1099, Saladin had always shown other religions great respect, handing the site of the crucifixion, the Church of the Holy Sepulchre, back to the Christians. The keys were given to a Muslim family with whom they remain – Wajeeh al-Nuseiba being the present incumbent who opens the church to pilgrims every morning.

Richard Lionheart, the 'splendid savage', never returned to the Holy Land, dying at Châlus in France in 1199 and missing out on the Fourth Crusade, announced the previous year by the newly installed Pope Innocent III.

Innocent III was clearly a pontiff determined to create all the right conditions for paradise on earth. One of his first appointees was a papal legate, Rainier da Ponza, who was a disciple of Joachim of Fiore. Then in 1201 the Fourth Crusade got under way with a promise from Rome of eternal life and remission of sins for all involved. This back-fired, however, when the crusaders fell upon Christian Byzantium and looted Constantinople on 13 April 1204. In a drunken frenzy the crusaders defiled everything they could lay their hands on – churches, nuns and works of art. Only the Venetian contingent kept their heads, marching home with piles of treasure, including the four bronze horses that would stand above the door to St Mark's for almost 800 years until the relevant authorities decreed that atmospheric pollution was damaging them and ordered their replacement with fibre-glass replicas.

Five years later Innocent, who had declared himself a being below God but above man, detected a new menace to Christendom. The belief that the material world was a Satanic creation had first surfaced in Persia in the third century AD with the prophet Mani – the man Augustine had followed for a while in his youth. Now this belief reap-peared in south-west France among a group calling themselves the Cathars, 'the pure'. Peaceful and egalitarian by nature, the Cathars believed that perfection in humans was possible via the route of celibacy, austerity, a vegan diet and much contemplation.[3]

For the Cathars heaven was inside the human heart, a personal relationship with God that resulted in perfection. But this was anathema to Innocent: he alone controlled the keys to the Kingdom. Ignoring appeals from Francis of Assisi for a peaceful resolution, he launched a Crusade in 1209, promising the knights involved land and absolution. For a non-violent sect, the Cathars did well to cling on for many years in southern France, but the cost in human life was enormous. At Béziers 20,000 were murdered – 'Kill them all,' the papal emissary, Arnald-Amaury, reputedly said. 'God will know his own.' The pattern was repeated elsewhere: warfare, chroniclers said, had reached new heights of cruelty and barbarity. Armageddon had certainly come to Languedoc. The demise of the Cathars cut a link with Eastern thought and destroyed a peace-loving people. It also made very clear that the Catholic Church was determined to be in control of the roads to paradise.

While the crusaders were busy slaughtering and burning the Cathars, a very different menace was rushing towards Europe. A real Armageddon for all the apocalypticists. It was called Genghis Khan.

On first hearing of this pagan warlord in the east, there had been high hopes in Europe that he could be manipulated into destroying Islam. The Franciscans decided to send an emissary. After their founder's death in 1226, the order had, Houdini-like, quickly released itself from St Francis' doctrine of poverty and love and switched to the other side of paradise-seeking, the belief in a Chosen People finding heaven on earth after Armageddon. One of their friars, William of Rubruck, eventually set out, hoping to convert the Great Khan – by then Genghis's grandson Mongke. It was, you might say, one of the more ambitious diplomatic missions ever undertaken. William did reach the Khan's capital in the Karakorum in 1254 and took part in learned discussions with other religious embassies who had come to convert the Khan: Nestorian Christians, Buddhists and Muslims were all there. In William's own account he acquits himself admirably, but the Khan was unimpressed and sent him home –

paganism was still to his liking, while his real love was conquest and plunder.

During his stay at the Mongol court, William noted the rumours of Assassins in the area, sent from Alamut to murder the Khan. In 1256 the Mongols moved decisively to root out the Nizaris who had dared threaten them, marching to within three days of Alamut. There they paused, probably recognizing the immense task ahead: the Nizaris had many castles, all capable of withstanding long sieges. Resorting to guile, the Mongol leader, Hulegu, tempted the Nizari Imam, Rukn al-Din, out of his Alamut bolthole with sweet words, then loaded him with presents – safety for his family, a princess to marry and 100 she-camels. One by one the fortresses capitulated without a fight, leaving only Alamut. However, after a short siege in early December 1256, even that fastness realized the futility of resistance. In the words of the chronicler, Juvayni, who was with Hulegu's forces: 'all the inmates of that seminary of iniquity and nest of Satan came down with all their goods and belongings.' Three days later the Mongols burned it down.[4]

With resistance finished, Rukn al-Din was superfluous to requirements. He and his family were 'kicked to a pulp and then put to the sword'. All were killed except one small boy, who in legend became the ancestor of the current Nizari Isma'ili leader, the Aga Khan. Islam's biggest and most significant example of millenarian madness was finally over.

Despite the Mongol attack, Alamut residents played a key part in the survival of the rational knowledge and mystical revelations produced by those Muslim renaissance scholar-poets. One man, Nasir al-Din Tusi, a learned and clever young philosopher working within Alamut, managed to switch allegiance and become a trusted confidant of the Mongols. He had been schooled in Nishapur, like Omar Khayyam, and was a brilliant astronomer. Sent by the Mongol leader Hulagu to Marageh (now in Iran near the Turkish border) he devised the most accurate astronomical tables ever made and was integral to the rebirth of knowledge after the devastation.

Tusi's change of allegiance was too clever for some: rumours spread that when the Mongols took Baghdad and captured the Abbasid caliph, it was Tusi who helped solve the problem of how to murder such a noble specimen without spilling his saintly blood – roll him in a carpet and beat it was the answer. Though he had supposedly dropped any previous allegiance to the Isma'ili cause, it's hard not to imagine Tusi deriving a little pleasure from the demise of the Sunni Abbasid caliph, for so long the arch-enemy of the Alamut Assassins.

South of the Elburz mountains, in the long broad valley that links Tehran and Tabriz, stands an immense domed mausoleum, the Soltaniyeh. It was built as a tomb for Oljaitu, one of the early Mongol rulers who had converted to Islam. After the absolute catastrophe of the Mongol invasion – every living creature, cats and dogs included, was slaughtered in some towns – had come a revival. According to Professor Robert Hillenbrand, expert on Islamic art and architecture, this is one of the finest buildings in Asia, but it is scarcely visited by non-Iranians.

When built between 1304 and 1315 it was the highest dome in the world at 174 feet, its size even more impressive for the lack of buildings around it. Recent hypotheses as to the architect of this behemoth suggest it was Rashid al-Din, son of a doctor at Alamut.[5] If correct, it would be fitting to imagine the violent millenarianism of Hasan Sabbah had finally been transmuted into great art and science, the apocalyptic extreme become serene harmony. The construction was famed throughout the Islamic world, reputedly inspiring the Taj Mahal.

Worked into the patterned walls of the tomb's octagonal main hall are glorious extensive proof that all the spiritual harmony and geometric perfection devised since Pythagoras had survived the catastrophe that had engulfed Muslim society. Pentagrams and octagons stretch across the walls with the name of Muhammad and Imam Ali worked into the pattern so cleverly that the calligraphic effect is scarcely visible. Each shape often produces other forms – six-, seven-, eight-, nine- and ten-sided – all integrated with incredible ingenuity and heading back to that essential unity. The geometry is a visual unfolding of the quest for perfection, and in each change and development can be read new levels of spiritual attainment.

The Muslim artists had always looked for that mathematical harmony: $1 + 2 + 3 + 4 + 5 + 6 + 7 = 28$, the number of days in the lunar month and the number of letters in the Arabic alphabet through which God revealed his message in the Qur'an. The wonderful clarity and elegance of line and form in buildings like the Soltaniyeh was also worked into wooden doors in Cairo, the ceramics of Samarkand, carpets from the Caucasus, tiles from Persia and in the hand-written Qur'ans. In some cases they managed to do what was mathematically impossible: resolve all the shapes from three-sided up to ten into a unified single pattern, the artistic equivalent of the alchemy of the soul that the mystics were working towards. This achievement stands, like the tip of an iceberg, on a vast foundation of insight, mathematics, poetry, geometry, astronomy and analytical thought that survived centuries of religious bigotry and schism, survived the loss of libraries and books, survived even the self-inflicted damage of those who would hate their way to heaven.

Soltaniyeh is a ceramic three-dimensional Qur'an, mimicking the book's style of endlessly repeating the same message from new angles, examining the truth from all quarters, building buttresses and columns and arches and domes until the whole single geometric truth is done, a Pythagorean and Islamic marvel. Omar Khayyam had put it into words:

> Ten laws with stages nine and heavens eight,
> with seven planes, six reasons thus relate:
> Five senses, tenets four, triad of soul,
> In pair of worlds have thee as One in state.

There would be later flowerings of Islamic culture, notably in Safavid Persia and Mughal India. There would be other great buildings too, and other Islamic attempts to find perfection. But in many ways the great days of Muslim paradise-seeking were over. In the West Muslim influence on knowledge tended to be downplayed: Islam was sexy, cruel, thrilling, fanatical and many other things too, but it was rarely thought to be learned. Islamic heaven, went the common view, was no better than a brothel run on principles of self-indulgence and sexual gratification. The highly erotic *Arabian Nights* stories would later confirm these long-held opinions. (As with the Qur'anic paradise the original was a good deal less saucy than might be supposed, but European translators made sure their customers would not be disappointed: spicing up the soup with extra helpings of cross-dressing and silky promiscuity.)

When Raphael came to paint his School of Athens on the walls of the papal rooms in the Vatican, he would include only one Muslim in all the worthy philosophers: the Andalucian Ibn Rushd whose influence within Islam was minor.[6] Within 150 years of Oljaitu's tomb being finished, Brunneleschi's dome in Florence had superceded it in stature while the Renaissance rediscovery of the classical world had brought a new dynamism to the search for human perfection. It was in Europe that the race for paradise had started anew and this came at the very time when Islam appeared poised for ascendancy.

On Tuesday, 29 May 1453, the Ottoman sultan, Mehmet II, still only 21 years old, walked into the great cathedral of Saint Sofia in Constantinople and heard the *fatiha*, the declaration of Islam: 'There is no God but God and Muhammad is His messenger...' The vast church with its dome 109 feet across had been built in 537 by one of Byzantium's greatest emperors, Justinian, and his first sight of the finished church had elicited the awestruck response: 'Solomon, I have surpassed thee.' Here had hung part of the True Cross retrieved by

Helena, along with Christ's swaddling clothes and the table of the Last Supper. Regardless of thuggish behaviour by certain crusaders, it had been one of Christendom's holiest sites and even described as the New Jerusalem. Now it was Muslim.

Having said his prayers, Mehmet crossed the courtyard and explored the halls of the Palace of the Emperors founded by Constantine 1,123 years earlier. As he did so, according to the chroniclers, he muttered the lines ascribed to Omar Khayyam:

> The spider weaves the curtains in the palace of the Caesars;
> The owl calls the watches in the towers of Afrasiab.

The Byzantine empire, the great bulwark of Christendom against the Eastern heresies of Islam, had finally fallen. At its best it had been what Robert Byron called 'a triple fusion' — of sturdy Roman body, brilliant Greek mind and mystical Oriental soul. At worst it was despotic and corrupt, staggering through dozens of incompetent emperors, even an empress who declared life unfair because three orifices were insufficient to satisfy a woman (the incomparable Theodora, wife of Justinian).[7] But finally it was reduced to a city state, then a palace, then nothing.

Within two months news of the fall of Byzantium reached the farthest corners of Europe and was everywhere greeted as an unparalleled disaster. The Ottoman sultan was a child-eating monster, a Prince of Satan, a debauched voluptuary and an insatiable sodomite — all these despite the fact that travellers who met him days after the fall found a cultured, sober individual with a keen interest in history. In fact this evil menace would treat non-Muslims with dignity and respect: persecuted Jews from Iberia would flee to what had become Istanbul in their thousands. That did nothing to help the image of Islam in the remaining Western Christian areas. When the Ottomans swiftly added Greece, Albania, the Crimea and other Black Sea territories to their conquests, the fear and loathing only grew.

There would be worse to come for the Christians, and prodded by these anxious times, the millenarian tendency, bubbling away since the Crusades, began to blossom again. If cataclysm and disaster preceded Armageddon and the ultimate restoration of paradise on earth, as prophesied, then the faithful should be ready. Ironically, many Muslims were also convinced that time was due to end, in their case for the simple calendraic reason that they were approaching 1000 Hijra, AD 1592. The fall of what they referred to as *madinat al-kufr*, the City of Unbelievers, was a step closer to the edge.

The anxieties in Christendom triggered by Islamic advances were boosted in the 1490s by the emergence of a horrible new disease. Sufferers were covered in stinking scabs and sores, sometimes they became crazed and their flesh was eaten away. The cause was well-known: 'a fit Sauce for that sweet sin of Letchery', as one unsympathetic observer put it. The affliction spread with terrifying speed through Europe, reaching northern Scotland by 1497. Physicians and herbalists seemed powerless to treat it – even the most exotic and expensive treatments, rhubarb among them, failed miserably. At first it was called the French Pox, except by the French who dubbed it the Neapolitan Pox. It was not until 1531 that the term syphilis was coined. Quite probably it had been brought from the New World by Columbus's men; one tale was that it was the diabolical result of carnal relations between men and llamas.

In Florence a charismatic Dominican friar, Girolamo Savonarola, had begun to preach in San Marco about the End of Time. He received visions and direct messages from God. With the Islamic threat, the syphilis epidemic and finally the French invasion of 1494, his hellfire preaching of the Last Days was terrifyingly convincing. Within three years he was in total control of the city, ordering the infamous 'bonfire of the vanities' when works of invaluable Renaissance art were destroyed. A year later he was discredited and burned too, but the millenarian fears were unstoppable now.

Prophets and prophetesses crowded forward to proclaim that the world was coming to an end and those gifted with 'the spirit' must shoulder responsibility for preparing the earth to become paradise. Part of this, some muttered, would involve annihilation of the godless. In Nuremburg, Andreas Osiander revised and republished parts of Joachim of Fiore's writings. Martin Luther himself, growing up in those times, became convinced these were the Last Days. The Turks, he would later declare, were sent by God to punish the wicked world.

The years at the close of the fifteenth century were filled with forebodings for Europe and Christendom. Only the fact that Armageddon would be followed by the reward of paradise gave any solace to the believers. And yet what of the three conditions widely believed to be necessary for the Kingdom of Heaven to come down to earth? The Jews remained stubbornly unconverted, while the defeat of Islam looked increasingly improbable. The glorious days of the Crusades were long gone and diplomatic missions to far-off pagans like the Mongols had clearly failed. Only in Spain was there much cause for celebration with the reconquest of the Iberian Peninsula well under way. Some optimistic souls hoped that there might come a last great attempt to rid the world of the Muslim menace, but then quite unexpectedly came a staggering new discovery that would profoundly change the direction of paradise-seeking: America.

6

Christopher Columbus Discovers Eden

In July 1498 a Genoese sailor stood on the forecastle of his ship, his eyes reddened and bleeding, and tried to check the reading from his primitive compass. For weeks his fleet of three tiny vessels had been sailing westwards and his close observation of the instrument did not appear to make any sense, the needle unexpectedly swinging through 90 degrees. There were other troubling signs: the air temperature was curiously steady and mild, the Pole Star had changed its course in the heavens, and the sea had filled with curious pine-like branches laden with small fruits. In fact so much of this vegetation had crowded around the fleet that the sailors had panicked, believing they were about to run aground. The admiral checked the compass readings once again and finally came to a bizarre conclusion: 'It was,' he noted later, 'as if the seas sloped upwards.'

This was no ordinary journey: the admiral of the small fleet was Christopher Columbus and this was the third of his four voyages of discovery, an expedition that had ventured far to the south of his previous missions. Confronted by his erratic compass and all the other signs, he would later write to King Ferdinand and Queen Isabella of Spain: 'I have found such great irregularities that I have come to the following conclusions concerning the world: that it is not round as they describe it, but the shape of a pear, which is round everywhere except at the stalk, where it juts out a long way; or that it is like a round ball, on part of which is something like a woman's nipple.' This extraordinary theory was about to have an even more extraordinary corollary: Columbus's discovery of that great earthy teat, a place he was certain must be the Garden of Eden.

Having sailed south-west for around 480 miles from the Cape Verde Islands off Africa's west coast, Columbus was becalmed for over a week in scorching temperatures. When a breeze finally sprang up, he dared not sail farther south, perhaps fearing worse heat, almost certainly afraid of mutiny. Although he was staking his reputation on the view of the Greek scholar Erastothenes that the equatorial zone was habitable by humans, there was a widespread medieval belief, no doubt muttered among the crew, that the 'torrid zone' would burn men alive. Somewhat judiciously then, the admiral turned due west. At midday on Tuesday 31 July the lookout spotted three mountains away to the north-west. Falling to their knees, Columbus and the whole crew recited the '*Salve Regina*' and prayed. There was no doubt that the Lord had saved them with these peaks symbolic of the Holy Trinity. It was duly named Trinidad.

After stopping to take on water, the fleet cruised to the extreme western corner of what proved to be a verdant and fertile island. Here they anchored while Columbus analysed the tricky situation ahead: a six-mile-wide passage between Trinidad and Gracia, the name given to the land they could see to the west. Fierce currents and hazardous reefs made the admiral fearful that they could neither retrace their route nor safely continue. But there was a more urgent danger too. 'Late at night standing on the deck I heard a terrible roar approaching.' Within seconds a terrifying wave 'as high as the ship' came rushing at them. 'Even today I can recall my physical fear that the ship might be swamped when it broke over her,' Columbus wrote.

It must have been a tsunami. No tidal bores are known in that area. But the ships miraculously rode up the massive swell and crashed through the crest, all surviving. The significance of the place seemed all the greater.

Next day the fleet braved the channel and came into a broad calm sea. Columbus ordered water to be drawn up and found it to be sweet and fresh. He was actually approaching the mouth of the Orinoco river, and his expedition had just become the first Europeans to see the mainland of South America — his previous two expeditions having only encountered islands.[1] For Columbus, however, a passing suspicion that this was a new continent — registered in his log a few days later, then subsequently retracted — was swamped by the awesome truth of the moment. The signs were all in place. The massive quantity of fresh water was the final proof. They were approaching the nipple of the earth, the original Garden of Eden: 'these waters may flow from there [Eden] to this place I have reached, and form this lake,' he later wrote. 'All this provides great evidence of the earthly Paradise, because the situation agrees with the beliefs of those holy and wise theologians and all the signs strongly accord with this idea.'

Not for the last time, the New World was mistaken for paradise, but Columbus went further than anyone else — he believed these were the outskirts of the actual Garden of Eden. The ships moved along the coast marvelling at the fertility and beauty of the land. Canoes came out to greet them and Columbus noted the finely proportioned people who wore pearls and gold on their necks and arms. They gave the navigators maize, fruits, drinks and tame parrots. The latter were not new to Columbus, but their presence was significant. The Europeans thought all animals could speak before the Fall: now here they were on the very doorstep of Eden and talking birds appeared. Sadly neither the parrots nor the Indians spoke Chaldean, the language Columbus expected to find in the east and for which he had brought an interpreter.

Sitting in his tiny cabin off the mouth of the river Orinoco, Columbus was convinced that the Bible had been vindicated: he had found the Garden of Eden in the east, just as it claimed. This recognition had surprisingly little to do with his well-thumbed Vulgate Bible. Eden is in the East, it informed him, and is a well-watered place where a river divides into four: Pishon, Gehon, Euphrates and Tigris.[2] (The fact that these four were known to be extremely far apart, possibly hundreds of leagues, was not a problem. There was a rather convenient theory that at some point each of the four great rivers disappeared underground, emerging far from their one true Edenic source.)

Faced with this sketchy information, Columbus was reliant on other sources to fill out the picture. He had certainly read Ovid's *Metamorphoses* with its description of a Golden Age when men lived together peacefully without laws in a perpetually fruitful rural idyll. There were other classical paradise myths too: Arcadia, for example, was a rough-hewn place of innocence and rugged virtue, while Elysium was a more refined type of perfection, a home for the dead on the banks of the Oceanus river. Many features of these classical myths had been incorporated into Christian iconography, often by artists looking for visual representations of religious themes.

On his first voyage Columbus had seen Ovid's words come to life on the coast of Hispaniola (modern Dominica / Haiti): 'The inhabitants of this island, and all the rest I discovered or heard of, go naked, as their mothers bore them, men and women alike.' Not only that, but they had no sense of property, something that amazed the admiral. 'They are so ingenuous and liberal with all their possessions that no one who has not seen them would believe it. If one asks for anything they have they never say no. On the contrary, they offer to share to anyone with demonstrations of heartfelt affection, and they are immediately content with any small thing, valuable or valueless, that is given to them.' No Christian could fail to wonder if this was akin to the poverty of Christ, a notion that had been declared heretical in 1322, or the communistic approach of the early Church.[3]

The evidence available to Columbus was overwhelming. Eden was in the east; it produced prodigious quantities of fresh water, vegetation and fruit; it was warm and talking birds flew out of it; humans living in proximity tended to be happy and forget about private property and clothes. The explorer drew no more fanciful a conclusion than any other man would. In the words of the scholar Valerie Flint, he would have been foolish 'not to have thought of the possible proximity of this Earthly Paradise'.[4]

Having reached such a staggering conclusion, Columbus did not attempt to press on and reach Eden itself, somewhere just beyond the coastal belt. He had read his Bible and knew that the Garden was guarded by cherubim, left there to guarantee its sanctity with a flaming sword: 'no one can enter except by God's leave.' There was also a more pressing and practical reason: the food supplies he was carrying for colonists left during earlier voyages to Hispaniola were starting to rot. Consequently the admiral ordered the ships to sail north, passing through the straits he named the Dragon's Mouth and out into the sea that would be named after the tribe who dominated it, the Caribbean. So it was that Columbus gave up paradise for a cargo of smelly biscuits and a few barrels of Spanish red wine, destined for men who, he was soon to discover, hated him.

The fleet followed the coast west to Margarita Island and then turned north to Hispaniola. It was a tremendous feat of navigation, but it earned no gratitude either from his men or those colonists awaiting supplies. Columbus was hated and resentments were high. They said he was a new Christian, a Jewish *converso*, and a lesser man for his impure blood.

There is no proof of this, but his Genoese origins, commonly cited, are certainly not unassailable fact. He wrote in Castilian, the favoured language of a *converso*, and he salted it with Catalan and Portuguese, not Italian. Curiously the main merchant backers of the voyage were *conversos* themselves – around 70,000 chose to stay and risk the Inquisition. They put up half of the capital for the operation, undoubtedly hoping to gain in return some much needed credit in high places. But one thing more than any other aroused deep feelings against Columbus. He had enticed everyone west with promises of gold, yet no great quantities had been discovered. Disappointment and despair were making men bitter.

Shortly after the fleet's arrival the new governor, Bobadilla, took the astonishing step of arresting Columbus, apparently for financial irregularities. The great admiral, confidant of Queen Isabella and discoverer of Eden, was sent home in chains. This indignity appears to have pushed Columbus further towards religion, and for such a devout man, there could be no obsession greater than the issue of the Messiah's return and the restoration of paradise on earth.

For much of the fifteenth century Christian Spain had been attempting to satisfy the first condition of heaven on earth with a war of conquest against a section of its own population, the Jews. The building of synagogues was banned in 1465, the wearing of identifying clothes ordered in 1476, and the isolation of walled ghettoes begun in 1480, 'where they might live on in their error, and be stung with remorse for it', as the edict stated. Jews were forcibly converted to Christianity, but fear that these *conversos* were secretly practising Judaism led Ferdinand and Isabella to start an 'inquisition' where the converted could have their faith tested. By 1486 around 600 had been burned to death in Seville alone, and thousands had fled. The witch hunt only served to increase fear and intolerance. On 31 March 1492, the same day Columbus agreed the terms of the first voyage with the monarchs, the Jews were ordered to leave Spain within four months. The wording of the document has a familiar ring to it, the sort of weasel words governments still use, as though granting a favour when actually perpetrating an injustice: 'We permit and authorize all Jews and Jewesses to carry all their goods and property out of all our said realms and seignories by sea or by land, provided they consist not of gold or silver or coined money, or other things prohibited by the laws of our realms...'

Some 130,000 left,[5] mostly going to Portugal from where they were expelled in turn four years later, large numbers heading for Istanbul, the newly installed jewel in the crown for the Ottomans. The mass exile of Jews didn't actually satisfy the supposed criterion for heaven creation – conversion – but the Jews had generally proved distressingly intractable on that score and so expulsion would have to suffice.[6]

As far as the second condition went, the defeat of Islam, Ferdinand and Isabella were in the vanguard. A decade before Columbus set out on the first voyage they had announced a Crusade to rid Iberia of Muslims. To pay for this they taxed the Church and also obtained a papal bull giving them the proceeds from the sale of indulgences, the system by which sinners could buy their way into heaven a little more quickly than they deserved. It was from this Islam fighting fund that the other half of Columbus's expenses on the first voyage came. The discovery of the New World, in fact, was financially tied to a grand plan of Christian conquest – 'taking Islam in the rear', as historian Felipe Fernández-Armesto puts it. Columbus, the curious and obsessive mariner who had been hawking his madcap plan around the courts of Europe for eight years prior to 1492, had fortuitously found himself perfectly in tune with Spanish monarchial ambition.

Whatever the mariner's own origins, he was a devout Christian who fervently believed that the millennium, the thousand-year paradise predicted in the book of Revelation, was only a few years away and that his mission was to help achieve that goal. We don't know to what extent millenarian belief swayed him before 1492, but later in the decade he was certainly urging Ferdinand and Isabella to spend any profits from his expeditions on the third condition of heaven-in-waiting, the recapture of Jerusalem.

The monarchs already had the empty title King and Queen of Jerusalem, and there were rumours that Joachim of Fiore, Richard Lionheart's seer in Sicily, had predicted that a Spaniard would rebuild Zion in the Holy City – rumours that may well have started with Columbus. Joachim's apocalyptic view of history, much admired by Columbus, was hugely influential, and by the 1490s expectations of the Last Days were running high. The very term 'Middle Ages', coined in 1469 to describe the previous period, implied that the human drama had now moved decisively into its final cataclysmic act. For Columbus, in the words of historian Richard Kagan, 'his "enterprise of the Indies" heralded... the end of time itself'.[7] Forget about exploration, mapping and the increase of human knowledge, Columbus's objective was nothing less than the restoration of paradise on earth. Unfortunately the failure to discover large quantities of gold or make converts with the prestige of a Great Khan made his ambitions seem foolish. Any prospect of encircling Islam or underwriting the recapture of the Holy City was looking increasingly unlikely. Perhaps, then, there was an element of defensive strategy in his claims about the Garden of Eden: he was certainly a man in need of good news.

Back in Spain after that disastrous third voyage, and having refused to have his chains cut off, Columbus wrote: 'God made me the messenger of the new heaven and the new earth of which he spoke in the Apocalypse of St John.' In Granada from the summer of 1501, he waited for an audience with his royal backers, brooding on matters of paradise and prophecy. Few people had taken much note of his amazing discovery of Eden, and there was no consensus that he had visited the Orient. When he first arrived in Cuba, the Indians had given clear signals that it was an island, but he persisted in claiming it was part of mainland China, even making the crew swear an oath to that effect. With no conclusive proof forthcoming, however, the doubts had surfaced, threatening his position and status. His religious mania increased, leading him to mystical self-examinations. The discovery of Eden was forgotten and he began to think deeply on his new obsession – the paradise to come, the New Jerusalem.

As the months of waiting for a royal audience went by, he started work on his *Book of Prophecies*, a collection of writings concerning 'when the world must end'. He gathered material from the Bible, from theologians and from his own letters, all designed to show that heaven on earth would be here soon. Each day of Creation, Columbus believed, represented a thousand years of earthly life for mankind, hence there would be 6,000 years before heaven arrived on the Sabbath. He calculated there were just 155 years remaining before this great paradisical millennium began, and that the discovery of the Indies was pivotal in hastening its onset. The hero of the story, as far as Christopher Columbus could work out, was none other than Christopher Columbus.

His source for his conclusions, he freely admitted, was the Bible. In the *Book of Prophecies* he recorded candidly: 'I have not availed myself of reason, or of mathematics, or of maps of the world. What mattered was the accomplishment of what Isaiah prophesied.'

When Ferdinand and Isabella did finally grant him an audience, on 17 December 1501, he shuffled in wearing his chains, hoping to pile on the melodrama by handing over his *Book of Prophecies*. But he did not. Perhaps he was wary: once before, the courtiers had laughed when he pressed for a new Crusade on Jerusalem, and already he had the reputation of an old-fashioned crank. It was, in all events, unnecessary, because suddenly he was back in favour again and no extra self-justification was required. A fourth voyage was announced, with Columbus once again in command.

He sailed in March 1502, the *Book of Prophecies* going along too. The admiral, never the most balanced of individuals, was now in a heightened state of religious excitement, spiced up with rampant paranoia about persecutions and plots.

This last expedition proved to be the most arduous yet. Somewhere in the western Caribbean, for a period of 88 days, the fleet was driven by storms, the pumps unable to cope, the men starving and rebellious, the admiral blinded by blood oozing from his eyes, sometimes raging from the mast-top against the heavens, sometimes receiving visions. It was pure madness and Columbus's account is full of wild imagery. Rain deluged down on them, Indians tried to kill them, lascivious enchantresses came aboard to ply the admiral with magic powders. The explorers were lost and beyond any hope of rescue. At night the lightning turned the sea to a boiling cauldron and the crews longed for death.

Eventually they managed to hide their ships up a central American river and then the storm threw up a sand bar and walled them in. Cannibal war parties gathered in the jungle, held back only by their fear of gunfire. (Cannibalism was a recurrent fear in Columbus's writings though there was only hearsay evidence for it.) Gold was collected in large quantities, but fevers and sickness were reducing the crew while the ships rotted under them. After three months they abandoned one of the vessels and forced a way out into the sea, but when all the men went back for water the storm rose up again and trapped them.

Alone on the outside Columbus climbed to the crow's nest, and railed at the heavens, only to hear God chastising him for weakness. Hadn't he delivered the Israelites out of Egypt? The admiral was deep in his own apocalyptic narrative now – wandering like Job in a wilderness of troubles, with only faith to save him. 'Be not afraid, but of good courage,' said God. 'All your afflictions are engraved in letters of marble and there is a purpose behind them all.'[8]

After two failed attempts to escape the coast, they managed to limp across to Jamaica where they landed, unable to continue in such holed and broken vessels. Some of the crew absconded and Columbus despaired: 'May Heaven now have pity on me and earth weep for me...alone in my troubles, sick, in daily expectation of death and surrounded by a million hostile savages full of cruelty.'[9] One of the few men left whom Columbus could trust, a nobleman called Diego Méndez de Salcedo, went on by canoe to Hispaniola to bring help.

Columbus was saved and made it back to Castille, broken in health, still raving against his detractors and persecutors, some imagined and some not. He died in Valladolid on 20 May 1509, steadfastly believing that Cuba was part of Asia, also that he had located the Garden of Eden somewhere to the south of it, and that Christ was coming soon, thanks to his own efforts. His bones – and chains – were initially buried in Valladolid, but soon they were transferred to Seville, then to Santo Domingo in the Caribbean, then to Havana, then finally back to Seville Cathedral.[10]

The curious irony is that in his mistaken discovery of Eden, Columbus did mark a turning point in paradise-seeking. His talk of new crusades to encircle Islam looked increasingly like medieval obsessions, the rantings of an old man from another age. At the Spanish court some mocked him when he asked Ferdinand and Isabella to spend the profits of his voyages on the recapture of Jerusalem. Even in the navigator's lifetime there were those who said the lands in the west were a New World, notably a Florentine clerk named Amerigo Vespucci who had sailed to the Caribbean in 1497 and to Brazil in 1499. Within a year of Columbus's death, it was Amerigo for whom the New World was being named.

The wonderful possibilities of this land of America would draw European minds away from the old struggles between Islam and Christianity (though Hernán Cortés, conqueror of Montezuma's Mexican empire between 1518 and 1521, would always refer to the temples his men looted as 'mosques'). Other explorers appear not to have taken Columbus's claim about the Garden of Eden particularly seriously. No one set sail planning to filch a pound of apples from the Tree of Life. Yet Amerigo Vespucci would use the language of paradise, as would men like Arthur Barlowe and Philip Amadas, the first Englishmen to see North Carolina in 1584: 'We found the people most gentle, loving and faithful, void of all guile and treason and such as live after the manner of the Golden Age...The soil is the most plentiful, sweet, fruitful, and wholesome of all the world.'[11]

These explorers did not claim the New World *was* Eden, only an approximation to something long ago lost, but the focus for paradise-seekers had shifted away from the apocalyptic fever of religious battles in the Holy Land and towards nature and America. Suddenly Jerusalem did not *have* to be recaptured and all its inhabitants put to the sword.

Suddenly God's earth had wider spaces and was filled with novelties and distractions. For Western Europeans paradise-seeking and the search for human perfection were about to accelerate rapidly and in directions that were often totally unexpected.

PART III

New Edens in an Old World: Sixteenth and Seventeenth Centuries

Engraving by Theodore Galle after the drawing, *America* by Johannes Stradanus (Jan Van der Straet) depicting Amerigo Vespucci landing in the New World. Published c.1580.

It was a grey day of low cloud. What I was about to do was, to some extent, dangerous. But at ten years old that was less of a consideration than being caught. New baseball boots helped – the type with rubber soles and a patch to protect the ankle-bone. Grip is very important if you want to climb up to heaven.

The spire of the Mormon church behind our house had fascinated me from the day I first saw it at the age of six. There was a soaring pillar of pale brown brick. Attached to it was a single column of white concrete blocks, about two feet square and recessed on both sides. They gave the effect of a ladder, supported on one side and heading towards the sky. I knew of Jacob's Ladder in the Bible, but I did not know the legend of it rising above the Temple Mount in Jerusalem, the same spot where Muhammad found it in his vision. Nor did I know that, on Judgement Day, some say that everyone will come to that place – specifically the great white rumpled rock that lies under the Dome of the Rock mosque – and be sent up, or down.

The Mormon building intrigued us boys. It had no fence around it, simply a long apron of lawn, and it was built for car convenience. The lawn surrounding it had a ring road and there was dedicated parking that doubled as a basketball court. In 1970 in Nottingham it was both alien and alluring.

The assault on the ladder required some planning. There was a caretaker whose location had to be checked, then there was a tricky plinth of brickwork that was at least eight feet high. I hauled a length of wood up the grassy bank and rested that on the plinth. That was a good start. There was a lightning conductor to wriggle my fingers under and the corner of a low-slung roof gable to press against. After a few false attempts I made it on to the narrow ledge where the concrete ladder began, already panting heavily from the effort required.

I was a good climber. At two my father had rescued me from the roof of the bungalow in Cumbria where we then lived. At seven the Fire Brigade rescued me from a tree. Two years later I was being helped from a vertical rock face by a group of mountaineers who found me on a ledge with a stolen washing line. By ten, however, I could climb a rope dangled from a tree: I was ready for this ultimate challenge.

Within a few blocks I had realized that coming down would present problems. The recesses, intended to give the impression of rungs on a ladder, were cambered slightly to shed rain – and small boys. I struggled upwards, exerting far more effort than I could possibly maintain. Come, the building had said, you too can get to heaven with us. Trespassers will be prosyletized. I was simply taking the offer at face value. I eased up another level. Only the grip on my boots made this possible and I was thinking that tightening my laces had been a very good idea.

I knew very little about heaven, but I did know it was coming soon. Jesus, I'd been told at Christadelphian Sunday School, was about to return to earth where he would establish paradise. The sect had given up on setting exact dates after failures in 1868 and 1910, although my mother said she had once heard a very persuasive lecture on the dangers of 1952. Now the signs were all too clear. The apocalypse was upon us. I quite definitely did not expect the year to end without Jesus Christ putting in an appearance.

My fingers were losing their skin on the rough concrete, but I managed a few more rungs. My cheek was pressed hard on the wall. Now about 30 feet up, I had reached a point where I had to admit defeat. What had looked to be so easy was rapidly becoming a nightmare. I stopped moving just short of the point where the ladder ended and became a simple concrete spike.

Far away, across the rooftops of the houses, green clouds of leaves were billowing in a light breeze. Did I know those woods? They were unfamiliar and yet apparently close. Why had I never found them before? I had climbed all the trees in Willow Wood – and been rescued from one of them – but these trees appeared different, a new and previously unknown playground. There was something heartening in this discovery: my literal-minded climb towards heaven was not a total failure.

I gingerly let one foot slide down to the rung below. The fact that descent was always a greater challenge than ascent occurred to me. Why didn't someone teach you to go down before they taught you how to get up? Why was getting to the top more important than getting to the bottom? My arms were trembling uncontrollably now, from the constant effort of holding on. I began to go faster, knowing that the time left to me on that wall was rapidly diminishing. The concrete scraped my face and I could feel real fear, fluttering like a trapped bird inside me. There was blood on the ends of my fingers. When I felt the ledge with my foot, all my strength disappeared and I jumped backwards, falling in a heap on the ground.

7

New Routes to Paradise: Relics and Indulgences

Entry to paradise has been a vexed question for most of human history, and the distressing silence of the dead on the matter has given prophets and seers an opportunity to guide their people. Following the Babylonian captivity in the sixth century BC, the Jews began to shift from the notion of *sheol*, a place for all Jews after death, to *gan eden,* the gardens of delight, a reward for good behaviour. The Greek Elysian Fields had already become a reward for a good life in the works of Pindar, a poet who produced triumphal odes for tyrants and Greek cities alike in the fifth century BC. With the coming of Christianity, Jesus added some nuances of his own – 'And again I say unto you, It is easier for a camel to go through the eye of a needle, than for a rich man to enter into the Kingdom of God' (Matthew 19:24). This teaching flew in the face of experience from previous centuries: hadn't the wealthy been able to perform better and more perfect sacrifices to please the Deity/deities, thus ensuring their continued success in this life and the next?

One method of procuring divine favour in Christianity was pilgrimage, a method given papal blessing in 1300 when Pope Boniface issued a bull announcing full remission of sins for pilgrims to Rome in a Holy Year. It's called a plenary indulgence and is still used. In such transactions, Thomas Aquinas had said, the moral debt owed by a pilgrim was paid in full from the vast stock of merit accrued by Jesus and the Virgin Mary. Within a hundred years this particular indulgence was on sale for the price of a trip to Rome. A century later armchair pilgrims were saving huge amounts of money – the indulgence costing around one-fifth of the trip. In some senses this was business as usual: after all, a pagan sacrifice to the gods was effectively a payment. The significant development was the involvement of money. Now the securing of a place in paradise had become a commercial transaction like any other. Paradise was a commodity.

Another means to speed one's departure from Purgatory to heaven was to visit a holy relic – a practice thought to have begun in Rome because it slid neatly into pre-Christian ancestor-worship. Viewing, touching and praying to the relics – usually accompanied by a financial donation – would buy time off from punishment.

Frederick the Wise of Wittenberg had his relic collection painted by Lucas Cranach the Elder in 1509 when it numbered over 5,000 pieces, including a thorn from the Crown of Thorns, a twig from the Burning Bush and a crumb from the Last Supper. A decade later the collection had grown to 19,000 items. By visiting particularly powerful relics on the relevant saint's day, and making the relevant donation, devout sinners could save themselves almost 2 million years in Purgatory. Not that everyone was impressed by such claims: Boccaccio had lampooned such superstitions mercilessly in the *Decameron* (1358) with Father Cipolla brandishing a feather from an angel's wing and the finger of the Holy Ghost. Chaucer had his Pardoner cheerily admitting his relics were fakes – the sheep's shoulder bone had not come from Jacob's flock, but it was a great way to drum up cash. Dip it into the soup, he told anxious husbands, and your wife will never stray.

Collectors were undeterred. Not only would ownership have benefits after death, but in this life they could earn a valuable income for the Church from pilgrims. With that at stake, collectors could be quite determined in their mania. The Bishop of Lincoln, on pilgrimage in Europe, bent down to kiss a bone from Mary Magdalene and bit the end off, secreting the precious morsel in his cheek unnoticed. The thirteenth-century saint Elizabeth of Thuringia lost her nipples and hair. In 1554 a Portuguese relic collector took his chance while kissing St Francis Xavier's foot to snaffle a beatific big toe – supposedly the blood still ran although the saint had been dead for two years. A Xavier hand was sent to the Pope, his intestines went to Japan. Public expositions of the embalmed corpse were stopped after another holy toe was harvested.

The profiteering and deceit surrounding the business of such relics were blatant. As Bamber Gascoigne memorably puts it: 'At the height of the Middle Ages there were no less than fifteen foreskins of Jesus being worshipped in various churches around Europe.'[1] There were also sufficient True Crosses to reforest Canaan, but the most important was that of Helena, mother of Constantine. In 327 on a pilgrimage to the Holy Land, the doughty 72-year-old had managed to unearth the Cross close to the site of the crucifixion.[2] When a dying old woman was lowered on to it, she recovered – Carbon-14 dating for the pre-scientific period. The cross was carried off in triumph to Constantinople, where there was already a significant collection of relics. Inside a 100-foot-tall porphyry column brought out of Egypt were kept Noah's Ark-building axe, Mary Magdalene's ointment jar and the leftovers of the loaves with which Christ had fed the multitude. The figure of Apollo placed on top of the column had its haloed head altered to be Constantine's; into his hand was put a sliver of True Cross. The relics had become props in the production of the Perfect Supreme Human.

Three centuries later the Cross was centre-stage once again. Part of it had been kept in the Church of the Holy Sepulchre in Jerusalem and from there it was looted by the Persian general Shahr-Baraz. The Byzantine emperor, Heraclius, went to war to recover it. This action, finally successful in 627, exhausted the two empires and laid the way for the Muslim forces to sweep through Egypt, the Levant and Mesopotamia, capturing Persia 20 years after Muhammad's death.

The new religion soon developed its own interest in relics: Saladin's men took part of the True Cross hostage and when some crusaders were allowed to visit it, their reverence was noted. Hairs from Muhammad's beard became popular – there are about 60 in the Topkapi Palace, along with the Prophet's holy sandals (size 4 or 5 in an English shoe, I'd guess). Among the lesser items there are Abraham's cooking pot, Joseph's turban, the skull and arm of John the Baptist and the stick of Moses – the one used to tap rocks and get water. At the mosque of Mehmed II, built in 1463, there is a tooth of Muhammad kept inside the octagonal pavilion where the Ottoman sultan is buried.

Tombs of prophets and holy leaders were important pilgrimage shrines. At Najaf in Iraq was the last resting place of Muhammad's son-in-law Ali, though another tradition claimed his corpse was loaded on a white she-camel which wandered until it dropped dead in Mazar-i-Sharif, northern Afghanistan. The exquisite mosque of Hazrat Ali now stands on the spot in a grove of white mulberry trees at the centre of town.

While venerated footprints, teeth, hairs, foreskins and so on appear to be more or less common to many religions, the actual sale of forgiveness and consequent entry to paradise seems to have been a Christian phenomenon. You could even get a receipt for your indulgence: several of the earliest printed documents are exactly that. Caxton ran them off by the thousand, the earliest dating to 1476 when he also printed *The Canterbury Tales*. A nadir was reached in 1517 when Johann Tetzel sold indulgences sufficiently powerful, he claimed, to excuse raping the Virgin Mary. There was even a story, repeated in John Osborne's *Luther*, that Tetzel had sold an indulgence for a crime yet to be committed, a sort of futures market in paradise tickets. Appropriately it was Tetzel who was robbed by the purchaser on his way home.

In that same year on the eve of All Saint's, 31 October, a day when relic-worship and profiteering reached an annual frenzy, Martin Luther marched up to Wittenberg Castle Church, home to Frederick the Wise's 19,000 holy relics, and nailed his 95 theses to the door. In terse straightforward language that would become the hallmark of the new way, Luther spelled out his objections, denouncing those who believed 'that so soon as the penny jingles into the money-box, the soul flies out' of Purgatory and that, 'the papal pardons [are] so great that they could absolve a man even if he had committed an impossible sin and violated the Mother of God – this is madness'.

There was no doubt in Luther's mind that 'those preachers of indulgences are in error, who say that by the pope's indulgences a man is freed from every penalty, and saved'.

Luther was chasing away the self-appointed gatekeepers to paradise. He wasn't interested in the sugary sops thrown to the masses: 'be confident of entering into heaven rather through many tribulations, than through the assurance of peace.'

Luther wanted a return to the true values of Christianity: simplicity and faith as opposed to the venal business of trafficking in redemption. Just as modern Islam has a strong Golden Age, yearning for the days of Muhammad and the early imams, Luther and the other reformers yearned for the Golden Age of the early Church and its reliance above all on Scripture. They also wanted a return to the pessimistic view of humanity proposed by Augustine. Christianity, they said, had been polluted by scholars like Erasmus with his view that humans were not completely and utterly worthless, totally corrupted by the Fall. The very notion that such worms could do anything to save themselves was preposterous. Origen had been wrong to suggest that eventually everyone would go to paradise, even the Devil. Mankind was bad and the majority were damned to hell for eternity.

Theologians and historians have generally described this position as 'bleak', something of an understatement, but there were gloomier theologies. The thirteenth-century Cathar heresy, as we've seen, had all Creation, including mankind, made by Satan, while Theodore Beza, Calvin's protégé, would claim mankind were all damned *before* the Fall (making the Good Lord something of a match-fixer.) For Luther,

Calvin and Beza, hope was only to be had in the salvation of God's grace, something over which man had no control – it was bestowed irrespective of an individual's sins or good works. The logical outcome, one that Luther stopped short of, was that some people, the elect, were saved for paradise, most were not. Calvin didn't like speculation on the subject, but let slip that around one in a hundred had a hope. Others said there were a limited number of seats in heaven and most were already taken.[3]

Luther believed that on Judgement Day the earth would be cleansed by fire and then the saved, the saints, would find a renewed Eden, a garden where even 'stinking creatures will be most delightful and have a wonderful fragrance'.[4]

It was not visions such as this that caused controversy, but the Church reforms Luther suggested – remove the Pope, for one – and the way he lived. Undoubtedly one of the most attractive characters of the Reformation, this abrasive German radiated good-hearted humanity, living life at reckless speed – indeed, he did think time was running out and hurried with his translation of the New Testament into German because he wanted as many people as possible to read it before the world ended. He married an ex-nun, had six children and took in four orphans. Rome hated this 'child of Satan'. A ferocious storm of abuse and hatred came raining down on the German, often from quarters Luther had thought might be sympathetic. King Henry VIII wrote a diatribe against the reformer, or at least tried to – he couldn't maintain concentration and had to ask Sir Thomas More to finish it. The learned More appeared to be just the right kind of eminent intellectual who might debate and discuss with Luther. In fact the author of *Utopia*, the gently amusing satire on perfectionist aspiration, when faced with Luther's assertions, became a foul-mouthed bigot whose written riposte is smeared with references to faeces, rectums and sex with nuns. But then More had done well from the Catholic empire, and whatever else Luther was doing, he was certainly threatening that hierarchy of knowledge and patronage.

Elsewhere, however, the reformist message was received more favourably. Albrecht Dürer became a fervent admirer of Luther after a spiritual crisis in 1519. His 'Four Apostles', presented to the city council at Nuremberg, shows Saints Paul, John, Mark and Peter in simple robes and posed without the usual haloes. Each was intended to represent one of the four humours – sanguine, choleric, melancholic and phlegmatic – which were believed to relate to the four elements, the basis of Creation (and the number that was the Pythagorean basis of universal harmony). The painting also symbolized the new reformed Church: balanced, just and egalitarian.

For Dürer it was the culmination of a lifetime searching for harmony and proportion. He had started by experimenting with simple grids through which he depicted a scene on to paper, then he had tried five-fold symmetry, nine- and ten-sided figures, then semi-regular nets, constantly striving for that mathematical solution to artistic representation. But in the end, he decided, a true and final perfection was impossible without that dark spark of revelation and chaos. He dropped calculation and used freehand 'tracery patterns'.

In 1504 he had unveiled a masterpiece, the etching of Adam and Eve in the Garden of Eden, showing the original couple standing in front of the tree of life. A parrot eyes a bunch of grapes behind Adam's head, the bird and the fruit both symbolic of Eden. At the couple's feet a mouse sits quietly with a cat. All the animals are instantly recognizable as Dürer creations: inside the graceful Renaissance beauty lurks an unsettling Gothic beast. His abilities are best seen in Adam and Eve: the couple seem to leap from the page, pulsing with life and energy. Jan van Eyck had painted Adam and Eve 72 years earlier in his altarpiece for Ghent Cathedral, but his orig-inals look soft and pliable, a hippy couple who have lost their tent at a rock festival. Dürer's manage to appear strong and capable in their garden, ready for anything, as if they might just throw caution to the winds, strangle that serpent and keep the apple. Here were an original couple who seem to know that paradise without knowledge is not really paradise at all, an optimistic Adam and Eve who were ready to reach out and grab the possibilities of a new age and make a paradise of their own.

8

The Collectors

If the sheer volatility of those times was sufficient to suggest to many that the Last Days had arrived, there were others who responded differently. The idea of a scientific botanical garden, like many great ideas, seems to have occurred to a large number of people at the same time in the late 1530s and early 1540s. But it was Padua that first took action. On the instigation of a Venetian nobleman, Daniele Barbaro, a group of local men signed an agreement to collect all the useful medicinal plants in one place for the purposes of identification and education. They set aside a circle of land, placed a fountain in the centre with four paths radiating out towards the cardinal points. No doubt they were aware of the symbolism of that choice: the four corners of the earth, the four humours and elements, the central water source, as in Eden. Within the quadrants, small stone-rimmed patches of earth were laid out in neat geometric patterns. The hope was to plant specimens of similar character in adjacent plots.

Previously herbalism had been largely in the hands of monks, but knowledge was now moving inexorably out into society to a new breed of interested parties. The world of healthcare and medicine, so basic to human happiness and contentment, was loosening its ties with religion and religious scholars. Where previously the monastic garden had been the source of material for herbalists and the reservoir of knowledge, at Padua this link was breaking down. In fact the baton of knowledge was passed in a very literal way: Benedictine monks gave the *orto botanico* some of its earliest specimens, including aloe veras from Mexico. From now the search for that essential element of any paradise on earth – good health – would fall increasingly into the hands of secular scholars.

At Padua they put a high wall around their garden and steadfastly began collecting. One can only marvel at their optimism: it takes about ninety seconds to stroll across their garden – the space available can hold only a tiny fraction of the world's useful plants. The classification, too, is naïve, positively archaic. And yet the garden is miraculous. A bold attempt at paradise-building: all the world's medicinal plants in one new Eden, a perfect collection tilting at the ambitious goal of perfect health and a solution to all medical problems. At Padua a modern age of paradise-seeking stepped from the shadows of Christianity and its earlier impossible ideals of eradicating Islam and converting the Jews.

Much of the new interest in collecting was inspired by all the novelties that began appearing, many of them botanical. The first European potatoes were grown at Padua, alongside the first lilacs and sunflowers.[1] Following Columbus's discoveries and those of Diaz and da Gama to the east, a golden age of exploration had begun and a huge variety of new plants, animals, minerals, exotica, even humans, came flooding into Europe. For a time there was concern that these new discoveries, unmentioned by the Bible, threatened its authority (a concern so grave that biblical scholar Benito Montano simply added an appendix to his Bible giving the 'original' Hebrew place names of New World locations. In the nineteenth century the Mormons picked up the idea, claiming that the American Indians were a lost tribe of Israel.) Such objections, however, were soon brushed aside in the stampede to explore and discover yet more.

In Munich Samuel Quiccheberg (1529–65), artistic consultant to Duke Albrecht V, a staunch Catholic, wrote the manifesto for the new collectors, declaring that each cabinet of 'curiosities', the *kunstkammer*, was a microcosm of God's Universe and a means to gain universal knowledge.[2] He suggested a division into man-made artificialia and natural objects, a classification system which was readily adopted. Things which crossed the divide, however, were especially prized: giant nautulus shells perched on gilded snails and being ridden by the carved figures of naked Moors, coconuts inscribed with biblical scenes, ostrich eggs made into ornate drinks' containers – the interest in transformations was stimulated by a book that had influenced Columbus, Ovid's *Metamorphoses*.

In some senses this activity marked a change to a symbolic approach to paradise and the start of secularization, but at the time collectors were very aware of the message in Genesis: 'Behold, I have given you every herb bearing seed, which is upon the face of all the earth, and every tree, in which is the fruit of a tree yielding seed; to you it shall be for meat.' And again: 'And out of the ground the Lord God formed every beast of the field, and every fowl of the air; and brought them unto Adam to see what he would call them…'[3]

For these collectors, gathering God's Creation and naming it was a literal attempt to recreate Eden, not just symbolic. Collecting and cataloguing were steps to regaining paradise through universal knowledge.[4]

There were other religious overtones that had deeper roots. The purchase of an indulgence had been a way for the wealthy to convert excess riches into spiritual credit. Clearly a collector who gathered the best examples of certain types, then removed them from any normal function and placed them in a special place, believing that God would approve of this, might derive similar spiritual satisfactions. Psychologically, collecting fulfilled that need to make a sacrifice and claim a ticket to paradise.

If this new collecting was scarcely more free of religious motivation than relic-hoarding, and still inextricably linked to paradise-seeking, it did at least have the intention of ordering and cataloguing, a major factor in the coming Enlightenment and scientific revolution.

Francis Bacon stated the practical objectives for gentlemen of means in 1595 when he exhorted them to gather around themselves:

a most perfect and general library ... a spacious, wonderful garden, wherein whatsoever plant the sun of divers climate, or the earth out of divers moulds, either wild or by the culture of man brought forth ... this garden to be built about with rooms to stable in all rare beasts and to cage in all rare birds; with two lakes adjoining, the one of fresh water the other of salt, for like variety of fishes. And so you may have in small compass a model of the universal nature made private. The third, a goodly, huge cabinet, wherein whatsoever the hand of man by exquisite art or engine has made rare in stuff, form or motion; whatsoever singularity, chance, and the shuffle of things hath produced; whatsoever Nature has wrought in things that want life and may be kept; shall be sorted and included. The fourth such a still-house, so furnished with mills, instruments, furnaces, and vessels as may be a palace fit for a philosopher's stone.[5]

If the old collecting of relics had related to a paradise in the next life, Bacon made clear that the new craze had more to do with perfection in this life and on this earth. A site such as Padua's *orto botanico* was certainly an attempt at a 'model of the universal nature', and in wrestling a new and ordered paradise from the myriad of new specimens, knowledge of the earth would be increased. This was a road to paradise, not the place itself, and presumably most thought that the final step would only be taken with Armageddon. But now there was optimism and hope: mankind would take control, have dominion, as Genesis promised Adam, and work its way gently forwards to a new Eden.

South Lambeth Road is not the most memorable of London streets. It starts near the MI6 building and heads south-west parallel to the river through a mish-mash of buildings. After a small park on the left and a dog-leg, it straightens up by the Victorian red-brick library. The shops and cafés on the left have Portuguese signs, the adverts in the Asian corner shop are in Spanish and Portuguese. Stand there by the library's battered doors and face east, towards the Café de Estrela. You are looking at paradise, or at least a brave attempt at it.

Not literally, of course. The coffee is good, but not that good, and the three-storey London terraces that occupy the residential streets behind may be fine examples of the type, though scuffed by the traffic at this end, but they hardly meet the exacting standards of perfection. This bold stab at paradise is one of those that has been lost.

The streets off South Lambeth Road were not built until the second half of the nineteenth century. In 1899 Walter Besant could recall an area 'wonderful for its loveliness', where wild heathlands were separated by gardens and orchards. Further back in time, a map of 1681 shows countryside divided into small fields and little in the way of housing. Several parcels of land are marked as the property of one Elias Ashmole, the same who would later give his name to the Ashmolean Museum and a man who will reappear in this tale.

At the outset of the seventeenth century, this rural area began to gather some interesting new residents. Simon Forman, astrologer, was one, Francis Moore, alchemist and the originator of *Moore's Almanac*, was another. With the river between it and the city authorities, Lambeth appears to have drawn eccentrics and foreigners from the start, not always reputable ones either. Guy Fawkes stored his gunpowder in a Lambeth house in 1605 and some years earlier one Richard Roose, a cook, had fiendishly poisoned 19 people. Somewhat appropriately his sentence was to be 'boiled in oil'.

This was the darker side; for most Lambeth was a place for simple pleasures. Samuel Pepys was typical: he and his family enjoying a boat ride, then a stroll before stopping by an inn and tucking into powdered beef, cakes and ale. In Pepys' lifetime there would be a spa and pleasure gardens (Canaletto painted them in 1751), but in the 1630s the main attraction was a curious exhibition. It had opened up in one of the houses, and quickly developed a reputation that drew in those with an interest in the wondrous wide world beyond England's shores. Billed

as the Ark, it was the cabinet of curiosities put together by John
Tradescant and son, the foremost gardeners, plant-hunters, and
collectors of rarities in England. Their vast and varied compilation of
oddities, wonders and curios was becoming known as the best in the
country, partly through Tradescant's innumerable aristocratic contacts
who had contributed many of the items. This was where Samuel
Quiccheberg's injunction to collect a new universe was at its apogee.
Tradescant had an Eden in his drawing room, and another in the
garden.

Visitors started arriving soon after the Tradescants moved here in
1629. Two sons of the Earl of Salisbury came upriver, spending nine
shillings 'going by water and for seeing John Tradeskin's antiquities'.
Poets mentioned it and foreigners were soon treating it as an essential
part of their tour.

In 1634 a group of three men came up the river hoping to see the
Ark. Thomas Barlowe had recently returned from the east, having
sailed to Persia, Surat and Sumatra. His friend was Peter Mundy, a man
who had completed several voyages east, travelling through central
India with trade caravans and once returning overland from
Constantinople. Two years earlier he had visited Akbar's tomb near
Agra and written a description of that Islamic paradise garden. He had
also seen the Taj Mahal in its early stages of construction.

Mundy was wealthy, having just closed his accounts with the East
India Company, but he was not about to settle down to the usual
country estate of the returned nabob. His appetite for adventure
undimmed, he had arranged a passage to China with a new venture
called the Courteen Association, an enterprise that had the backing of
several experienced merchants and sea captains, plus that of the king.
(Charles I had promised them £10,000, but they would never get a
penny of it.)

The identity of the third individual is not recorded, but we can
imagine it was someone equally well travelled, perhaps another
hopeful adventurer awaiting the Courteen fleet's departure. Its

commander, Captain John Weddell, was certainly known to Mundy, Barlowe and Tradescant.[6]

The group were passing time, seeing the sights. They went to the Tower to examine 'a Unicorne's horne, about 1½ yards in length'. The existence of these fabulous Eden residents was not as widely accepted as it had been in medieval times, but there was still great interest. Two thousand years after he had written the first description of it, Ktesias, physician to the Persian kings, would have been pleased to see his fanciful beast still running. Mundy was wise enough, however, to suggest in his journal that the exhibit could be from a sea creature. (It was a narwhal tusk.)

In what was fast becoming a London tradition the three men hired a boat to take them up to Lambeth for viewing the Ark. The river was an essential part of the show: marvellous, but unpredictable, entertainment. The watermen were a notoriously riotous bunch, brawling with each other and their fares, hurling abuse across the water and generally behaving scandalously. People loved it. 'The conversations you hear are most entertaining,' wrote César de Saussure, a Swiss traveller who visited at the close of the century, 'for I must tell you it is the custom for anyone on the water to call out whatever he pleases to other occupants of boats, even were it to the King himself, and no one has a right to be shocked.'

A couple of miles upriver from London Bridge, with its grisly display of criminals' heads on poles, they disembarked at Faux Hall (now Vauxhall) and took the track south-west along the hedgerows, passing the grand house of the recently deceased Dutch ambassador, Noel de Caron. The neighbouring property was much less splendid, but it was the place they had come to see.

At its heart John Tradescant's home was a simple sixteenth-century farmhouse, and yet visitors would see that large sums of money had recently been spent improving and extending, expelling all traces of the dark and dusky vernacular. A new brick wing and some fashionably tall chimneys had been added, plus four bays of Venetian glass at the front. Glass was all the rage: light pouring into rooms through handsome windows framed with harmonious pilasters and pediments, illuminating all the new fancy goods that trade was bringing.

Over the Tradescants' garden wall were glimpses of trees, and not the common English varieties but unusual species gathered from Europe, the Levant, North Africa and the Americas. The latter region would be well represented when John's son started visiting Virginia, but for now specimens came from friends, men such as Captain John Smith, the colourful adventurer who had gone out to the Virginia Colony in 1606 and been twice saved from death by the Indian princess Pocohontas. Her father's cloak would find its way into the Ark (and is still there).

The three men passed through the gates, formed from two whale ribs arched over, and into the garden. Mundy mentions it only briefly, 'a little garden with divers outlandish herbes and flowers, whereof some that I had not seene elsewhere but in India, being supplyed by Noblemen, gentlemen, Sea Commaunders, etts'. In Tradescant's own list published in 1634, he catalogues around 750 plants to be found in his garden, plus around 169 fruit varieties, including 48 apples.

Mundy and his friends were more interested in the contents of the room where the Ark was kept. Here John Tradescant the Elder had amassed a collection of objects that would excite the curiosity of even the most experienced traveller. Mundy mentions a cherry stone carved with 80 faces and 'pictures to bee seene by a Celinder which otherwise appeare like confused blotts'.[7] There was much more besides: 'A natural Dragon, above two inches long', 'Boots from Babylonians', 'Edward the Confessors knit gloves', 'Birds of Paradise...some with, some without legges', 'A bundle of Tobacco, *Amazonian*'.

The shelves and drawers, arranged very much as if in an apothecary's shop, were packed with vast numbers of natural and man-made objects. The larger pieces were probably hung from the ceiling – some that survive in Oxford's Ashmolean Museum still have the relevant holes. Georg Christoph Stirn, a German student, who visited in the summer of 1638 lists what caught his eye in a crazy, haphazard tumble of colour and variety:

> a picture wrought in feathers, a small piece of wood from the cross of Christ, pictures in perspective of Henry IV and Louis XIII of France…a sea parrot, a toad-fish, an elk's hoof with three claws, a bat as large as a pigeon, a human bone weighing 42 pounds, Indian arrows, an elephant's head, a tiger's head…the robe of the king of Virginia, a few goblets of agate, a girdle such as the Turks wear in Jerusalem, the passion of Christ carved very daintily on a plum-stone.

That fragment of the True Cross is a telling piece: the timber that had exhausted the efforts of Byzantium and Persia, killed thousands in its wake, been dragged by the Emperor Heraclius himself along Jerusalem's *Via Dolorosa*, and no doubt convinced many a believer that a brief contact had hastened entry to everlasting bliss, was now tossed in between two pictures, a sign of how much had changed.

Stirn's list is valuable, and no doubt the chaotic jumble is what he saw, but the fact is that the Ark possessed the beginnings of order, a classification of plants, animals and human industry that would grow and develop into the systems that scientists, librarians and curators recognize today.

Mundy makes no mention in his journal of meeting Tradescant the Elder that morning, but none of the few contemporary accounts speak of being shown around by the owner. There were, in any case, several servants. Captain John Weddell would have warranted different treatment. He was a celebrity, having assisted in the storming of Hormuz in the mouth of the Persian Gulf, and we know that he gave items to the Ark because he appears among the benefactors in a 1656 list. His maverick personality and enquiring mind must have appealed to Tradescant, the man who was interested in everything. The captain had brought all sorts of curiosities back from his four long voyages to the east, once even importing a group of wide-eyed Madagascans for whom he wrote the first English-Malagasy dictionary. A surviving cargo manifest of his reads like a paradise packing list, a glimpse into the exotic lost world of those times when so much was new and astonishing: 'narrow baftas, 5000 corge, broad baftas, dutties Dulka, seriahs, necanees, dimitties, quesos cullered, thred tapseels, semianos, chuckree (rolls of four), callicoe lawnes, amber-trees, indigo bales, gum-lac, aloes socotrina, preserved ginger, quilts of cuttany, bloodstones in baskets, Lahore carpets, pepper.'

Weddell may well have provided a prize rarity, the 'dodar', as he had stopped in Mauritius in June 1630. Certainly, he would have mentioned it to Tradescant as something lacking in the Ark. The dodo was eminently suitable for an Edenic collection: its lack of fear and gentle nature had suggested to many visitors a beast before the Fall, a lost denizen of paradise. Sadly the same characteristics also suggested lunch – the birds' amiable sloth made them an easy target for hungry sailors.[8]

By 1681 the dodo was extinct, but the Tradescant exhibit would ensure a literary afterlife: in the nineteenth century the remains of the Ark were in Oxford and Charles Dodgson, a stuttering maths professor, became fascinated by the bird, presumably because of the Do-do-do-dodgson connection. Whatever the reason, it became a character in the tales he told Alice Liddell, later to be published under the pseudonym Lewis Carroll.[9]

It is significant that Tradescant termed his collection the Ark. It was intended to be comprehensive and intended to preserve. The desire was to make whole and complete, also to show the breadth and variety of God's Creation.

Tradescant was far from being alone in his inspired collecting endeavours: Ole Worm had started a significant collection in Copenhagen, Morin had one in Paris, Rembrandt gathered exotica in Amsterdam, Abraham Ortelius, the Antwerp cartographer, had a *kunstkammer* containing a tortoise shell large enough for ten men to dine around it. Jan Brueghel the Elder painted the cabinets; every inquisitive soul in Europe was doing it, every nobleman, every sea captain and merchant, they were all busy collecting. And Tradescant had an army of admirers and well-placed benefactors to help, a list that reads like the cast of a Ben Jonson comedy: Mr Gasper Calthoofe, Rowland Bucket, Mr Stone, Messers Green, Brown, and White, Mr Gage, Mr Pette and Doctor Bugg, Sir Clipsby Crew, Sir Dudley Diggs, Sir Butts Bacon and Mr Woolfe, plus the king, a charm of courtiers, a fleet of sea captains and a packet of merchants.

Peter Mundy and party, well travelled as they were, found themselves entranced. The day slipped away in examining specimens. Their concentration itself is a marvel to us who are so accustomed to museums and displays of staggering variety. Mundy declared that there was not sufficient time to do it justice. His account shows how quickly the collecting mania had become part of a new order that united such disparate professions as sea captain and gardener. A new aristocracy of knowledge was emerging and with it came change: all these new and wonderful things would forever alter ideas of perfection and of paradise.[10]

Tradescant's origins are obscure, but what we know for certain is that on 1 January 1610 he joined the staff of Robert Cecil, first Earl Salisbury, at Hatfield House in Hertfordshire. His wages were £50 a year, a very handsome figure for a gardener.

This was a superb opportunity. Like his father before him, Robert Cecil was immensely powerful and influential, a scheming fixer skilled in negotiations, politicking and duplicity. His hunched back had earned him the nick-name 'Pygmy' from James I, but Cecil was a giant when it came to self-advancement and enrichment. When he concluded the treaty to end England's war with Spain in 1604, he emerged with a fine pension paid by Spain.

At the time of the accession of James I, Cecil's family seat was Theobalds (pronounced 'tibbalds'), a colourful and ostentatious extravagance that would make any modern oil-soaked sheikh proud. It had a hall ceiling painted with the signs of the Zodiac across which a mechanical sun moved during the day, while at night the stars came out. On each side were six artificial trees so cunningly life-like that birds were known to fly in the open windows, perch there and sing. There were galleries filled with portraits of every notable the world had ever seen and a vast mural map of England.

Cecil's life was a microcosm of the possibilities that the new age held. He loved curiosities and exotica, avidly gathering strange objects from all over the globe, including a parrot who dined at table with the guests. Plants and gardens were another of the man's passions, as Tradescant would discover. For James, coming from the impecunious Scottish court, Cecil's house, gardens and their contents were a miracle, a symbol of all the wonderful excess and gilded magnificence that his new kingdom offered. He decided to have it.

The Pygmy agreed. He didn't have much choice and there were compensations, including the old hall at Hatfield where Elizabeth I had once lived, virtually as a prisoner, until news of her accession was brought. Cecil decided to build a new house, the most magnificent in England, and he required gardens to match.

Many elements of the house remind the modern visitor of the Jacobean interest in the original Garden of Eden. At the library door is the parchment roll as long as a cricket pitch that details Elizabeth I's pedigree back through William of Normandy to Adam and Eve. In the winter dining room next door, a bedchamber in Robert Cecil's day, is a 1543 copy of Albrecht Dürer's 'Adam and Eve' by Martin Coffermans, a pupil of Dürer. Perhaps most striking though are the carved hermaphrodites holding up the gallery in the great hall: winged, bearded and with breasts, they were to be found in many Jacobean houses, looking strangely akin to the magical *buraq* that carried Muhammad on his visionary journey to Jerusalem. This was an age, like that of Muhammad in Mecca, when a fascination with dualities and unification engaged many minds.

Cecil was fated not to live much longer, but he had set Tradescant on a course that would occupy almost three decades. On the first of many overseas journeys, he plundered the nurseries of the Low Countries for fruit trees – cherries, quinces, medlars, apples and pears. Several were species new to England, including the Archduke variety of cherry which remains available today. He bought tulip bulbs and lime trees by the hundreds, gilliflowers (carnations), roses, anemones, mulberries, red currants, and two arborvita trees, a species introduced from Canada probably from Jacques Cartier's voyages of 1534–42. In Brussels he discovered more flowers new to England: the Anemone hepatica, the Martygon pompom and two irises. In Paris were orange trees, figs, myrtles and a pomegranate.

After Cecil's death in 1612 Tradescant found new patrons and continued the astonishing flood of imports, all the time augmenting the Ark too. Off Archangel on a Russian expedition he found the Muscovie rose and, some say, the European larch. Into his sea chest went a snake's skin, a Russian vest, various boots and stockings, plus 'shooes to walk on Snow without sinking'. A voyage to North Africa netted him the wild pomegranate tree, 'Argier apricocks', also new kinds of rock rose. Perhaps it was on this journey that he gathered the Cos lettuce for which he is often credited.

Sir Humphrey Slaney, a Guinea Company merchant, sent him the Smoke Tree or Venetian Sumach – a very popular British garden variety now – and Asian plane trees, the same species that provided shade in the Afghan gardens so beloved of the Mughal emperor Babur.[11]

Some specimens were undoubtedly already found in Britain, others not. Familiar plants such as the strawberry tree, Pyracantha and Virginia creeper all probably came to us via Tradescant and his son, also named John. In other cases Tradescant was the man who first managed to derive seed from plants brought back by others – his extraordinary abilities in the garden were famous – and so made him instrumental in propagating and spreading species.

Having solved the problem of getting new specimens more successfully than any previous plant-hunter, Tradescant faced the vast labour of naming them correctly, as Adam had supposedly done in Eden.

The sheer quantity of types and varieties flooding into Tradescant's hands must have seemed overwhelming at times. In 1629 his friend John Parkinson mentioned that he had 20 sorts of vine, 'that hee never knew how or by what name to call them'. Early herbals had made do with common names, but this could not suffice. Tradescant used two-word Latin names, but so many introductions were coming that names often had to be changed. The common garden plant Dame's Violet went through 13 names before 1753.

This vast task required more than just names, of course, but a classification system that was scientific and usable. In this Tradescant would not be the man to finally achieve what Adam had managed. Carl Linnaeus, the Swedish naturalist, would set the pattern in 1753 with a binomial system that Erasmus Darwin, Charles's father, would popularize in his *Love of the Plants* (1789). The system, modified and extended, is still in use today. But essentially the naming continues: new species are discovered still, and others have to be reclassified. The building of Eden through naming of parts would prove far more monumental a task than anyone could have imagined in 1600.

Tradescant's patrons may not have cared particularly what things were called, only that they had them first. There would have been much satisfaction, no doubt, in bestowing gifts of previously unknown species on your friends and connections. For Tradescant there were networking benefits too, but he seems to have been particularly zealous in distributing seeds, cuttings and specimens. They poured out into the wider community, working a revolution in the contents of English gardens. John Tradescant had become the first man to travel overseas specifically to seek useful and beautiful plants in large quantities, then bring them back, plant them and propagate them himself. This was entirely different to previous venturers who had happened upon new species and chosen occasional specimens to take back home, or to herbalists who had built impressive gardens with specimens sent to them. Tradescant gathered all kinds of plants, from tiny and innocuous (ironically his name is best known for being attached to one of the most forgettable, tradescantia) to the large and imposing.

The effects were remarkable: gardens, agriculture and diet were being radically changed. This revolution came at a time when the Protestant faith was looking to transform the moral landscape too, and in the new plants some would see the germ of an idea: the greening of England and a new Eden to match the new humans who deserved to live in it. Plants would bloom where none had before. Nothing was deemed impossible, the welcome weed of optimism raced unchecked through the orchard and the vegetable patch. All kinds of plants from all quarters would grow harmoniously in England just as Francis Bacon had proposed. There would be delight and entertainment in natural surroundings for the aristocrats, fruit and vegetables for all the masses. In botany at least, God's earth had never seemed so promising, so full of goodness and fertility. Tropical fruits might even be cultivated inside houses, providing exotic tastes in the dead of English winter. Perpetual Spring could be achieved and Eden remade in England's fair and pleasant land.

9

The English Eden

The flood of Eden-yearning, paradise-hunting and plain utopianism in some hearts in the early seventeenth century did not,
on the evidence, have much hope of engulfing the majority. For a
start, the omens were always bad. In 1618 a comet was spotted and
20,000 starlings were said to have dropped dead from the skies after
a massive aerial battle over Ireland. Three years later ice floes
appeared in the Thames 'like rocks and mountains', and Parliament
opened on 30 January with James, crippled by arthritis, carried in by
chair. Scaffolding holding spectators collapsed and many were
injured. Elsewhere, John Tradescant deposited in his Ark a small vial
marked, 'Blood that rained in the Isle of Wight'. This was a time of
signs and wonders, a time when a vengeful God, the God of Ezekiel,
was ever ready to reveal himself: 'I will judge thee according to thy
ways, and will recompense thee for all thine abominations.' In a
chilling sign of God's displeasure, a fishmonger in Cambridge cut
open a large cod and found in its belly a religious tract, *A Preparation
For The Cross*.

Plague broke out in London at the time of James I's coronation in
July 1603 and by the end of that year over 30,000 would be dead. If
that was not suffering enough, there then came a second plague, this
one of puritan hellfire preachermen who would climb the trees in
graveyards and comfort the bereaved with the news that this was
God's judgement on their loved ones' abominable immorality.
Carpenter-cum-tub-thumper Nehemiah Wallington identified a few

of the offending practices: 'Whoredoms, adulteries, fornication, murders, oppressions, drunkeness, cozening, lying, the contempt of the Gospels with slandering, mocking, flouting, chiding, silencing and stopping the mouths of God's prophets and servants, and other gross secret sins.'

Minister James Godskall offered an Ark to those who would be saved, except, unsurprisingly, the Ark was made not of 'corruptible wood', but 'fervent prayer' and the running into it was to be done on 'spiritual legs'. As ever in times of stress and change, those who were religious blamed the baleful nature of events on a lack of religion in others.

Corruption, both physical and moral, obsessed the doomsayers. In the London theatres, audiences were treated to blood-fests of vengeance and hate. Tarantino would have loved it – they used pigs' blood, lots and lots of it, on stage. Fingers were cut off in *The Changeling*, a poisoned skull appears in *The Revenger's Tragedy*, stranglings and insanity in Webster's *The Duchess of Malfi*, there were fatal stabbings by the fistful at every turn. It was feverish and ghastly; performances in which 'human beings are writhing grubs in an immense night', as Rupert Brooke put it. Even those who condemned such abominable liberties were not immune. The hypocritical, self-righteous puritan became a stock stage character.

Ben Jonson summed up the corrupted mood of the age in *Volpone*, probably written in the winter of 1605–6, only weeks after the Catholic conspiracy to assassinate King James had given Protestant England a fearful glimpse into the abyss (a glimpse that Robert Cecil deliberately ensured was a good long look, milking the Gunpower Plot for every ounce of benefit, maybe even orchestrating events and evidence). In Jonson's brilliant and savage satire the hero Volpone, the Fox, debases his enemies through their love of gold – one even offers up his wife for rape – but in the process Volpone progressively reduces himself too. The irony of the play is that the hero, like the other greed-struck characters, believes himself rising on the social scale, improving his position. But paradise cannot be reached via riches and, as it appears to approach, it actually recedes.

In a London without clean water or air and little in the way of efficacious medicine (one suggested remedy for dysentery, 'the bloodie flux', was to insert hard-boiled eggs), the wish for light and order and cleanliness was in many hearts.[1] At the Jacobean court, there was certainly a desire to show the harmony and righteousness of the ruling order. James was fond of masques, a peculiarly Jacobean love, a kind of dinner-dance-theatre with audience participation, a spectacle of wealth – and a conspicuous consumer of it. In these shows James found something profound: a complex allegory of the harmony and order of society with himself at the centre as all the courtiers danced around, arranged by rank. In Ben Jonson's *A Masque of Blacknesse*, performed in 1605 with stage sets and costumes by Inigo Jones, Queen Anne herself appeared as the Queen of Aethiopia dressed in see-through shimmering gauze, blacked-up and sitting in a sea-shell on what was apparently a moving ocean. She and her ten attendant ladies had to be saved from their blackness by a great white monarch – guess who? The saviour duly saved. The Spanish ambassador, pretending to be impressed, bent to kiss the queen's hand, risking a black mouth; the tables collapsed from weight of food. The entire performance cost £3,000, a king's ransom.

The style and atmosphere of these Jacobean extravagances is beautifully expressed in a portrait of Lady Elizabeth Pope in the Tate Britain collection. Painted in 1615, this dazzlingly fashionable lady stands dressed for a masque before an arcadian landscape, her hair loose and one nipple shyly peeping from her pearl-embroidered cloak, an exquisite distillation of innocence and knowledge.

For those who attended the events they were undoubtedly powerfully symbolic, their dances and ceremonies allegories for social harmony and beauty. Like bees in a hive, dancing around their queen, the masques revealed and celebrated the social order.

Ben Jonson further developed the genre by introducing an anti-masque, an antithesis in which all was chaos and darkness, until the forces of light restored harmony. The finale came with the restoration of the Golden Age, James at the helm, a recapitulation of the ancient myth of paradise regained after good triumphs over evil.

But this type of paradisical-yearning was never much deeper than a man's purse. Voices were raised against the cost and wastage. The mood, at least in devout Protestant circles, was for something more genuine and pure, something whose effects went through society, not just a privileged elite. With hindsight James's masques look as out of step as Marie Antoinette's apocryphal, 'Let them eat cake.'

The urge towards a New Jerusalem was expressed as new covenants, new settlements or plantations as they were called, new communities with new ways of ordering their existence. It was largely a Protestant phenomenon, evidenced by a desire for a plain, honest, straightforward life of work. (Luther specifically condemned the idleness of monks and nuns: 'man was created not for leisure but for work, even in the state of innocence.'[2]) The mood was for improvement and perfection, of the self, of the land, of the family and of the religion. This new Perfect Human was slightly different to that of the Italian Renaissance and a whole new set of self-help books was needed to advise. One that reflected the new ideals was entitled *The English Husbandman*, by Gervase Markham, first published in 1613.

The book reads like a DIY guide to becoming a Robinson Crusoe in an English country gentleman's residence. Markham tells how to plant and grow orchards, graft trees, raise animals and doctor them, everything, in fact, that a smallholder might need to know. It was information that many people must have already possessed: country folk scarcely needed to be told how to rear pigs. But this information was all laid out in a rational and practical way suitable for the discerning intelligent mind. Markham even presented plans for house and garden, all devised according to the latest thinking on orientation of rooms, entrances, lawns (*plats* in those days), fruit and vegetable production. The designs reflected his readers' aspirations and values, but they also built on an interest in harmonious living that went all the way back through the Renaissance to the Greeks. (Books on Feng Shui would be the contemporary example.)

Markham was aiming at a new audience, individuals wealthy enough to own land and yet determined to muddy their own hands. The nature of his readers is revealed best in his advice to the good wife, exhorting her to keep her fingernails clean, to be chaste and demure, and to be 'far from vanity of new and fantastique fashions'. This was no aristocratic lady tending her flowers. Markham had discovered a thirst for knowledge a notch or two down the social scale. The result was something of a primer for sober, self-help puritanism.

Among the Puritans, the choice of garden activities often showed a religious frame of mind. Bees, for example, were fast emerging as one obsession of the times: their strangely ordered world, with asexual reproduction and each individual happy in its role, an ideal in itself. Bees were innocent and therefore symbolic of Eden. According to the expert apiarist of the age, the Reverend Charles Butler, they hated the stench of copulation, stinging anyone who smelled 'unchaste'.[3]

Another obsession was the apple and most leading pomologists were also Puritan divines. One of them, Ralph Austen, declared it was a Christian's duty to cultivate apples and thus regain paradise. Austen was a passionate eccentric who lived inside a house painted entirely green and spent all his time beseeching his fellow man to plant trees and recreate Eden.

But it was not only eccentrics who succumbed to the mood. Francis Bacon wrote that a garden 'is the purest of human pleasures

...the greatest refreshment to the spirits of man'. Notorious later for other refreshments to the spirits – such as keeping a brace of catamites to warm his bed – Bacon was as fanatical a gardener as any, and an optimistic one. He goes on to describe how one can create a garden that blooms all year, using the plants that are available. For January and February, 'the mezereon tree, which then blossoms; crocus vernus, both the yellow and the gray; primroses; anemones; the early tulippa; hyacinthus orientalis; chamaïris; fritillaria. For March, there come violets...the yellow daffadil; the daisy; the almond-tree in blossom; the peach-tree in blossom.' By September the fruit is coming: 'grapes; apples; poppies of all colours; peaches; melocotones; nectarines; cornelians; wardens; quinces.' Running through the other months in equally fertile style, he concludes, 'These particulars are for the climate of London; but my meaning is perceived, that you may have *ver perpetuum*, as the place affords.'

It seems astonishing now, this hope of year-round abundance, but they were sustained by an ignorance of the difficulties, the cascade of new species, and belief in a new Eden. In that time of heightened millenarian hope, even the art of grafting came in for the allegorical treatment. It was to fruit trees what divine grace was to man, an act of creating perfection. God was still there, smiling on our efforts, yet the new road to paradise was going to be built by our own labour – that good, noble puritanical work ethic – and if the language still beat to the rhythms of religion, the idyllic destination was becoming ever more worldly and secularized. Even labour itself was undergoing a subtle transformation: it had once been a sign of our fall from grace, now it was to be the means of our recovery.

Many years later, when the blind John Milton wrote the final lines of his epic, the sentiment he captured was the sentiment of those earlier times, his youth.

Adam and Eve, having been evicted for their sins from paradise, shed a tear, but the Archangel Michael comforts them with the

promise of a 'paradise within thee, happier far'. Down the cliff and out
into the plain they go, wiping away their tears.

> The world was all before them, where to choose
> Their place of rest, and Providence their guide;
> They, hand in hand, with wandering steps and slow,
> Through Eden took their solitary way.

In the summer of 1628, the year before Tradescant moved into his
house in Lambeth, a ship from the Baltic landed on the east coast
carrying an unusual passenger who would do much to promote the
idea of the English Eden. Samuel Hartlib was a young man with a
powerful sense of his own destiny. However, as so often in the story of
paradise-seekers, he would achieve something magnificent yet see the
dreams he harboured fail. Hartlib's fate was that his Edenic efforts
would deliver an enormous and indispensable boost to the scientific
revolution in England; it was also his fate to be almost completely
forgotten, dismissed by far lesser mortals as 'a fanatick'.

On that day when Hartlib landed, however, he had yet to achieve
anything. In one pocket he had a valuable list of contacts, and in
another, we can safely assume, the Bible. And if there was one verse in
his Bible which meant more to that young man than any other, it was
Daniel 12:4: 'many shall run to and fro, and knowledge shall be
increased.'

It was a prophecy of the End, when those 'that sleep in the dust of
the earth shall awake, some to everlasting life, and some to shame and
everlasting contempt'. It was also a rallying cry to speed a new Eden
on earth by increasing the stock of knowledge. As Hartlib well knew, it
was a rallying cry that Sir Francis Bacon had used in 1620 to preface his
Novum organum, a book that urged a new and scientific frame of
thinking on the reader. 'And surely it would be disgraceful if, while the
regions of the material globe – that is, of the earth, of the sea, and of
the stars – have been in our times laid widely open and revealed, the

intellectual globe should remain shut up within the narrow limits of old discoveries.'

Bacon was two years dead by the time Samuel Hartlib arrived in England, but the young man was burning with excitement at the task ahead. Coming from Elbing,[4] a Baltic port with a tradition of reformed religion, he was on a mission to find a backer for a new utopian settlement, Antilia, that he and the members of his secret society had been planning for some years. The place was a utopian daydream, but one that appeared on maps throughout the fifteenth century. Columbus thought he had sighted it on his first voyage. By Hartlib's day, any possibility that Antilia might be discovered was gone, but the hope of establishing a plantation under that name endured. This reflected the deep change in attitudes: paradise was no longer to be stumbled upon, but built.

Hartlib was no crackpot, at least not by the relaxed standards of the time. He came from a well-connected Hanseatic League merchant family with English kin – his father having taken an Englishwoman as his third wife – Samuel's mother.

Arriving in London, he probably lodged in the area around what was known as the Steelyard, long since lost under Cannon Street Station, an area where the Baltic merchants had been bringing their goods for over 500 years. Hartlib had money and connections to help him. Sir Thomas Roe, ambassador to the Mughal court of India and benefactor of John Tradescant's Ark, was known to him.

With the almost messianic energy and zeal that he displayed all his life, Hartlib threw himself into his task. It was, no doubt, a convivial and amusing one at times. London life centred on taverns and alehouses, places filled with all types of humanity from whores scouting for business to itinerant ministers ready to rail against the sins of Sodom while champing on slivers of salt beef from plates on the bar and knocking back pints of wine (watered down by the unscrupulous landlords). The taverns served set-price dinners, a popular option in a city where few private houses had a kitchen.

Some were already becoming the stuff of legend: the Boar's Head which stood near London Bridge (where the statue of King William now stands in Eastcheap), reputedly the memorable drinking den of Shakespeare's *Henry IV Part I*, with its barman who spoke so little they said he had 'fewer words than a parrot'. Then there was the Rhenish Winehouse, in the Steelyard itself, where Pepys would enjoy lobsters and prawns the year before the Great Fire – a good place to pick up news of home for Hartlib, though that was nearly all bad with northern Europe torn apart by the Thirty Years War and the armies of the Habsburgs threatening to over-run his home town.

Hartlib quickly put down some roots. On 20 January 1629 he married an Englishwoman, Mary Burningham at St Dionis Backchurch, then moved to Chichester and tried to set up a school where he could start to apply his principles of universal knowledge. Unfortunately it was not the success he had hoped for and by late 1630 he was back in London, living a few minutes' walk from the Steelyard. His zeal for the utopian settlement of Antilia was a little dented, but he had a new vision to sustain him: England as paradise – a paradise realized through universal education and the planting of orchards.

Visionary he was, but no idle dreamer. These were intended to be practical ambitions towards creating perfection. Unlike some who simply waited for Christ's return, Hartlib was convinced action could contribute to hastening the Kingdom. He set about encouraging promising individuals. His correspondence went out to the Americas, central Europe and the Near East, while at home he made contact with luminaries such as John Milton, Andrew Marvell and Oliver Cromwell. Letters were copied by scriveners and sent out to other interested parties. With all these friends and acquaintances, the Hartlib house soon became a shelter for any deserving sectarian fallen foul of either European Catholicism, or the increasingly anti-Puritan Stuart state.

This formidable attempt to build a community around himself was an essential part of his philosophy. For Hartlib, the return to Eden was also a return to the communal spirit of the primitive Church. At some point he had come under the influence of a charismatic preacher called Jan Komensky, 'Comenius', a Czech who had produced a well-known mystical classic, *The Labyrinth of the Word and the Paradise of the Heart*, in 1623. Comenius extolled a faith called pansophism that was largely a revival of the teachings of Pelagius – the British monk who had fallen foul of Augustine back in the early fifth century.

Pelagius had said that perfection was attainable in this life and that it was a Christian duty to achieve it. With some effort, people could live the simple honest life of Adam and Eve, revelling in natural beauty and even enjoying sexual pleasure. The Church believed it had quashed these heretical ideas, but 1,200 years later, they found new life in Comenius who adapted and developed them. He was convinced that if scientific knowledge could be gathered and disseminated to all people, then basic evils like hunger would be defeated and a foundation laid for paradise on earth. Everyone would live that simple honest life of Adam and Eve. His views on universal education were revolutionary, inspiring others to spread the message. Comenius's effect on Hartlib was profound, enthusing the young man with the hope that Eden could begin to be re-established on earth, if only knowledge was harvested and spread more efficiently.

As Hartlib's range and influence grew in London, so did his interests. One concern of his circle of New Eden enthusiasts was a universal language. Clearly Eden must have had one tongue spoken by Adam and Eve, perhaps by all creatures, parrots and unicorns included. In the previous century Johannes Goropius Becanus had suggested ancient Flemish, which was no more ridiculous than any other proposal. (This resident of Antwerp also convinced himself that the Garden of Eden had been somewhere between the rivers Scheldt and Meuse.)[5]

The universal language was believed to have survived the Fall and the Flood, but to have been destroyed, or at least damaged, at Babel. Though Latin had advantages as a replacement, it was indelibly stained for the Protestants by long association with popish observances and traditions. What was required was a simple, plain tongue in which men could say what they meant. Several ideas were advanced, including one based on music.

Hartlib's interests widened. He corresponded on bee-keeping, diet, horticulture and education. Nothing escaped his eye: he visited Gaspar Calthoofe, a man named as a Tradescant benefactor (actually Caspar Kalthoff, a Dutch inventor) and observed his machine for 'boring into brasses and iron as if it were wood'. Kalthoff's lifetime quest for the secret of perpetual motion no doubt intrigued Hartlib. Sponsored by the Marquess of Worcester, Kalthoff applied for several patents and claimed to have devised a steam engine for pumping water. A popular outing was to inspect this marvel at Vauxhall and go on to Tradescant's Ark and garden.

Orchards and fruit-growing were paramount in the Eden hunt. John Evelyn was so in love with apple orchards he believed that time spent under the blossom helped promote longevity. Ralph Austen, the owner of the green house, sent 'raspy' wine and Hartlib wrote back to thank him, taking the opportunity to declare that the heaths and moorlands of England 'may be turned into pleasant Gardens and orchards: I am fully satisfied from scripture grounds.'

As well as being a passionate pomologist, Austen was a radical Puritan with pedigree – his cousin Henry Ireton would later sign Charles I's death warrant. Hartlib helped him publish his *Treatise of Fruit Trees*, together with a religious tract, *The Spiritual Use of an Orchard*. Five hundred copies were printed and soon sold out.

One of Hartlib's new friends in the late 1630s was George Plattes, an engineer who had built the water supply for Theobalds, the Cecils' old family seat. Plattes' theories on fertilizers and tree-planting impressed Hartlib and the pair did further work on utopian schemes abroad, eventually publishing a prospectus for a utopian settlement named Macaria in 1641. There was a spate of utopian fiction at the time as England marched towards civil war and a time of ambitious conjectures about possible futures. With Parliament and monarchy and religious sects often at loggerheads, utopian literature offered a chance to expand political arguments and theories. Even so Macaria stands out as a bracingly practical document, shorn of any of the usual literary and narrative devices. Hardly radical to a modern reader, but revolutionary then, it made the prescient suggestion of a state with a restricted king and Parliament supreme. Probably it was printed for distribution to members of the Long Parliament which had convened in November 1640.

The 1630s had proven to be difficult times for the Puritans. For all his faults James I had been an adroit manager of religious factions, delicately balancing the interests of those who would narrow the gap between Canterbury and Rome, and those who looked to Geneva and Calvin. His son Charles was much less skilful, and married to a Catholic. As the Anglican establishment shuffled towards High Church grandeur – stained glass and episcopal splendour – the Puritans were squeezed out. When the Reverend Alexander Leighton imprudently called the queen an 'idolatress' and called for the episcopacy to be abolished, his punishment was savage. After first being ceremonially stripped, he was whipped and pilloried, then his nostrils were sliced open, both ears cut off, and SS – sower of sedition – branded on his forehead. A £10,000 fine was levied and he was dragged away to the Fleet Prison. Archbishop Laud was said to have been joyful. Puritan William Prynne fared a little better: he objected to stage plays and for that lost part of both ears and £5,000. From the Tower he issued a second pamphlet describing bishops as 'devouring wolves'. This time he lost more of both ears and was branded before a crowd of 100,000.[6] The radical belief in a New Eden for England was faltering and the urge to find heaven elsewhere grew stronger.

Samuel Hartlib stuck to his mission: England was not irredeemable. His was the way of love and compassion, dedicated to inclusivity and communication, but an increasing number of Protestant hardliners had begun to denounce the Jacobean regime and urge flight to the New World.

10

The Separatists Head for America

During the early years of James I's reign, in the north Nottinghamshire village of Scrooby, a postmaster called William Brewster and a preacher, John Robinson, had begun to believe in departure: the evil around them had become so hostile that godly folk must remove themselves. (One gets an idea of Brewster's world view in his choice of names for his children: boys, Wrestling and Love; girls, Patience and Fear.) There were others who agreed: preachers like John Smyth of nearby Gainsborough who would later come to the conclusion that no error in the Word of God could be tolerated: his lengthy sermons, therefore, should be in Hebrew, Greek or Aramaic – the original biblical languages – irrespective of the fact that no one in his congregation understood them.

The Separatist theology was radical, even revolutionary: their ideal was the early Church of Antioch where no priests and bishops were allowed and the Holy Spirit guided the faithful. This primitive democracy, however egalitarian, extended no further than the borders of their small Lincolnshire communities. In the words of St Peter, they believed they were 'a chosen generation, a royal priesthood, an holy nation, a peculiar people' (I Peter 2:9). The remainder of mankind was damned to hell. No matter that they were not militaristic, their language was violent and the killing would be done by their God, the vengeful Lord of Ezekiel, not Jesus's compassionate Father. Like all the apocalyptic dreamers before, including the Assassins' Hasan Sabbah, their paradise was to be built on blood and bones.

Chronicled by a member of the Separatist flock, William Bradford, the holy quest of these pioneers becomes an epic struggle against the monstrous machine of the Jacobean state. 'Religion has been disgraced,' wrote Bradford in his *Of Plymouth Plantation*, 'the godly grieved, afflicted, persecuted, and many exiled; sundry have lost their lives in prisons and other ways. On the other hand sin has been countenanced; ignorance, profaneness and atheism increased, and the papists encouraged to hope again for a day.'

Bradford's account undoubtedly exaggerated the hostility, but there was persecution. The Archbishop of York, Tobias Matthews, offered them compliance, imprisonment or exile — mild for the times but oppression all the same. With persecution came confirmation that England was indeed the Babylon of Revelation, and the faithful Separatists were the captive Israelites. This very literal application of Scripture to their own lives had another consequence: the site of the New Jerusalem, paradise, was out there, waiting for them.

They had a first attempt at leaving in 1607, hoping to reach Amsterdam. These were times when permission to leave was required so they did it in secret, boarding a boat off the Lincolnshire coast and paying exorbitantly for the pleasure. In a situation that the hapless asylum-seeker might recognize today, the captain promptly had the men robbed, the women groped and the whole lot taken back to port where they were thrown in gaol for a month. Next year they had more luck, reaching Amsterdam, a haven of religious tolerance, but still not the place they needed for total religious freedom. Bradford and Brewster tried Leiden, earning a living printing religious tracts and manufacturing fustian and moleskin.

During these lean years, news of the Americas gave them much cause for thought. Then in a book entitled *Description of New England*, published in 1616, they found just the place they were looking for. The author was Captain John Smith, the bluff Lincolnshire yeoman and Tradescant's friend, who had set pulses racing with an account of his rescue from death by Pocohontas the Indian princess. Pocohontas herself had subsequently been rescued from pagan hell and turned into a good Christian, marrying the settler John Rolfe and travelling to England.[1]

Smith had depicted the New World in a positive light and urged colonization of Massachusetts – a place he described as 'paradise'. The possibility that America might be a new Eden was readily absorbed by the Separatists over in Amsterdam and Leiden. Convinced that this was the place for them, they contracted a London merchant to take them across the Atlantic.

The *Mayflower* sailed on 6 September 1620 with 102 passengers on board, including Williams Bradford and Brewster and 39 other Leiden folk. The rest were Anglicans, many of whom would nevertheless join the Separatists in the 'Mayflower Compact' – an agreement to work together and obey their own laws. After a tough nine-week voyage they landed in a natural harbour that Smith had named Plymouth and immediately began building, against all odds, their godly community.

By 1629 the numbers of emigrants were rising fast and they included people of means. It was one of those Puritan gentry, John Winthrop, another of Hartlib's correspondents, who famously gave articulate expression to the Puritan dream. The speech is often quoted, but worth reading again for its power and vision.

We must entertain each other in brotherly affection. We must be willing to abridge ourselves of our superfluities, for the supply of others' necessities. We must uphold a familiar commerce together in all meekness, gentleness, patience and liberality. We must delight in each other; make others' conditions our own; rejoice together, mourn together, labor and suffer together, always having before our eyes our commission and community in the work, as members of the same body. So shall we keep the unity of the spirit in the bond of peace. The Lord will be our God, and delight to dwell among us, as His own people, and will command a blessing upon us in all our ways, so that we shall see much more of His wisdom, power, goodness and truth, than formerly we have been acquainted with. We shall find that the God of Israel is among us, when ten of us shall be able to resist a thousand of our enemies; when He shall make us a praise and glory that men shall say of succeeding plantations, 'may the Lord make it like that of New England.' For we must consider that we shall be as a city upon a hill. The eyes of all people are upon us.

When Winthrop landed, having delivered these stirring words aboard ship, he found a small colony stricken with disease. Paradise, the city on the hill, was not going to come easily. The sheer physical hardships of a new environment played their part, but it was also – to borrow Alain de Botton's phrase – because they had arrived in paradise and inadvertently brought themselves.[2] The dictatorial instincts of governors were matched by the rebellious streak of feisty colonists. By 1636 the governor of Boston, Henry Vane, found himself weeping in frustration at all the splits and dissensions. Fortunately there was a vast continent behind them: some radicals trekked off to Rhode Island, others sailed away for the Caribbean. This would be the key to the new paradise-seeking: that empty American horizon, always ready to absorb another group of hopeful pioneers, always offering the promise of a fresh beginning.

Despite the setbacks and the hostility of the land, the Puritans would eventually prosper. They believed in their mission to build that 'city on the hill' and this ultimate objective was served by the Puritan character. All that labour, thrift and simplicity, developed and honed since the Reformation, was bent to that higher purpose. While hard work had once been seen as man's punishment for sinning in Eden, now it would be an essential part of his salvation.

11

The Birth of Science

Back in England more and more Puritans were leaving for the New World: 20,000 or more in the 1630s, equivalent to the population of England's second city, Norwich.[1] Samuel Hartlib was certainly well-informed of the New World — he corresponded with Winthrop and among his circle was an alchemist, George Starkey, who had been born in Bermuda and lived in New England. The constant news of like-minded souls abandoning England, added to an oppressive political climate, must have raised many doubts and debates, but Hartlib stuck with his adopted home. In 1640 a little financial respite came when he was left money in the will of the influential Puritan preacher, John Stoughton, a man who had prophesied the coming perfection of harmony in the celestial spheres when the earth would increase its fertility and children would learn without effort. In February 1641, Hartlib wrote to Sir William Waller: 'mee thinkes the tyme drawes neare that this Great desideratum all soe shall bee fulfilled for some noble ende which Gods providence aymes at.' Waller was a Puritan and MP for Andover, soon to become a hero of the Civil War.

Volatile and dangerous times had come: mobs marched on Westminster and a poster was found on the doors of Parliament denouncing bishops as 'the limbs of Anti-christ'. As summer edged in, smallpox and plague broke out.

In 1642 Hartlib was busy hosting a visit by his mentor, Comenius, part of a plan for a new London University. The pair even inspected Chelsea College as a possible site, but these were no longer times for their brand of a quiet ride to paradise. The king had fled London and the rhetoric of preachers had become even more violent: in Parliament the Puritan Stephen Marshall called for the massacre of Roman Catholic children.

The Civil War fizzed into life on 23 October at Edgehill, an indecisive action, but one that ended the skirmishing and heralded real battles. One effect was to encourage some of those Puritans who had gone to America to return and fight for Parliament. Others who had never escaped received a second chance: the Reverend Alexander Leighton, slanderer of the queen, was led out of the Fleet, a doddering wreck. He was put in charge of Lambeth Palace, now a prison for the overly popish. In 1644 Hartlib's old friend, George Plattes, dropped dead in the street 'for want of food'. The End could hardly be far away. In the Parliamentary army there were those who thought the millennium very close now, and that it was their job to force it into being. These Fifth Monarchy Men based that belief on the book of Daniel in which four terrible monsters rise from the sea and devour humans. The four, Daniel was told, were monarchies that would rise and fall before paradise came with the fifth monarchy of Christ. This sect was strong in the Parliamentary army and abroad: Hartlib's younger daughter would marry a Fifth Monarchy man from Utrecht. All believed paradise on earth was imminent. The Civil War threw up many similar groups, all more or less dragging paradise into politics and revolution, all borrowing the language of religion and Joachim of Fiore's Last Days ideology. The hunt for paradise and perfection on earth had become feverish as old standards were questioned and found wanting.[2]

For the Tradescants the outbreak of hostilities was a disaster. John Tradescant's son, also John, had become King Charles's gardener but, with his patron gone, the situation was bleak. Hartlib had taken great interest in the family's work, noting in his diary the purchase of Tradescant senior's first botanical list in 1634. A visit to Lambeth was undoubtedly made, probably one of many. Hartlib remarked on the

Spanish Cane that Tradescant had originally acquired in 1632 as proof that tropical plants could flourish in England, a hopeful sign for any aspiring Eden-maker. When the elder Tradescant died in 1638 his son was in Virginia on the first of several plant-finding missions to the Americas. Hartlib was fascinated by the American specimens. The burgeoning Ark, too, met with his approval, but with Tradescant's income suddenly curtailed, the sale of the rarities looked inevitable. Typically, Hartlib's response was farsighted, suggesting that for £100 a year to recompense Tradescant, the collection could go to Cambridge University rather than fall into private hands, a fate contrary to the purpose of universal education and enlightenment. In Hartlib's unerring and egalitarian instincts we can see the germ of the modern public museum, the final end of the collecting mania, the temple where all those sacrificial objects could be held.

Tradescant was indeed thinking of selling the Ark and Hartlib's proposal was persuasive – it would allow the collection to remain intact and accessible. But now Hartlib's selfless hopes were threatened by the arrival on the scene of a character whose deviousness was matched only by his determination. The road to modern museumhood for the Ark had yet a few twists.

Elias Ashmole, son of a Lichfield sadler, was a successful London solicitor who had studied astrology, mathematics, natural philosophy and astronomy at Brasenose College, Oxford. During the Civil War he sided with the Royalists, but escaped any retribution after Charles's execution put the seal on Parliamentary victory. A favourable second marriage to a rich widow gave him opportunity to indulge his interests in alchemy and botany – an indulgence only temporarily interrupted when one of his stepsons attempted to murder him.

Ashmole met John Tradescant the Younger for the first time in 1650 and within two years Mrs Ashmole, rather strangely, had moved in with the Tradescants at Lambeth, leaving her husband in Blackfriars. The bumptious solicitor was a frequent visitor, however, and soon began to cast his eye upon the rarities. He took on the task of cataloguing them, and eventually paid for the list to be published, complete with glaring errors. He seems to have been ambitious, ingratiating and keen to aggrandize himself. To him the Ark must have presented an opportunity to establish his own name as a man of science and letters, if only he could wheedle his way towards ownership. Hartlib's reasonable suggestions were poison to him: the Ark gone to Protestant Cambridge and his name nowhere mentioned – dreadful! Ashmole wanted a public museum too, but after a period in the hands of a conscientious private owner – his hands, of course – and then a grandiose bequest to Oxford. It would be the most fabulous sacrifice ever, like a Scythian king slaughtering his horses for the gods; Ashmole would enter the pantheon for it.

Tradescant's wife Hester would have done better if her husband had taken Samuel Hartlib's advice, but perhaps her husband was not much of a man for business. When the son of Ole Worm, the great Danish collector, visited the Ark in 1652, the father noted to his son, 'I have previously heard that he [John Tradescant] was an Idiot.' Certainly the plant-hunter did not show much perspicacity with his new friend Mr Ashmole.

Through the difficult decade of the 1650s, however, nothing was decided. The Ark remained open to visitors and Hartlib had apparently no cause for concern. His own life was exceptionally busy now that the Puritan saints were in charge of the country. The chief saint himself, Oliver Cromwell, asked the renowned networker for weekly briefings. Life should have been improving: the papishly pagan festival of Christmas was banned, the theatres were closed, even those diehard bacchanals of dancing, feasting and fornication were on the wane and hopefully about to disappear altogether. In Oxford, Ralph Austen had helped purge the university of Royalists and was making plans to plant extensive orchards in the area. Unfortunately, not everyone agreed with the saints; disillusionment and rumours of rebellion were rife.

Hartlib's financial worries eased when Parliament voted him a pension of £100 per year though it appears not to have been paid very regularly. Quite how he survived is a mystery. For the most part he seems to have relied on irregular donations from patrons.

During this period he became friends with Robert Boyle, a wealthy and pious aristocrat with a passion for alchemy and God. Other rising stars drifted into the circle: William Petty, a mathematician and economist; John Wilkins, warden of Wadham College and proponent of a universal language, and Henry Oldenburg, a young Hartlib protégé almost equal to his mentor in voluminous correspondence across Europe. Everyone who met Hartlib spoke of his honesty, sincerity and discipline. John Evelyn visited him at home and left a portrait of 'honest and learned Mr Hartlib...The Master of Innumerable curiosities', his conversation dashing from subject to subject – first the perfumed decorations on German stoves, then a new kind of copying ink. John Milton declared that he was 'a person sent hither by some good providence from a farre country to be the occasion and incitement of great good to this illand'. It was Hartlib's extraordinary ability to make contacts and bring people together which would have a massive impact on the future of science.

In particular he encouraged Boyle, writing long epistles to him which reveal an astonishing range of interests. He passes on recipes for making saltpetre, new ways of butter and cheese production, methods of growing clover and enriching the soil, where to buy antimony, the benefits of glass stoppers for chemical bottles, the effects of a remarkable new beverage called 'coffee' which makes his brain 'clearer'; he sends copies of letters from other scientists and discusses the possibility of a universal medicine. In an age when secrecy was prized and everyone had some wonderful invention that could never be disclosed, Hartlib's openness was a remarkable development in itself. Boyle responded with fervour and chemical experiments: '[I] fancy my Laboratory a kind of Elysium,' he wrote to his sister, Lady Ranelagh, another close friend of Hartlib.

The lab may have been an Elysium for the enthusiastic Boyle, and it did give us his Law of Gases, but generations of children had cause to rue some of the other discoveries that went into his popular handbook of medicine. For sore throats the great scientist recommended, 'a drachm of white dog's turd', mixed with honey of roses, 'a linctus, to be very slowly let down the throat'. The father of Alexander Pope owned a copy, and poor little Alexander, never a strong child, probably tasted that one along with the cure that involved dry powdered faeces blown into the eyes three times a day.[3]

Hartlib's own medical problem looms large in his diary and letters. In the back rooms of the house, his son-in-law Frederick Clodius was working day and night over alchemical recipes, assisted by 'an expert ancient old laborant'. Top priority was a cure for Samuel's kidney stones and the poor man was constantly acting as a guinea pig for new and obnoxious remedies. A stream of visitors and house guests helped distract the patient. Sir Kenelm Digby calls to suggest a plan for a 'universal laboratory', Mr Dalgarno pops in for a chat about universal language – every other caller seems to be a seeker of some great panacea or paradise. And despite his pain Hartlib engages with everyone, discusses their dreams, passes on letters and ideas that might help. Occasionally he walks down to St Paul's Churchyard, hunting out books for Boyle.

Universal is a word that crops up again and again: universal medicine, universal language, universal laboratory, universal index, even a universal compost. The Renaissance interest in universal rules governing beauty and harmony had exploded into every aspect of life, but there was a new and distinct emphasis: everything was by experimentation and observation. Hartlib designed a perfect 'mannorhouse', set in a circular estate with tidy segments for each crop.[4] He promoted clover and crop rotation, advances that had worked in the Low Countries. This was an eminently practical brand of paradise-seeking and the new agricultural practices turned England from an importer of corn in 1638 to an exporter by the Restoration – and that in a time of devastating civil strife. At the centre of it all, like the grand house in his ideal estate, stood Hartlib. Of all new patents issued to inventions in the 1650s, the great networker was somehow involved with more than half of the items.

Hartlib's quest was now to open the way to discovering all these universals with an academy for the advancement of natural philosophy, what we would now call science. Boyle became involved, as did John Milton.

But as the decade wore on and optimism about the Republic faded, Hartlib too seems to have sunk a little. In 1656 pain from his kidney stones kept him housebound and then in November 1658, a couple of months after Cromwell had died, so did Samuel's wife Mary. Hartlib moved house then, joining his son at Axe Yard where Samuel Pepys lived, himself a rare survivor of kidney stone removal. Now approaching 60, Hartlib remained industrious with his letters, but the public mood was swinging against such visionary Protestants as himself, powered by the ineptitude of the government and an unpopular army. Talk of a New Jerusalem in England was out of fashion. In London a restoration of the monarchy was rumoured. Charles was reported to be waiting off the coast of Ireland and strange portentous signs were seen in the London night sky, 'a blazing star with a great tail in the form of a rod, and afterwards of a sword, appearing over Whitehall', wrote Hartlib.

His friend John Milton, deep in the dictation of *Paradise Lost* at this time, wrote, 'to creep back so poorly as it seems the multitude would, to their once abjured and detested thraldom of kingship, not only argues a strange degenerate corruption suddenly spread among us, fitted and prepared for a new slavery, but will render us a scorn and derision to all our neighbours'.[5] Despite such sentiments, Royalist pamphlets appeared on the streets; one of them ridiculed Milton and called for his execution along with the regicides.

The Ark and its future were still in Hartlib's thoughts. In 1657 he had noted: 'John Tradescant has no roomes for his Rarities but Oxford hath roome enough.' But while Hartlib's hopes and powers were fading, Ashmole, the old Royalist, was sensing victory. On the evening of 16 December 1659, he moved decisively, taking his old friend John Tradescant for some drinking, so much drinking in fact that the befuddled botanist was persuaded that Elias Ashmole was his best and worthiest friend. As the evening wore on, a document was pushed under Tradescant's nose and he signed.

Some time later that night, Hester was disturbed by her husband arriving back in South Lambeth with four men she had never seen before. Ashmole had discreetly withdrawn from the field at this point. Still worse for drink, Tradescant pulled out the document and insisted his wife sign it in front of the four witnesses conveniently on hand. Only afterwards did she realize its contents concerned her own interests: her husband had gifted Ashmole the Ark, the transaction to be completed after the deaths of herself and her husband. Not only that, the deed made no mention of a university, it was to go to Ashmole as a private collector. Next morning, sobering up rapidly and furious with himself, Tradescant cut his seal and signature from the document in the belief this would invalidate it. He was wrong. Ashmole, the solicitor, had his witnesses and had only to wait. Little wonder that Pepys described Ashmole as 'a very ingenious gentleman'.

That following spring, amid scenes of great rejoicing, drunkenness and attacks on Quakers, Charles II was proclaimed king. The men who had signed his father's death warrant were hunted down. Oliver Cromwell and Henry Ireton were beheaded, posthumously. Samuel Hartlib found patrons harder to find and some of the men who had been his close confidants were moving away from him. A split was emerging between those who could progress in the new climate and those who could not. As a foreigner and a well-known utopian visionary, he could not easily do what so many did: swallow their pride, make their peace, and slide into the new regime. His response was to withdraw into new plans for founding utopian Antilia on Bermuda. But in October 1660, he announced that he had been misled and there was no chance of establishing it. 'The name and thing is as good as vanished.' We don't know what prompted such a dramatic retreat, probably the non-appearance of promised funds. Even with his characteristic good humour, the hurt and disappointment come through. 'A friend of ours always suspected that it would appear to be but words,' wrote his friend John Worthington.

It marked the end of Hartlib's dreams. Quite suddenly utopias were no longer the rage and the science he had encouraged was in the hands of a new elite, many of them known to him but less fulsome in their correspondence these days. A month later, on Wednesday, 28 November 1660, a group of philosphers and thinkers met at Gresham College to hear Christopher Wren present a paper on astronomy. Afterwards a few of those present discussed forming an academy for the advancement of experimental philosophy. Robert Boyle, John Wilkins and Henry Oldenburg were all there, but Samuel Hartlib was not. The new body bore the distinctive marks of his own proposed academy, but this one would be called the Royal Society, the powerhouse of the scientific revolution to come. The king was needed as a figurehead and the ambitious new organization needed to distance itself from any taint of the previous regime: poor Samuel Hartlib was a Puritan embarrassment. He was dismissed by some as a 'fanatick', but he knew where the impetus had come from: 'I look upon this society as a previous introduction of the grand design here represented,' he noted to Worthington.

Henry Oldenburg, the first secretary of the new Society, fulfilled the central networking role that Hartlib had pioneered and was true to his old mentor, always speaking of the new Society as if it was Hartlib's own, with its ideals of benefiting all mankind.[6] But in the meantime, very quietly, the man who had done more than any to lever the Society into life had quietly disappeared. His old friend from Elbing, John Dury, stood by him to the end. His wife wrote: 'I can with you say, the day of wanting money brings with it a loss of freinds [sic].' In mid-February 1662, he despatched a letter to the man who had inspired his lifelong work, Comenius, declaring he was sick of life and it would be his last message.

On 10 March 1662, Comenius sent an anxious reply, enquiring after his old friend, but Hartlib had died the same day. He was buried without pomp at St Martin's-in-the-Fields. Pepys did not mark the day, but remembered that one night he had stepped forward for a carriage at the same time as Hartlib's son. The young man apologized and strode away into the shadows. A few years later he fled the country to avoid the debtors' prison – it was the last that would be heard of the family. With Hartlib's death an era of incredible paradise-seeking had ended.

The following month John Tradescant died, leaving a will that clearly stated: 'I give, devize, and bequeath my Closet of Rarities to my dearly beloved wife Hester,' and on her death, 'to the Universities of Oxford or Cambridge, to which of them shee shall think fitt at her decease.' There was no mention of Mr Elias Ashmole, but within a month the man was taking legal action to recover his property, studiously mentioning the Tradescants' debt to him for compiling and publishing the catalogue. Hester strongly contested his claim and the case eventually came to court in May 1664.

The intervening period had been a good one for the oily Ashmole. He had acquired the court post of Windsor Herald from Charles II and was now a formidable adversary with powerful friends. When the case was heard, by the Lord Chancellor, the Earl of Clarendon, Hester was humiliated. The judgement declared that the cabinet of rarities 'in or about his said house att South Lambeth' was rightfully the property of Elias Ashmole and that Oxford University had no claim. Not only that but a commission, stuffed with Ashmole's friends, was formed to catalogue the rarities to prevent any embezzlement. Hester was to be questioned on oath to ensure no items had been hidden or sold.

Hester still had possession until her death, but it seems Ashmole was impatient. He paid several visits, checking presumably that his inheritance was not being diminished, then in 1674 he bought the house next door and moved in. The lonely old lady now began to feel the strain of this intolerable man. She told friends that he had cheated her of her estate and had even made a doorway in the garden wall ready to remove objects. Ashmole sanctimoniously forced her to sign a legal recantation of these allegations. The Ark was now closed to the public.

There cannot have been a stronger contrast between the two at this time. The solitary widow in the huge darkened house with its bizarre collection overflowing the rooms. Next door, the self-appointed bastion of science and letters, his house alive with visitors from the new Royal Society and the court. Hester's mental state does not appear to have improved and the end was close. On 4 April 1678, Ashmole recorded in his diary, with a withering lack of emotion, 'my wife told me Mrs Tradescant was found drowned in her Pond.'

Within the month Ashmole had let himself into the house and removed the family paintings, stolen them effectively, as they were never included in the Ark. He began to speak of 'my Rarities'. In July, John Evelyn recorded visiting 'Mr Elias Ashmole's library and curiosities at Lambeth', without a mention of Tradescant. There is a gentle hint of waspish condescension in Evelyn's verdict. Ashmole is 'industrious in astrology but not learned...he shew'd me a toad included in amber.'

The social-climber, however, knew his game. Within the year he had the lease on the house and garden in his pocket. The Ark was open once more, not to the public, but to Ashmole's friends and the sort of people he hoped to impress. In February 1683 he started sending specimens to Oxford to go into a new building located between the Sheldonian Theatre and Exeter College (now the Museum of the History of Science). He had achieved his ambition of becoming the great benefactor. John Evelyn returned to Lambeth and dined with his 'old friend'.

Not everything arrived in Oxford: pieces disappeared, the books apparently found their way into Ashmole's own library – exactly the problems of private ownership that Hartlib and John Tradescant had foreseen. Most iniquitous of all was the name of the new institution, the Ashmolean Museum. It was one of those hideous injustices that history plays on some people: Columbus, overlooked in the naming of the New World in favour of a clerk, would have sympathized.

These days the Ashmolean is on South Parks Road and it has a room dedicated to Tradescant's Ark, a tiny flavour of the original with Pocohontas's father's cloak among the objects on display. Sadly, although it can claim to be the first modern British museum, the standards of museum curating were not always as high as they are now. In 1880 a cache of gemstones, carvings, crystal globes and a silver hookah were found lying in an outhouse open to the street. As for the poor extinct dodo, he became so decrepit that someone threw him on a fire in 1755 and only a beak and a leg were salvaged.

Ashmole died in 1692 but a few visitors kept coming to see the house and garden in South Lambeth. John Aubrey noted that a Balm of Gilead tree (*Cedronella triphylla*) still grew and that the whale ribs at the gate were there. In spring 1749 a William Watson FRS found the house uninhabited and ruined, the garden overgrown, but some trees surviving. A swamp cypress continued to thrive and a strawberry tree. There was not much to remind anyone that this had been one of the most important gardens of England, the first nursery for hundreds of new species that would help spin the dreams of an English Eden. In 1773 a historian, Dr Ducarel, was living in the house, but the garden had clearly further fallen into neglect. 'It were much to be wished,' wrote Ducarel, 'that the lovers of botany had visited this once famous garden, before, or at least in, the beginning of the present century.'

In 1880 the house and garden were swept away by redevelopment, but the church of St Mary's, where the Tradescants worshipped and were buried, survives and is now a Museum of Garden History. The area around their tombs is planted solely with species that appeared on the 1656 plant list. The rehabilitation of the Tradescant name has continued over the years and now their place in the history of science is assured.[7]

Not so Samuel Hartlib. Despite his Herculean efforts towards education, knowledge and progress, his visionary ideas on universities, museums and language, the long-time London resident has never been honoured. His papers disappeared and were only unearthed by chance in 1933 when they were discovered in a wooden chest, tucked away in the office of a London solicitor. Hartlib had never made his utopia come true, nor an Eden of England, but in the attempt he had foreseen how Tradescant's Ark and other 'cabinets of curiosities' would escape the shadowy world of freak shows and holy relic collections to become a scientific museum dedicated to universal knowledge. More significantly, his circle of visionaries, eccentrics and genuine genuises had emerged, under his guidance, as the first modern scientific society. What is remarkable is how these two great achievements of the Enlightenment had started with paradise-building impulses. And if no one cared to make connections between religious ideals such as pansophism, it did not mean the ideals were dead. Like a ghost in the new machines of science and progress, the myth of paradise lived on.

12

The Decline and Fall of Witchcraft

In 1661, shortly before he became the Royal Society's secretary, Henry Oldenburg travelled to the continent and took time to visit a Jewish thinker called Benedict Spinoza. What he heard from this unpublished lens-grinder must have been profoundly shocking: the entire universe, God included, was governed by natural laws, Satan and his minions were dismissed as absurdities, so were Jesus's miracles and the Resurrection. Not even Thomas Hobbes had dared say that if scientific laws of nature existed, then they applied universally without exceptions (though Muslim philosophers had suggested it some 700 years before). Spinoza said it. Happiness, contentment, paradise on earth and in this life – they all depended on science and rationality.

Spinoza's family, intriguingly, had previously been the victims of someone else's paradise fantasy, fleeing from Portugal in the early sixteenth century and setting up as merchants in the haven of Amsterdam. They did well and had a comfortable lifestyle, if dependent on the vagaries of ship arrivals, and occasionally their disappearance. In 1656 Spinoza eventually plucked up the courage to abandon this life, not only severing business ties but leaving the synagogue and many friendships behind him. The religious authorities then expelled him for 'evil opinions'. The young man, it was muttered with disbelief, was an atheist and his shocking habits were said to include having the Bible next to the Qur'an on his bookshelves. Spinoza had set himself up as a philosopher, using his time between meditation and reading to indulge a fascination for telescopes and microscopes – hence the lens-grinding.

Spinoza's opinions and ideas fascinated Oldenburg and they corresponded regularly, but there was a limit to how far the friendship could go. When Spinoza later wrote asking him to distribute a few copies of his new book in England, the secretary of the Royal Society suggested Spinoza send them to a Dutch merchant in London – and no need to mention Oldenburg's name anywhere in the parcel. Proximity to such a man, whose name was now commonly associated with the dreaded new disease of atheism, could be dangerous.[1]

For Society members, their science and rationality was certainly never intended to be the foe of religion, quite the reverse. Boyle was hoping to show the existence of 'spirits' in the air at the same time as he studied the laws of gases and vacuums. Isaac Newton, a closet alchemist, kept quiet about his own experiments in the supernatural and wrote copiously on theological matters. Other members of the Society proposed experiments to prove that poltergeists, spirits and demons did exist. If only these evil apparitions could be scientifically proven, they reasoned, then science would be shown not to be religion's enemy, but rather its helpmeet in revealing God's majesty. Joseph Glanvill, fellow of the Society and earnest proponent of the new science, collected well-attested and reliable examples of the black arts.

Ironically it was Christian ministers, not scientists, who did more than anyone to roll back belief in supernatural occurrences. The Westphalian preacher, Balthasar Bekker, tried very hard to do away with superstition yet keep Satan alive. Enraged by reports of a witch trial in Beckington, Somerset, in 1689, he set about disproving nonsense such as hauntings, exorcisms, pacts with the Devil and so on as both non-scientific and irreligious. The Great Beguiler didn't need those minions. His book *The World Bewitched* (1681) became a bestseller and unleashed a storm of other publications. To his acute embarrassment, Bekker discovered that everyone thought he was attempting the *coup de grâce* on Satan, something he had never intended.

There was a tide in this affair: belief in diabolists, hell-hags, polter-geists and sundry sprites was draining away like water from a reclaimed East Anglian fen. Revealed religion had raised the issue of paradise on earth, and now it was science and reason that had taken on the task, leaving that very religion, with all its supernatural nonsense, high and dry. In Leiden, gleeful atheists issued a commemorative medal showing the notoriously unattractive Balthasar Bekker whack Old Nick over the head with a large club. Years later Voltaire consoled Bekker's memory with the thought that his ugly face would always remind people of their dead foe, Satan.[2]

In 1703 a preacher in the Dutch Reformed Church, Frederik van Leenhof, published a programme for reaching earthly perfection via rationality entitled *Heaven on Earth*. There were no demons or witches, but no Messiahs and divine Providence either: heaven was a state of mind achievable by everyone (as was hell). The book caused a furore in Holland, Germany and the Baltic states. Leenhof was predictably attacked and vilified as a 'spinozist' – by then a term of abuse heaped on anyone suspected of atheism.[3] Eventually the Church defined the principles to which they objected and made him sign a condemnation. These horrifying beliefs included:

- body and soul are the same thing and not separate
- there are no creatures outside Nature such as demons and spirits
- there are no absolutes of good and evil, only man-made distinc-tions to keep the ignorant obedient
- there is no such thing as divine revelation, and consequently the Bible has no more authority than Plato, Cicero, Epicurus and others.

In 1737 the statutes governing witchcraft in England were finally repealed, causing John Wesley to rail: 'the giving up of witchcraft is in effect giving up the Bible.' Satan was dead, rationalism triumphant, religious authority on the back foot. 'The number of those who call themselves unbelievers increases,' moaned the Bishop of Durham, 'and with their number, their zeal.'

A Golden Age for reason was beginning, an age for opening things up and letting in light. No one put their finger on the mood quite so wittily as Voltaire. Scooping his hero Candide into a South American paradise like an Enlightenment Columbus, he had him delighted to find a distinct lack of religious authority, asking the inhabitants: 'Then have you no monks among you, to teach, dispute, govern, intrigue, and burn people who disagree with them?'

'Do you take us for madmen?' came the reply.

With Satan unseated, many turned their attention to knotty questions such as original sin and the nature of the Trinity. Under this pressure, the Protestant faith splintered. Unitarians declared Jesus just a man, Deists said God existed but never interfered – Moses, Jesus and Muhammad were all imposters. Mortalists – like Hobbes – said death was a sleep that would end with the Second Coming.[4] In educated society miracles and supernatural occurrences were gently pushed back into biblical times – those days were gone, rational religion reigned. Only at the fringes was there interest in the *parousia* – speaking in tongues and prophecy. The seventeenth-century experience in England had left deep suspicions regarding prophetic visionaries and those 'enthusaists' touched by the Holy Spirit.[5]

In France the intellectuals pushed the boundaries farther back. Julien Offray de la Mettrie made the universe entirely mechanistic and godless, with man no more than a complex machine. Few were prepared to go that far, not least because it tended to land you in disgrace or prison. Mettrie was forced into exile and died, appropriately, from over-eating. The more acceptable view was of a Supreme Being whose existence was discerned in the marvellous design of his Creation.

At that time, there appeared little common ground between the radicals and the mainstream, and yet there were several points where they shared ideas. Joachim of Fiore would have been pleased to note that everyone was still living in a state of crisis, convinced they were at a moment of historical transformation, the end of an era. Not only that but for the religious, paradise – the goal of history – was just around the corner, and for anyone else there was now something called 'progress', an unstoppable force that would lead to perfection, also just around the corner.

In an essay on apocalyptic ideas between the Reformation and the French Revolution, Robin Barnes wrote: 'In millenarian hope lay the seeds of the modern idea of progress, while apocalyptic disillusionment moved in the direction of practical skepticism and agnosticism.'[6] If a few were now thinking that the paradise to come would be secular and man-made, it was nevertheless still the child of Christian mythology.

13

Selling the American Eden

While science and reason were the great new gods of philo-
sophical enquiry, there was another force to be reckoned with,
one that was inextricably linked to the discovery of the New World:
nature. Columbus had inadvertently sent European paradise-seeking
up an entirely new path in that respect. Previously the Garden of Eden
had largely figured in the visions of the paradise-to-come by way of its
qualities (Adam and Eve's perfect and immortal bodies, their relationships to each other and to nature, their ability to communicate, and so
on). Christians had generally believed that the kingdom on earth
would be a New Jerusalem, a city where those qualities would appear.
As for Eden, it was essentially an abandoned plot, a perfect one of
course, but not exactly the place of prophesied return.

With America, however, came reminders of what that original
garden might have been. 'In the beginning, all was America,' wrote
John Locke.[1] The miraculous fecundity of this pristine New World
staggered colonists. Men spoke in awe of its great forests where
endless supplies of timber were available (822 million acres on the
North American mainland in the early 1600s). Some found it
disturbing, even frightening, but no one denied it made good houses,
furniture, boats and fires – better fires 'than many noblemen in
England can afford', wrote Francis Higginson in 1629.[2] On Caribbean
islands the trees were so huge they could defeat colonists. On Barbados
in the 1640s, the cavalier refugee Richard Ligon was amazed by the
variety of trees, many bearing fruit: banana, orange, guava, citrus,

plum, plantain, pomegranate, papaya and pear. The mainland to the north might not match that tropical fecundity, but it managed more than adequately with specialities of its own: cranberries, chestnuts, walnuts, hazels and hickory nuts. Rootling around this natural larder were fat turkeys and over-sized deer. Across the skies ducks flew in vast flocks, 'seven miles long'. Off the coast sailors imagined walking to shore on the backs of the fish. (By 1672 over 200 varieties had been identified off New England alone.) An anonymous English traveller reported catching turtles so large they took 16 strong men to carry them to the dining table. Everyone was swept up by this Edenic imagery, no matter how religious they were. Thomas Morton, in England after being arrested by New England Puritans for erecting a maypole and allowing dancing, wrote of 'sweet crystal fountaines', and 'millions of turtle doves'.[3] If some of these reports played on ancient myth, it was not so much Arcadia as Land of Cockayne – that medieval paradise where pigs threw themselves gladly into pies and rivers flowed with good Burgundy.

And there was land, staggering quantities of it. No crusader heading off to the Holy Land could ever have dreamed of so much good country to expropriate. The land had residents to be sure, but these Indians – the word Columbus used for the tribes he encountered – were child-like in their naïvety and easily pushed aside.

Initially the American tribes became part of the Eden mythology: they were noble savages whose innocence in business and ownership served as a reminder of what man had lost in his fall from grace. Everyone knew the stories of how they had sold Manhattan Island for a handful of wampum beads, and how they thought copper kettles were living beings. At the Massachusetts settlements the tribes had been friendly in the crucial early years, showing the colonists where to fish and how to grow maize. By 1625, however, the English were demanding an extra 12,000 acres of land – a bizarre request as far as the Pemaquid tribe were concerned, since they believed land could not be owned.

As the forests were felled, clear streams muddied, and wildlife hunted out, the tribes became anxious: what kind of humans were these new arrivals, with their terrible rapacious thirst for riches and destruction? All down the eastern seaboard the tribes began to rebel and attempt to throw the English out. Soon they were no longer noble savages, but ignorant brutes. Disease defeated many of them: the natives around Boston, reported John Winthrop in 1634, 'are neere all dead of the small Poxe, so as the Lord hathe cleared our title to what we possess'. Over the following three centuries the Lord did much more clearing of title as settlers drove the tribes back.

Winthrop's chilling and businesslike approach was matched by the philosophy of John Locke who argued for a 'natural right' to use 'inferior creatures' in the accumulation of wealth. The American Indians had not established their right to the land, Locke argued, for 'as much land as a man tills, plants, improves, cultivates, and can use the product of, so much is his property.' This argument stretched right back to Genesis 1:28: 'Be fruitful and multiply, and replenish the earth, and subdue it.' On those last two words would be built a fine new edifice of capitalism. In political philosophy, or self-justification at least, the colonists were becoming more sophisticated and their vanquished competitors disappeared. Most left behind only their names, at first as towns and geographical features – Miami, Ottawa, Potomac – but later, poignantly, as commercial products – Winnebago (a camper van), Kickapoo (a soft drink) and Pontiac (a car).

To the south, in the Caribbean, paradise soured even faster. The original tribes were killed off by new diseases and savage treatment, the peoples leaving us just a few words of their language (words that say a lot about their lives: hammock and barbecue in particular.) Their verdant islands were clear-felled for sugar cane plantations. By 1654 Bermuda had a timber shortage and there were only a few patches of the woods that had held vast trees – the Royal Palms had reached 200 feet. A decade later and there was nothing but a few inaccessible specimens in gullies. Visitors commented on the lack of birds.

One thing not in short supply was the local hooch – kill-devil, they called it. By 1641 the Reverend John Wilson estimated 'the Inhabitants have pissed out £15,000...by their excessive drinking.' Adultery and incest were said to be rife. Disillusionment and despondency among colonists were common when their high hopes on arrival were revealed as unrealistic dreams. Even those settlers who made a success of it were well aware of the drawbacks: vicious tropical storms down south, severe winters in the north, disease and privations that could wipe out settlements. In New England William Bradford described his flawed paradise as a 'hideous and desolate wilderness full of wild beasts and wild men'.[4]

Back in Europe, however, the re-formation of the paradise myth to include the American Eden ensured that the romance of the New World was strong. The poet Andrew Marvell, tutor in the house of former Bermudan settlers, the Oxenbridges, could spin out a seductive tropical idyll in his poem 'Bermudas', never having left Europe.

> He hangs in shades the orange bright,
> Like golden lamps in a green night,
> And does in the pomegranates close
> Jewels more rich than Ormus shows;
> He makes the figs our mouths to meet,
> And throws the melons at our feet.

The plants that came back from those western paradises were the closest most Europeans ever came to seeing this marvellous botanical vibrancy. Thomas Johnson exhibited bananas for the first time in a shop window in London in 1633, causing great debate as to whether these strange exotics may have been 'Adam's apples'. Thomas Verney, writing home from the Caribbean, suggested the pineapple for that role: 'King Jeames swore it was the apple that Eve cosned Adam with.' Others agreed that it was 'the nectar which the Gods drunk'.

After the Restoration in England, wealthy garden-lovers began to build hothouses to grow these new fruits, giving an extra tropical dimension to Sir Francis Bacon's idea of a year-round bonanza.[5] Such unnatural interference in God's seasons had once been considered nothing less than Satanic: a medieval alchemist named Ripley had been killed for the dastardly crime of making a pear tree 'fructify in winter'.[6] But those ancient fears had no place in the new ideal of an Everlasting Spring where human dominion over nature, a feature of Eden, was reborn in a flood of exotic imports – John Aubrey's estimate was 7,000 species in the 1680s. At Badminton in the Cotswolds Mary Duchess of Beaufort could place fresh papaya on her dining table at Christmas 1700; 20 years later the Duke of Chandos could astonish his guests with a cornucopia of tropical fruits, including avocado, custard apples and guava. The Earl of Burlington had pineapples and coffee grown in hothouses on his Yorkshire estates near Hull, then sped south by mailcoach and bestowed on friends. The eighteenth-century hothouse, or stove as it was known, was one of the wonders of its day: climate-controlled, ever bountiful and highly exclusive, a little Eden in itself.

Much of the wealth that allowed such extravagance came from slave-worked plantations. Vast new houses, such as Castle Howard near York and Harewood near Leeds, were financed with slave-economy profits.[7] The Caribbean island paradise had been dissolved into molasses, shipped back across the Atlantic and reassembled as stately homes with miraculous gardens. The Arawak Indians, had any of them lived to see it, would have noticed the stone pineapples on the imposing gateposts – it had always been a symbol of welcome and hospitality in their islands.[8]

The wealth of these few individuals was staggering: in 1715 the Duke of Newcastle earned £32,000 from his extensive lands at a time when £300 a year was sufficient to support a gentleman and £50 a vicar. The Duke of Chandos kept 93 household servants and a 27-piece orchestra. Burlington could happily return from his first Grand Tour in

1715 with a total of 878 trunks, plus a sculptor named Guelfi, a violinist, a cellist, several Italian craftsmen and two harpsichords. A year later he had a musician called Handel sent over too. With such mountains of cash available, the paradise-hungry aristocrat could lay on an endless cornucopia of plenty for family and friends. David Garrick, having enjoyed a lavish dinner at Burlington's expense, staggered back to his room and wrote a note to thank his absent host.

I must beg leave to inform your Lordship that I have at this present writing such a mixture of ale, champagne, florence, claret and cowslip wine within me, that my head may be in my pocket for any use I have of it – but how could I possible avoid being so free with the creature, in the company of Lord Langdale, his Honr., Mrs Langdale of Cliff, Miss Kitty and Monsr. Philip – a disagreeable circumstance indeed stopt the course of our wit and humour for five minutes – My Lord Langdale who had eaten three plates of soup, two of salmon, one of carp besides the head, two dozen of gudgeons, some eels, with macaroni, omlett and raspberry tart and adding to these, strawberry and cream, pineapple, etc., etc., etc., grew a little sick after the third bottle of burgundy, and I believe had left the maigre compound upon the table he took it from, had not a handsome dram of brandy come to his and our relief – You may imagine we were damped for a few minutes, till My Lord recovered his spirits again, and told us very seriously, that fasting days never agreed with him...[9]

From the very beginning of the modern period, in characters like Burlington we can see the route society was taking: the ever-present human desire for endless supply and plenty, that restless hunger for more, was to be satisfied through innovation, science, exploitation and spending. At first only a few individuals would benefit, though many were involved. Putting that first pineapple on Burlington's dinner table required teams of gardeners working for many years. Gradually, however, the spread of largesse was widened. Science could solve every problem. The York to London mailcoach bearing a pair of precious pineapples to a brace of baronets is now a Jumbo jet carrying 10,000 for the masses. The paradise myth was being transformed into a voracious capitalist monster, determined to have its Perpetual Spring, gobbling its way through the earth's resources at an accelerating pace. By 1650 around 2,300 square miles of North American forest had been cleared, a century later 80,000 and by 1980 an estimated 424,710 square miles.

As so often happens, it was the losers who saw the stark truth of what had been unleashed. As early as 1642 Miantunnomoh, leader of the Narragansett people declared: 'You know our fathers had plenty of deer and skins and our plains were full of game and turkeys, and our coves and rivers were full of fish. But, brothers, since these Englishmen have seized our country, they have cut down the grass with scythes, and the trees with axes. Their cows and horses eat up the grass, and their hogs spoil our bed of clams, and finally we shall starve to death.' He was correct. There was no room in paradise for the Narragansetts. Soon afterwards, they were wiped out.[10]

PART IV

The Modern Paradise:
1700–1945

Thomas Rowlandson, *The Harem*, c.1812 (photo: Philip de Bay)

A t the age of five I recall walking with my grandfather to the end of his road in the Lincolnshire town of Grantham and being held up to see over a wall into a garden.

'Isaac Newton discovered gravity in there,' he said. 'And it's gravity that holds us down on the planet and saves us all from spinning away into space.'

This knowledge had come to Newton, so Grandad said, when an apple fell on his head from one particular tree – over there, he claimed, with some poetic licence. Newton had certainly attended the school building near this garden, but no more. Grandad warmed to his theme: ever since then men had worn a belt on their trousers lest the gravity snatch them down. Knowledge, Tree, Fall. A five-year-old Sunday School boy could put these parts together, dimly perhaps, but sufficiently to stare at the garden in awe.

Our family had originally come from north Lincolnshire where most had been farm labourers. It was this area that sent so many across the Atlantic in the seventeenth century. Family photographs from the late nineteenth century show men in white shepherd's smocks pictured with their favourite dog, characters from a Hardy novel with fine moustaches and weathered faces. The women are shown standing in the door of country cottages, honeysuckle and ivy all around the walls, their hands folded across their aprons. For the children the annual highlight was not Christmas but Michaelmas when the pig was slaughtered. They would eat or use everything, 'except the squeak', salting the hams to hang from the pantry ceiling.

Further along the street, walking slowly, we looked at St Wulfram's church – 'finest steeple in England'. But he never mentioned the Roll of Honour for the Machine Gun Corps inside, or took us to see it. The Great War was not to be mentioned. On 30 November 1917 he had been near Cambrai, the small French town whose bishop, Pierre d'Ailly, had once enthused Christopher Columbus with calculations of where to find Eden. I wonder if Grandad thought about Eden on that particular November day – they said that phosgene gas had the delicate scent of new-mown hay about it on first inhalation, a gentle arcadian nudge before it burned the life out of you. He went temporarily blind and dumb, one of those men in grainy sepia photographs, clutching a rag over his face, hand on the shoulder of the man in front. In the previous ten days his machine gun unit had run through almost 9,000 rounds, and as lance corporal it was his finger on the trigger. Little wonder he never talked about it. Behind him the battle was almost over, settling into stalemate again. Ninety thousand had died.

He spent time in a sanatorium, emerging to take a job in Grantham as a gardener-chauffeur to the two old ladies who lived in Grantham House. Before the war the house would have had several servants, but not then. The conflict had broken the English country house tradition that led back to the start of the eighteenth century. Grandad trimmed the lawns, kept bees and took the old ladies for Sunday drives in the Rolls-Royce.

The house is almost opposite St Wulfram's and beyond its entrance was a high stone wall, impossibly high and mysterious to a five-year-old. Halfway along Grandad took out a large rusty key and opened a door that let into this wall. We came then into a passageway flanked on one side by the same wall and on the other by an impenetrable hedge. This led to a second gate and a garden full of flowers and vegetables and two ancient pear trees, a garden that was protected on one side by an ancient brick wall, on two by hedges and on the fourth by the river.

This was part of the old walled vegetable garden that once sustained the glory days of the house and to us boys it was a *paradeiza*, a walled and magical place of plenty. Grandad had kept it for many years, a connection with the house since the old ladies had died and he had retired.

We climbed ladders into the pear trees and dropped the fruit into sackcloth laid over the flowers. Later he would snooze in a deckchair outside the greenhouse with the missing panes replaced with pin-ups from the *Daily Express*. My brother and I would play along the grassy paths. There were no rows of vegetables or orderly borders of flowers: he grew everything mixed in together in a wild profusion, carrot tops sprigging from among chysanthemums, lilies and garlic in the shade near the river, runner beans and sweet peas entwined up the sunny walls. He was quite an orderly man in other respects, enjoying repairing clocks in his spare time, but in that garden he made no rules. This was the sanctuary he had made for himself after the war, the traditional retreat of enclosed garden that has never lost its appeal, nor ever gone away through all the New Jerusalems, Arcadias and Utopias. Despite all the promises and prophecies, no one has yet found a better place to be in touch with what the mythical Adam and Eve possessed in Eden – the harmony of man, nature and God.

When the sun dipped a little and the temperature dropped, he would wake up and pack the fruit and vegetables that we had picked into a wicker basket. Then we would head home, locking the gates of his paradise behind us.

14

The Comforts of the New Earthly Paradise

' All historians of paradise,' wrote A. Bartlett Giametti, '... have to face the fact that after 2,000 years their subject essentially disappears in the eighteenth century.'[1]

He was completely wrong about that. Paradise as an earthly, and earthy, obsession – a possibility thrown up by the Puritans' literal reading of the Bible – was just accelerating into new dimensions propelled by the wave of discovery. Europeans were finding and improving and extracting and cataloguing with their eyes firmly fixed on perfection. And never before had there been so many ways to answer those ancient questions about the perfect life as lived by Adam and Eve (the vast majority of people did still believe in them). In health, beauty, food and drink, the comforts of home, sexual relations, childbirth and almost every aspect of living, the burgeoning middle classes of Western Europe were faced with new opportunities. Delights, previously considered the sole preserve of the afterlife, were now available wholesale and the tantalizing prospect of perfection achieved through progress was dangled before those with some silver in their pockets.

In London three factors were crucial: population growth, the rise in incomes and the flood of imported luxuries from newly discovered territories. The chief beneficiaries, the middle and upper classes, were for the first time shopping in places that we would recognize. The dark and cramped outlets of Elizabethan and Jacobean times were fast being replaced with larger, more impressive emporia. Glance inside the bow-fronted windows and you might see displays set out on white cloths and lit by gilded candelabras. One German visitor recorded her evening visit to a lamp-lit Oxford Street: 'pyramids of pineapples, figs, grapes, oranges and all manner of fruits are on show. We enquired the price of a fine pineapple and did not think it too dear at 6s.'[2] The taste of paradise was there in such streets, even if the everlasting spring of the hothouse remained an aristocratic pleasure.

The purchase of life-improving wallpapers, furniture, crockery and fabrics increased rapidly. There were also books, curios, silver tooth-brushes, sedan chairs, musical and scientific instruments and new breeds of animal. The idea of selectively breeding horses in order to approach perfection was first mooted.[3] Furniture was a particular interest. Those New World forests of tropical hardwood and walnut were being tooled into fine dining sets, sofas, escritoires, four-poster beds and more.

Shopping for these kinds of items had moved beyond the mere satisfying of a need into a pleasurable activity in itself. Josiah Wedgwood opened a dazzling shop for his chinaware and was at the forefront of another new phenomenon: he cultivated his customers, offering quality service, pampering and reliable prices. Part of Wedgwood's genius was to listen to his customers and be alert to trends that could be exploited with new products. A fashion for one style of ornament would be followed by another, then another. In this way his shops created what would become a feature of mass consumption: a rolling thunder of desires. There was something else too: snobbery. Wedgwood refused to use the word 'shop', preferring to call his outlets 'warehouses' – an affectation that has not endured. Shop assistants in such high-class places learned to treat with disdain anyone of insufficient quality – an affectation that perhaps does linger. The upmarket shops moved to London's West

End and held themselves aloof. When luxuries were on sale, the shopkeepers discovered, an air of exclusivity was a great selling point and the gatekeepers to this new paradise were, of course, money and status.[4]

Among the gentry, anxious to have the best possessions, notions about what constituted perfection were being profoundly altered. The young Alexander Pope launched into the fray, calling on classical images of Arcadia and Elysium to press for change in what was considered beautiful. At the age of 16 he drew attention for the publication of his *Pastoral Odes*, then in 1711 his 'Essay on Criticism' caught the mood of the new aesthetics with precocious brilliance:

> First follow NATURE, and your Judgement frame
> By her just Standard, which is still the same:
> *Unerring Nature*, still divinely bright,
> One *clear, unchang'd*, and *Universal* Light,
> Life, Force, and Beauty, must to all impart,
> At once the *Source*, and *End*, and *Test* of *Art*.

The following year, his friend Joseph Addison was complaining about perfect geometry and formality: 'we see the marks of the scissars on every Plant and Bush.' 'Let the countryside come in,' he argued, with 'some small Additions of Art'. In fact there were quite substantial additions and a small number of wealthy intellectuals were dictating what they should be.[5] Paradise had become a thoroughly secular concern, the use of biblical and classical terms as metaphors deeply entrenched.

The gardens and parks of the gentry became less geometric: out went the knots and parterres of previous times and in came curves and asymmetry. Others began to remake their country estates into *fermes ornées*, self-conscious experiments in Arcadian bliss. This so-called primitivism, a retreat to a simpler rustic lifestyle, had long antecedents: Pliny the Younger had kept two villas for such purposes (named Comedy and Tragedy), Epicurus and Virgil had espoused the practice. In the late seventeenth century the retired diplomat William Temple did likewise. Most men made the pursuit of wealth their life's work, he wrote, a pastime that had the great advantage of never being satisfied. Wiser souls realized that happiness required them 'to place true riches in wanting little, rather than possessing much, and true pleasure in temperance, rather than satisfying the senses'.[6] Half a century later, most of those English aristocrats who espoused such views were only dabbling, but the fact remains that the eighteenth century hit a purple patch in this respect with its harmonious country houses and rolling parks. (Retreat to such well-staffed simplicity remains a very pleasant kind of paradise dream judging by visitor levels for such houses today and, perhaps, in the buoyant demand for country houses and barns in Britain – the new outflow from London to the country was around 116,000 in 2004.)

Later in the eighteenth century Jean-Jacques Rousseau would take this movement to its extreme. In a letter to the Duchess of Portland in 1767, Rousseau wrote: 'Men say, they make nature more beautiful – but I believe they disfigure her.' True perfection, he decided, was the wilderness. For many that meant North America, the most perfectly sublime example of wilderness.

At the same time, the nature of the Perfect Man took a parallel trajectory, taking in a pinch of the pioneer character. In the words of historian Roy Porter this individual, in England at least, began the eighteenth century as 'convivial conformist', but by the end, 'in the gospel according to Jean-Jacques Rousseau, it was in the unbiddable rough diamond that true value lay'.[7]

The perfect woman was also undergoing radical alterations. Journeys into remote and barbarous regions had convinced Enlightenment males that savage societies treated women appallingly, either as donkeys or sexual slaves. 'Can love exist in countries where women are beasts of burthene?' asked Joseph Banks, sailing the Pacific with James Cook. 'I think not.'[8] But Banks fell for a

Tahitian beauty himself and the allure of the naked, as well as noble, savage was obvious. Tales of women who confidently took sexual pleasure when they wanted it were common. Louis de Bougainville, calling at Tahiti in 1768, was thrilled by a bronzed goddess who insinuated herself on to his quarter deck, then casually dropped her robe. The effect was 'celestial', the island was a 'Garden of Eden'. His readers were agog.

Sex was one of the key issues about paradise that was thrown into the spotlight by the new freedoms. Many Christians of an Augustinian type were reluctant to even allow it a place, preferring to snipe at what they claimed to be Islam's rather licentious attitudes. But with secular paradise gaining ground, views on what constituted a perfect relationship were moving too. Sex in the eighteenth century was undergoing a revolution. As Roy Porter put it: 'The libido was liberated, and erotic gratification increasingly disassociated from sin and shame.' Early in the century a new type of bestselling book began to appear: usually translated from the French, often ignored by the literary world, always erotic, these *romans* were snapped up by an eager readership. Typical was Claude Prosper Jolyot de Crébillon's titillating volume, *Le Sopha* (1740), in which a man who had been a sofa in a previous life tells ten tales of what he saw. If this was paradise as a sexual debauch – everlasting springs – then it had a new and fascinating overtone; it was set in the Islamic world.[9]

There had been changes in the European relationship with Islam since the high tide of Ottoman menace. Back in 1587 Christopher Marlowe's *Tamburlaine* had the 'Scourge of God' burning the Qur'an on stage and almost immediately feeling the 'distemper' of punishment creeping up on him. Islam, the message seemed to be, was a potent force. A century later, after the Ottomans last threatened Vienna in 1683, there was a growing feeling that Islam was no longer so powerful, a feeling that grew as the Ottoman empire was surrounded by resurgent enemies: Russia in the north, the Habsburgs in Eastern Europe and Britain in the west. France had a different kind of relationship with the Ottomans, cultivating links and keen to find common cause against the Habsburgs. In 1670 a young scholar named Anthoine Galland was sent out to the embassy in Istanbul. Over the next few years he toured extensively in the Ottoman lands, searching out curiosities for the cabinet of his patron, Jean-Baptiste Colbert, finance minister to Louis XIV. As with Tradescant's collecting, there were remarkable and unforeseen consequences to this search.

Among Galland's finds in Syria was a manuscript of stories about an Arab sailor from Basra called Sindbad. On his return to France, Galland translated and published the work. It was an immediate success and, hoping to follow it up, Galland managed to get hold of another Syrian manuscript, this one from the fourteenth century and titled *The Thousand and One Nights*.[10]

Within the stories was a strong and exciting undercurrent of sexual licence, despite Galland's tendency to play this down. Between 1704 and 1711 they were published as *Les Mille et Une Nuits* and became hugely popular, a standard part of personal libraries – Edward Gibbon had three copies.

Hard on the heels of Galland came a horde of other books, many less circumspect about the erotic, often graphically illustrated. Many had an element of social satire and presented radical views. (Galland himself had added a speech against the arranged marriage – a common institution of the time in France.) These authors were influenced by Julien Offray de la Mettrie, the philosopher who declared the human to be no more than a machine. If vice makes you happy, argued Mettrie, then do it. Now in the harems and seraglios of Istanbul and the Levant, Europe was finding its idea of sexual paradise for bodies, male ones at least, that had been released from Christian constraint. (For women, Lady Mary Wortley Montagu suggested, there was the prospect of a different kind of release, from the bondage of strait-laced tight clothes into loose flowing robes.)

Denis Diderot, one of the leading intellectuals of the French Enlightenment, used the genre to write a biting satire of the French court portrayed as a sensual eastern idyll. The *roman à clef, Indiscreet Jewels* (1749), has a bored sultan (Mangogul/Louis XV) conjure up a ghost who gives him a ring with the power to make women confess their most intimate adventures. Rather surprisingly for the women involved, these confessions erupt from between their legs.

The Oriental genre was very popular: Henry Fielding owned such books, as did Swift. Lawrence Sterne had a copy of *Le Sopha* among his collection and when Hogarth issued his 'Marriage à la Mode' in 1745 he could place a copy of the book on the sofa beside the figure of Counsellor Silvertongue, a convenient symbol of the man's nature.[11] Authors would use ingenious devices to carry their action into the sexy Orient. Elizabeth Inchbald's farce, *The Mogul Tale*, which ran successfully at the Haymarket in 1784, had a hot air balloon taking off from Hyde Park Corner and landing in a harem in the east. There the Great Mogul proves adept at pretending to be cruel and sensual, while the Cockney hero gets drunk and falls in love with a concubine who turns out to be his own dear wife Fanny in disguise.

Views of Islam were shifting, though scarcely becoming more accurate. This saucy new dimension had more to do with European yearnings than Middle Eastern reality. The silken surfeits of the harem would now forever be part of the male sexual paradise on earth, while in heaven the *huris* were presented as no less sexualized. This seductive myth of the East caught on just as military threats faded. (And it grew in power: when Byron published his epic of harem-rescue *The Corsair* in 1814, it sold 10,000 copies in a single day, an unprecedented literary phenomenon.)

There were other revisions to Islam's image in the early 1700s: in France Henri de Boulainvilliers's *Life of Muhammad*[12] actually dared to present the Prophet in a flattering light. No other religion, argued Boulainvilliers, was as close to reason as Islam. This idea, needless to say, did not catch on as readily as that of a sensual eroticized Orient.

15

Creating the New Adam

The volatile forces that had wrought changes in attitudes to sex were also having an effect on those other paradisical attributes: perfect bodies. Fresh thinking about the human body was working to free people from centuries of Christian contempt for the aching miserable vehicle that housed their immortal souls. James Graham, a medical student from Edinburgh, was a man who epitomized the new optimism about scientifically enhanced health, something he matched with a very contemporary love of money-making and large doses of old-fashioned superstition and charlatanism. Graham was going to produce perfect humans ready for paradise and get rich in the process.

In the early 1770s Graham had gone out to America where, in Philadelphia, he was intrigued by Benjamin Franklin's latest experiments with electricity. The 'Prometheus of modern times', as Franklin was called, had proved that electricity was a basic element of nature and Graham became convinced that electrical stimuli were the way to health.[1] After catching up with Franklin in Paris during the summer of 1779, Graham settled in London and opened the Temple of Health, a fantastical and colourful palace dedicated to long life, sex and procreation. For 2s 6d patrons were promised a place that was dedicated to: 'the propagating of beings rational, and far stronger and more beautiful in mental as well as bodily endowment, than the present puny, feeble and nonsensical race of probationary mortals, which crawl, fret and politely play at cutting one another's throats for nothing at all, on most parts of this terraqueous globe'.

Graham's obsessive belief in the perfectibility of human beings was right for the times. (Across the Channel a decade later, it would be an obsession that the Jacobins would share, but as yet less helpful quacks like Graham had the field to themselves.) Aristocratic customers were convinced, including Georgiana Duchess of Devonshire who tried Graham's various potions in her desperation to become pregnant. Hugh Walpole was less impressed: 'The most impudent puppet-show of imposition I ever saw,' he commented.

As living advertisements for his new race of perfect Enlightenment beings, Graham employed nubile young women recruited through the newspapers, one of whom was a 16-year-old serving girl called Emma Lyon. In the words of Graham's promotional literature:

Precisely at eight o'clock the Gentleman Usher of the Rosy Rod, assisted by the High Priestess, will conduct the rosy, the gigantic, the STUPENDOUS Goddess of Health to the Celestial Throne. The blooming Priestess of the Temple will endeavour to entertain Ladies and Gentlemen of candour and good nature, by reading a Lecture on the simplest and most efficacious means of preserving health, beauty, and personal loveliness, and a serene mental brilliancy even to the extremest old age.

Stunningly attractive and delightfully shameless, Emma proved to be the star, shedding her clothes to enter a mud bath before entranced audiences. Graham could not hold on to such talent – as her fame grew she worked her way out of the *demi-monde* and up the social ladder: mistress to a knight and then to the Honourable Charles Greville, who sold her to his uncle Sir William Hamilton who then married her before she finally hooked Nelson. By then she was said to be still pretty but enormously fat – rather like, one might imagine, the rotund lovelies seen in the harem scenes of the artist Thomas Rowlandson.

For those with problems of procreation, and £50 to spare, Graham reserved a night to remember in his masterpiece, a gigantic 12-foot-long bed supported on 40 glass pillars with a domed canopy into which oozed perfumes and piped music. Under a mattress supposedly stuffed with rose petals and the tail hair of English thoroughbred stallions, were 15 hundredweight of magnets plus Hauksbee's Influence Machine – a device that generated static electricity. On the vast head-board, electricity was said to crackle and spark across the inscription, 'Be fruitful, multiply and replenish the earth.' With all this awesome power, Graham – the Frankenstein of the phallus – hoped to revive limp aristocrats, though the results appear to have been more hair-raising than heir-making.

Sadly, high running costs and relentless lampooning forced him out of business – there was even a West End play about him. Undeterred the doctor moved back to Edinburgh where he modestly announced that he had solved the problems of senescence and death. Mud baths were the answer. He gave public displays – with a naked and nubile assistant – and was repeatedly arrested. Now his interest in religion appeared with his Church of the New Jerusalem. He declared that time began at its inception and set off around the country, prosely-tizing for vegetarianism and nudism while condemning masturbation and woollen clothes. For a time he was incarcerated as a lunatic, then died in 1794 at the age of 49 from a burst blood vessel.

Graham's theatrical shows were denounced as quackery even at the time, but perhaps more for his irreligion than his fake science. He was actually something of a forerunner: mud baths, fresh air, electrical stimulation of the body and sex aids were all things he pioneered against scientific opinion. Most of all he had made the connection between science, paradisical desires and cash – today he would be selling breast implants and botox injections in health spas.

The years at the end of Graham's life were a time of bewildering change in Europe. The French Revolution had brought many paradise-seeking strands together: the secular production of the Perfect Man in his Perfect Society had, at last, grabbed itself a broad stage. When Tom Paine's *The Rights of Man* had appeared in 1791, then his *Age of Reason* in

1794, anybody could buy a simple, straightforward demolition of the Bible's claim to be God's word, plus a stirring call: 'the present generation will appear to the future as the Adam of the new world.'

In the Revolution Christianity was supposedly discarded: churches were vandalized and priests persecuted. Initially idealistic young men and women were drawn towards the light. On arriving in Paris to take up his seat in the new National Convention in September 1792, Tom Paine was feted as a hero, while William Wordsworth later recalled, 'Bliss was it in that dawn to be alive.'[2] His friends Southey and Coleridge felt the quickened pulse of paradise-seeking too, and started on plans to build a utopian settlement, 'Pantisocracy'. Not that France was ever entertained as a location: America reigned supreme as the home of paradise, no matter what the Committee of Public Safety might say.

Even at the time, more perceptive participants in the French Revolution, including Robespierre, knew that religion could not be dismissed so easily and that the Revolution would have to borrow the clothes of the old faith, if only to avoid a counter-revolution. In November 1793 Notre-Dame was renamed the Temple of Reason and opened with a procession led by the Goddess of Reason. But the borrowing went far deeper than that: the whole bloody spectacle marched to the same drum as the millenarians of previous centuries. The End of Time had come, Judgement was at hand, a new age of glory was beginning (with a new calendar) and those unworthy must be eliminated. The paradise myth had not only survived, it was driving the revolution to bring heaven down on earth. Even when the failings of the Revolution were obvious, the yearnings for what it had promised only seemed to increase. Rather than diminish paradise-seeking and attempts to build utopian communities, the Revolution had 'lit a passion which the most violent political revolutions had never before been able to produce'.[3]

Robespierre was right to think that religion would not be dismissed so easily. The incidence of prophetism increased in Britain in the 1790s as the same conditions that spurred intellectuals towards revolution were whipping others towards apocalyptic hysteria. For these people, the obsession with the Perfect Man, the New Adam, remained overtly religious and was centred on the figure of the Messiah.

In 1792 an obscure Devonshire woman, Joanna Southcott, started seeing visions of the future. Gathering devotees, she moved to London and announced that she would give birth by immaculate conception to 'Shiloh', the next saviour who would bring paradise with him. Her aim was 144,000 followers, a number – inevitably – found in Revelation.[4] Public excitement did bring around 20,000 converts, along with gifts like a gilded satinwood cradle, but sadly no baby Messiah. In December 1814, already at least two months overdue, Southcott died. Her autopsy must have been one of the more bizarre ever held: the room ringed by devotees expecting either a resurrection or the removal from her womb of the living saviour. Alas, despite the application of hot water bottles she did not arise, nor, it transpired, had she ever been pregnant. The sect continued to thrive, however, convinced that their own lack of faith had prevented the miraculous.[5]

In those turbulent times, there was a well-founded fear in Britain and elsewhere that religion was under attack. Something had to be done to protect the faith, mainly from atheism and materialism, but also crackpot prophetism too. Between reason and revelation there had to be an accommodation. In his 1814 Hunterian Lectures, John Abernethy, fellow of the Royal College of Surgeons, would suggest something 'analogous to electricity' as the essential life force previously known as soul. This mysterious substance was 'subtle, mobile, invisible' – it was also a red rag to more radical scientists. Two years later his former pupil William Lawrence, also a professor at the Royal College, used his own lectures to denounce this position and propose a completely materialistic theory of life. The influential journal *Quarterly Review* was outraged, accusing Lawrence of having a twisted brain and demanded the Royal College control this mad maverick. At the heart of the furore was a vital question: was religion either necessary or relevant any longer? If not, then man alone should get on with perfecting himself.

It was the daughter of Tom Paine's friend Mary Wollstonecraft who would distill these new unsettling developments into an electrifying stew of science and imagination, a book that would be a tribute to the effects of religion's melancholy withdrawal from the paradise dreaming of materialism. In *Frankenstein*, the new arbiters of perfection were science and reason.

Mary Wollstonecraft Godwin was intellectually precocious and still only 16 when the radical Percy Bysshe Shelley met her in the summer of 1814. They were soon spending hours together, no doubt discussing issues such as Abernethy's lectures on the essential life force. William Lawrence was a member of the intellectual circle cultivated by Mary's father, William Godwin, and Shelley himself was always fascinated by science and medical progress. Fourteen days after meeting the poet, Mary declared her unbounded love for him and offered herself, body and soul, forever. Shelley immediately went to her father William Godwin who tried to stop the romance. His own marriage had scarcely been conventional, but Shelley was already married with children.

On 28 July, Shelley, Mary and her half-sister Jane all eloped, taking a boat from Dover beach. Over the following weeks they walked to Switzerland where Shelley imagined setting up a community of free spirits – with characteristic generosity and unthinking cruelty he offered to include his estranged wife Harriet in the plan.

France was in post-conflict chaos, lodgings hard to find and they were permanently anxious about money, but Shelley turned the whole thing into a mad romance, behaving, so Jane recorded, 'as if he were Adam in Paradise before his fall'.[6] When they reached Lucerne, he started work on a story that had been brewing during those long walks. He provisionally titled it *The Assassins*.

Shelley had learned of the sect from Sale de Lisle's *Old Man of the Mountain* published in 1799, a book he had probably picked up on the way through Paris. The mix of paradise myth, communal retreat and violent idealism clearly had parallels with his own situation and his desires. A few years later he would write to Mary: 'My greatest content would be utterly to desert all human society. I would retire with you & our child to a solitary island in the sea, would build a boat, & shut upon my retreat the floodgates of the world.'[7] This ability to articulate timeless human longings, then go and attempt to live them, was the bedrock of Shelley's genius, and of his enduring appeal. The retreat to paradise appealed to him and that was how he saw the Assassins, not as starry-eyed vicious killers, but seekers of peace and perfection. In his version of their story he tells how they withdraw from the world to live in idyllic harmony, gradually realizing an incredible intensity of bliss in a world of complete love, sexual freedom and ecstatic pleasure. Was this, one wonders, what Shelley had in mind for himself as the trio plodded through the burned-out and ruined villages of France, sleeping in flea-infested straw and fighting off amorous innkeepers? For a man of his social class, as for his friend-to-be Byron, the normal ideal of paradise was an English country estate and a healthy cash-stream from land rents and Caribbean plantations. But in both men's poetry their paradises would prove to be the temporary refuges of remote islands and peaks, places that drove 'their imaginations to the outermost limits that mythology and modern travel allowed them to conceive'.[8] On that long walk south the Assassin myth became part of that drive for Shelley.

In his unfinished story, Shelley speculates on how the Assassins would cope with exposure to normal civilized society. They would, he decides, necessarily fall into conflict, unable to accept authority and driven to destroy the tyrants. 'The respectable man – smooth, smiling, polished villain whom all the city honours; whose very trade is lies and murder; who buys his daily bread with the blood and tears of men – would feed the ravens with his limbs.' The implications of Shelley's words echo down to the modern day: the idealist has no choice, no matter how far he or she retreats, one day justice will demand that 'his path through the wilderness of civilized society...be marked with the blood of the oppressor'. For all his atheism one can hear an Old Testament prophet in Shelley's words, thundering his disapproval and forebodings at the iniquities of the world, but now this Jeremiah carries a gun.

Shelley's own attempts to forge a new kind of community took further shape when the three were forced back to London through lack of money. Mary, now pregnant, was encouraged to become the lover of Thomas Jefferson Hogg, Shelley's friend from Oxford. Meanwhile Shelley spent more time with Mary's half-sister, Jane, now renamed Claire. The foursome did not last, however. Claire left to become Byron's mistress. In May 1816 a new coterie of individuals gathered in Geneva – Shelley, Mary, Claire, Byron and his doctor, Polidori – all enjoying boating and leisurely breakfasts. They visited Jean-Jacques Rousseau's memorial and Byron leased the house that Milton had once occupied overlooking the lake, the Villa Diodati. Claire was found to be pregnant and Byron assumed it was his, rather than Shelley's.

In mid-June a series of late-night discusssions at the villa began, often made more portentous by dramatic electrical storms over the lake. Science and theories of the origins of life were recurrent subjects, and at some point came the now legendary challenge to tell ghost stories. The pressure cooker of Shelley's social experimentation was boiling up. One night, provoked by a reading of Coleridge's macabre poem 'Christabel', he had a kind of fit. A few days later, Mary had a ghastly nightmare in which a 'hideous phantasm of a man' was awakened to life by mechanical means. This was the moment when the story of *Frankenstein, the Modern Prometheus* first came into existence.

The tale of Doctor Frankenstein who attempted to create his own New Adam, with tragic consequences, was published in 1818. *Frankenstein* tells how the creature receives a brisk education with four books, one of them *Paradise Lost*.[9] Despite this excellent start in life he turns out to be a murderous monster who cries out to his maker, 'I ought to be thy Adam; but I am rather a fallen angel, whom thou drivest from joy for no misdeed. Everywhere I see bliss, from which I am irrevocably excluded.' Instead of finding any happiness, Frankenstein and his monster — his child — steadily hound and destroy one another.

No doubt Shelley, the quintessentially modern individual who wanted perfection in his own world and had tried building it, saw in both the monster and its creator something of himself.[10] In this he was the first, but not last. At the very moment when science was about to step forward and revolutionize the earth, Mary had understood the full potential horror of man as a God who is bent on producing perfection.

16

Robert Owen and the Godless Millennium

On the evening of 14 May 1855, a meeting was held in St Martin's Hall in London at which a design for a great new invention that would bring universal peace was unveiled. The Devastator was a steam-driven machine that would hurtle across continents pouring explosive fire in all directions, killing indiscriminately and finally curing mankind of its love of violence. Its inventors, the inaptly named Mr Sweetlove and his colleague Mr Cowen, estimated that 100,000 lives per hour could be reaped. The presentation of their monster, however, they left to Mr Robert Owen, an 84-year-old who had never been known to raise his voice in argument, the mildest and most courteous of visionaries. After unveiling the design, Owen expressed the opinion that the Crimean War could be settled and a new moral order inaugurated simply by threatening governments with this iron-clad Armageddon. It was a bitter swansong for the man who had spent a lifetime working for co-operative utopias and along the way had also started the first adult evening classes, the first purpose-built children's playground, and a nursery school where – shockingly – corporal punishment was not allowed.

The urge to seek paradise on this earth knows no boundaries of class, race, sex or age. It seizes young and old, rich and poor, the wise and the foolish. It seized Robert Owen when he was young and poor, yet never left him while wealthy, nor while he was being very wise, nor while he was being extraordinarily foolish.

Owen had been born in 1771 into the working classes in Newtown, mid-Wales, apparently without any great prospects, certainly without any fleeting taste of the good life to spark his utopian ambitions.[1] Nevertheless, he was a bright boy and when he got his chance he took it, rising fast in the Manchester mill business. There he joined the city's Unitarian College, attending lectures and reading widely. As a youth he had abandoned all religions, the 'false imaginations of our early ancestors', but found that the space left behind was filled with 'the spirit of universal charity'.[2] In Manchester this sense of social responsibility found an intellectual framework to express itself.

It was probably at the college that he heard about William Godwin and his book *Enquiry Concerning Political Justice* (1793) with its ideas derived from John Locke on how children were formed by their experience. Knowledge, Owen decided, was acquired through our senses and whatever impressions and experiences impinged on us would form our character. Human beings, then, were malleable, and the agent of this, and the route to self-fulfilment, was education. In Owen, the pansophist ideals of Hartlib and Comenius were revived, but post-Enlightenment these ideals came without God.

Until 1798 Owen had little opportunity to put his beliefs into practice. In that year, however, he visited the extensive Scottish mills of the progressive Glaswegian capitalist, David Dale at New Lanark. Owen was impressed with the business, with the philanthropy, and with Dale's daughter, Caroline. Within two years he had bought the mills, adopted the philosophy and married the daughter.

He proved to be an adept manager and profits were healthy, but his real enthusiasm was now for reform. About 500 orphaned children were employed in the mill, each doing eleven and three-quarter hours a day which Owen cut by one hour, significantly less than such foundlings were expected to do in other mills. He opened a nursery school, the first of its kind in the world, where the syllabus included dancing and singing (for which he was condemned by one Quaker business partner – such frivolous pursuits were ungodly). As well as forbidding corporal punishment, he attempted to make learning interesting. True happiness, he taught the children, came through the happiness of others.

With the astonishing zeal and energy he displayed all his life, Owen pushed through many other reforms – often against the wishes of his workforce who were endlessly suspicious of his good works. Along with the world's first children's playground and adult evening classes came a pension scheme. Workers were encouraged – some said forced – to keep their tenement houses clean, to avoid drink and to educate their children. There were critics who said these were slave plantations reconstructed on an industrial scale. Owen ignored them. Although gentle by nature, he was not conciliatory, never wasting much time on anyone who disagreed with him. He was out 'to reform the world at a profit'.[3] At New Lanark the company shop sold goods to the workers who were paid in tokens. By purchasing in bulk, Owen managed to undercut other local outlets and still make healthy profits.

By 1816 Owen was moving towards a personal crisis. In a tour of other textile mills he was appalled by the conditions. Children as young as five were forced to work 16 hours a day, often crawling under moving machinery in thick fibrous dust and tremendous heat. Around a quarter of them were carrying injuries and deformities from work-related accidents. These wretches, he declared, were 'living human skeletons, almost disrobed of intellect ... they linger out a few years of miserable existence, acquiring every bad habit, which they disseminate through society.'[4] The tour electrified Owen: what had been benign philanthropy became something more passionate. When he found only resistance to change among mill-owners and in government circles, he became more radical. Incremental reforms were no longer sufficient, the system needed a revolution.

At the City of London Tavern on the night of 21 August 1817, Owen spoke before a packed crowd of radicals, clergymen and bullish free-traders. To their astonishment, and accompanied by some hisses, he rounded on religion, denouncing it as nothing but lies. Then he offered to end that 'long bondage of error, crime, and misery'. The new millennium began there and then. According to Owen's highly partial account, the audience were first thunderstruck, then burst into applause and cheering. The great crisis and misery, the Last Days, were now over, he told them, a new dawn had arrived, brought about by 'the invincible and irresistible power of Truth'.

Throughout August and September he kept up a furious pace, bombarding the press and spending £4,000 on spreading his message. The world was in crisis, everywhere men were slaves and misery reigned. But with his message came deliverance, paradise was at hand: there would be one nation, one language, swords would be turned into ploughshares, and spears into pruning hooks. All that was needed was for 'the minds of all men…to be born again'.

Owen had borrowed the Christian myth of paradise and turned it into a secular faith. In his ideals the plan of history begun by Joachim of Fiore was intact, despite the disappearance of God. History had been moving inevitably towards crisis, now resolved by Owen's arrival. (He always tried to downplay the obvious charge that he was claiming to be the Messiah.) Paradise could begin.

What possessed Owen suddenly to start using the language of millenarianism, we do not know. As a child he had certainly imbibed Christian values and read works such as John Bunyan's classic, *Pilgrim's Progress*. Then post-French Revolution, with prophets like Joanna Southcott and the rise of evangelical Christianity, talk of the Last Days was certainly in the air. Perhaps he thought it would appeal to the kind of people he needed to contact: Southcott had been unusually successful in attracting middle-class converts when such sects were normally associated with the disadvantaged classes in society.

The Owenite millennium, however, got off to a slow start with backers hard to find. The government was determined to keep a tight rein on any revolutionary activity, brutally suppressing dissent.[5] This was a time when even Sir Robert Peel's 12-hour maximum working day for children was vehemently opposed. Plans that advocated dishing out large tracts of land and money to grubby beggars – Owen suggested £60,000 for each utopian community – did not get a sympathetic hearing.[6] Having been the toast of philanthropic circles, Owen now found that his attacks on established religion had made him enemies. Typically he soldiered on, even handing out pamphlets at the meeting of the Great Powers in Aix-la-Chapelle the following year. (Tsar Alexander I coldly refused the offer.) Owen's beliefs were now overtly socialist, arguing that self-interest would not lead to individual happiness.[7]

In the summer of 1824 Owen heard of a group of religious settlers in America called the Rappites who wanted to sell their land and buildings. Suddenly all the utopian idealism, scientific progress and business acumen seemed to come together. He wanted to make perfect human beings, he wanted to make a perfect place for them to inhabit, and he wanted to make money. What's more: he knew he could do all three at the same time, and if England was not ready, the right place to go was America.

By October Owen had embarked for the New World and in the following January he agreed to buy the Rappite settlement at Harmony on the banks of the Wabash river in Indiana for $125,000. The Rappites were a millenarian sect, which may have influenced Owen's choice. (George Rapp, the German founder, was so convinced he would lead his flock to paradise on earth that as he lay on his sick bed, he muttered to them, 'If I did not know that the dear Lord meant I should present you all to him, I should think my last moment has come.' Whereupon he died.)[8] For his substantial investment Owen got 20,000 acres, a village on a grid plan (which is still there), four mills, a tannery, a textile factory, a brewery and orchards.

Owen's vision was of a new kind of urban and egalitarian paradise, a place without the false promises of previous paradises and one accessible to the mass of people. His colony would be built on a grid pattern with parks and a maze (just to remind the inhabitants that life was a series of challenging decisions). It was a time when many people were trying out life in idealistic communities and some of those who answered Owen's call were undoubtedly sympathetic to his message. For others, however, it was simply a meal ticket and, with a large operation to run, entrance requirements were ominously low. Not only that but Owen himself, the great motivator and enthusiast, was too busy to linger. Leaving his son William in charge, he dashed off to Washington where he spoke to Congress and the president, promising that his system would, in one generation, 'make the inhabitants a very superior race of beings'. 'The time is now come,' he told them, 'when the principle of good is about to predominate and reign triumphant over the principle of evil ... old things shall pass away and all shall become new.' The biblical reference (2 Corinthians 5:17) would not have been lost on President Monroe and the assembled representatives.

From Washington Owen went on tour, speaking in several cities and spending four days intensively debating with the 82-year-old Thomas Jefferson. The founding father declared himself convinced by the principles, but wondered how they might be practically implemented. Owen himself, like many a new arrival in the New World, had no doubts: he was fired up with enthusiasm and sketching grandiose plans for settlements. He imagined self-regulating and self-sufficient utopias, communities that would leave behind the flaws of the Old World. He added the businesslike touch of expecting them to be run with the efficiency of a good textile mill, and at a profit. He firmly believed this system would catch on and take over the world (an astonishing ambition, but less fantastic than that of his French contemporary Charles Fourier who believed his utopian communities in the United States would eventually result in a realignment of the planets).

At New Harmony there was an all-too-brief period of hope, but within a year discord emerged: one breakway became Macluria – after a new leader – another took the name Feiba-Peveli – after a bizarre system of translating latitude and longitude into letters. When Owen returned in April 1828 it was with his family, intending to settle at New Harmony. Instead he found himself winding things up. His great plan had failed, taking most of his fortune with it. (He had put in around $250,000.)

Owen himself was not disillusioned by the New Harmony disaster. It was not that he did not learn from the experience, he simply ignored it. He travelled on through America still keen to evangelize his faithless creed. One cannot help but admire the man: he was on the side of love in the paradise business, earnestly believing that wretched human beings were products of their environment. Good housing, education and humane treatment, Owen constantly repeated, plus a system of co-operation, would work wonders.

His optimism intact, he sailed for Mexico, where, with customary hubris, he asked if he might govern Texas. The Mexicans apologized for being unable to give him the state, but offered a 150-mile-wide strip of land all along the border with the United States, over 2,000 miles of it. Voltaire would have been proud of Owen's account of this journey – he had become a new Candide, marching ever onwards with trusting innocence sparkling in his eyes. The border zone was to be his 'Kingdom of Peace' run on Owenite principles with total religious freedom. The Bishop of Puebla, head of the Catholic Church, listened and smoothly offered any assistance. But when Owen set off for the United States again, the plan was swiftly strangled at birth by the Church. Owen lost no sleep, he was already on to his next struggle: a titanic debate with one of America's religious heavyweights scheduled for April of 1829.

At that time the small towns of the American frontier buzzed with self-made men, dreamers and quacks of every hue, religious, financial and medical. Before the 1849 California Gold Rush[9] one fad was to search for precious metals supposedly tucked away by marauding Indians or long dead conquistadores. A man named Walters toured upstate New York carrying a Latin copy of Cicero's *Orations,* claiming it held secret information on the ancient inhabitants of America and their treasure troves — information available, of course, at a price. Men would dig huge pits and trenches, desperate to find valuables, often working at night to avoid detection, but also perhaps because they used witchcraft and magic to assist them. If only a person with a knack for divining the spot marked X could be found, then you'd be making whoopee in New York City instead of watching your beans disappear up the sharp end of a dust devil.

Joseph Smith, founder of the Mormons, started out as one of these magic-assisted gold prospectors, later joining the arts of treasure-hunting and paradise-seeking in his discovery of the golden plates of the Book of Mormon.[10]

At that time pioneers were moving up the Ohio Valley, heading towards the line of the Mississippi. The census of 1800 showed a population of about a million spread across the frontier lands of central Kentucky, western Pennsylvania and the territories that would become Ohio, Indiana, Illinois and parts of Michigan and Wisconsin. Frontier life was not noted for its spirituality, nor were the established Churches doing any evangelizing. People had a suspicion of those home country institutions. 'Old World!' cries the trapper in James Fennimore Cooper's *The Prairie* (1826). 'That is the miserable cry of all the half-starved miscreants that have come into this blessed land since the days of my boyhood ... Were they to say a *worn-out,* and an *abused,* and a *sacrilegious* world, they might not be so far from the truth!'

Those that did attend religious gatherings showed a taste for the wilder and more ecstatic. The apocalyptic went down well and anyone with a good account of why the world would end violently and soon got a hearing. It was, after all, no more than anyone could expect.

Barton Stone, a Presbyterian from Kentucky, left an account of a revivalist meeting at which the congregation would fall down swooning then lie 'for hours together in an apparently breathless and motionless state. Sometimes for a few moments reviving and exhibiting symptoms of life by a deep groan or a piercing shriek or by a prayer for mercy most fervently uttered. After lying thus for hours ... they would rise, shouting deliverance.'

Stone regretted that sectarianism plagued the lives of these believers. His own sect was originally an attempt to unite the frontier Christians under the supremacy of the Gospels and the banner Disciples of Christ. The literal interpretation of Scripture was an important feature, and one very much in tune with the spirit of the age. This was a simple Protestantism that championed liberty and independence, spiced up with some fiery End of Time prophecy – religion that warmed the belly faster than moonshine. It was guaranteed to appeal on the frontier.

It was Stone's fellow Disciple, the Reverend Alexander Campbell, who had accepted Robert Owen's challenge to any clergyman to debate his proposition that 'all the religions of the world have been founded on the ignorance of mankind ... and that they have been and are the real cause of vice, dissension and misery of every description'.

A date was set in April of the following year and Owen hurried away from his talks with the Mexican government to reach Cincinnati in time for the showdown.

The Methodist Hall was chosen as the venue and by 9 a.m. on Monday 13 April over one thousand people had packed in, no doubt hoping for fireworks. In this Owen, at least, disappointed: he spoke very gently and calmly, smiling charmingly at the audience. A certain Mrs Trollope who was present found the experience strangely disturbing: the man was saying that the Christian religion was a fraud and its teachings nothing but fables, and yet she could not help but like him.

Campbell was made of sterner stuff. He punched relentlessly at Owen's theories of human nature and his plans for utopian settlements, then hammered home his message of the Gospel Truth, all backed up with a barrage of biblical references. The debate resumed next morning, and for six more days after that. At one point Campbell was on his feet for 12 hours. Even Owen had met his match. After the final points had been made, the audience – all one thousand apparently still present – were invited to vote on whether they would continue to support Christianity: 997 went with Campbell.

Typically, Owen was unabashed. Most of the audience had been with him, he reported, but had felt social pressure to vote with Campbell. Anyway he had to rush off, 'to reconcile the two greatest nations in the world',[11] Britain and America still being at loggerheads following the War of Independence. Whatever the truth of the matter, the fact was that Owen's secular paradise had not been a hit in the United States, the very place where he thought success was guaranteed. On the contrary, when it came to paradise-seeking, Americans were showing themselves to be firmly religious in their choices. Unfortunately for Alexander Campbell, Americans were also showing themselves to be adepts at schism. The smallest argument was easily settled by packing up and heading out to those distant horizons where things would be just perfect. In 1837 one of Campbell's more trenchant colleagues in the Disciples, a Virginian named John Thomas, began to wrangle with him on the subject of baptism. They both agreed that adult baptism should occur after an understanding of the true faith had been reached. But what if, enquired Thomas, that understanding was incorrect? Didn't that invalidate the immersion?

Taken together, an outsider might have observed, reason and religion are a recipe for schisms – an endless series of expulsions of the unworthy in the preparation for salvation. It was the story of Protestantism played out in a few small churches in the mountains of Virginia. At that point the two men were still speaking, but Thomas then decided that the immortality of the soul was a Greek invention not mentioned in the Bible. Soul, in fact, did not exist. We were material and we lived material lives. When we died, everything died. Only when Jesus returned would there be a miracle of resurrection, but on this earth. Then we would have our paradise. Thomas had taken an Enlightenment blade to Christianity and pared it down to its barest essentials.

Campbell expelled him, and the Christadelphians were born. Their values were those of the frontier: self-reliance, independence and simplicity; they avoided public office and refused military service. But crucially they did not withdraw completely from society. When Christadelphian missionaries arrived back in England, they had success in the Midlands while the mother *ecclesia* in America did not prosper.

While Robert Owen debated the future of mankind in Cincinnati and Washington, the settlers at the failed New Harmony site had to find a new means of survival. Those who were loyal to the cause drifted away and formed new utopian communities, some joined religious communities. Owen's son, Robert Dale Owen, helped set up a new venture near Memphis with the Scottish radical, Frances Wright. The aim was to settle freed slaves, some bought by the founders. When they added religious and sexual emancipation to the original charter, however, the community was condemned as a 'brothel'. Eventually it collapsed in 1830 and all the slaves were packed off to 'freedom' in Haiti. Other groups limped on, but as the years passed they would all fail. Within 25 years of him first setting foot in the New World, Owen's communitarian experiment in America, and those of many other paradise-dreamers, were effectively dead.

Owen was a man who had managed to combine elements of both sides of the paradise-seeking equation, the paths of love and of hate, but on balance he erred on the side of the angels. Even the madness of the Devastator was at least prescient, foreshadowing the insanity of

Mutually Assured Destruction, nuclear weapons and the long-range strikes of B52 bombers. At the end of his own days Owen had understood that a secular earthly paradise might still need a threat of Armageddon to keep it straight.

The failure of Owen's style of utopianism marked the end of a certain kind of patrician, philanthropic paradise-seeking that wanted to build large institutional communities – little more than idealized workhouses said the critics. The key failure was in the individuals themselves: the transformation of character needed for those joining a utopian community was simply too great. While Owen's educational beliefs allowed for a gradual improvement, his rhetoric was millenarian and that brand of faith always attracted those who expected themselves to be transformed in a great cathartic, and communal, upheaval. Owen's philosophy, admirable as it was, did not cater for that. There was no cleansing, not by bloody Terror nor by wild ecstatic ceremonies, and no one felt reborn. Significantly, many Owenites drifted into Shaker communities where they did get a combination of orderly workhouse-style life and enthusiastic religion.[12]

Owen's reputation would suffer for his failure in America, but he had made many important advances at New Lanark and his particular brand of optimistic hope in humanity had at least never got around to bloodshed. In Europe, however, the torch of utopianism would be carried on by men like Karl Marx.

Like Owen, Marx thought he would dispense with religion (and ended up creating something that had many of the attributes of a particularly severe and intolerant faith), but the religious paradise-seekers had certainly not disappeared. On the American frontier they were for the moment still the undisputed kings. And while Owen's brand of Godless faith had failed, the religious sects were far more successful and would leave an indelible mark on the United States. When Alexis de Tocqueville, the radical French nobleman, travelled around in 1831, he reported: 'In France I had almost always seen the spirit of religion and the spirit of freedom pursuing courses diametrically opposed to each other, but in America I found that they were intimately united, and that they reigned in common over the same country.'[13]

17

Religious America Tries to Build a New Adam

While the Owenites were busy with attempting to establish perfect communities in America, others were more concerned with that related paradisical obsession: the Perfect Human. A preacher named Lucinia Umphreville from Vermont moved the paradise agenda decisively towards a very modern obsession: the idea that a perfect partner existed somewhere for everyone. Umphreville's Perfectionism, as it was known, held that perfect partners would live together in a passionate and sexless union, akin to that of Adam and Eve before the Fall. The method of finding your perfect partner was to try and live together without sex. Failure meant saying goodbye.

Most Perfectionists were traditional enough to think the Original Couple had not had sex – hence the logic behind Umphreville's dating game. But others disagreed, saying that if Adam and Eve had made love, then it must have been without shame. In fact, claimed a young charismatic preacher called John Humphrey Noyes, when sex was done in a spiritual way, worthy of Eden, any shame amounted to blasphemy.

Noyes had been drawn to Perfectionism in the early 1830s by a certain Nathaniel Taylor whose motto was 'Follow The Truth Even If It Carries You Over Niagara.'[1] The huge revival of religious enthusiasm under way in the United States between 1820 and 1850 had not only started sects like the Christadelphians, it had encouraged an estimated 100,000 people to be part of utopian communities. Noyes soon set out to build his own, walking huge distances like some Old Testament prophet, spreading the word. His radical ideas on sexual relationships were grounded deep in Eden mythology and always well intentioned, but as they developed they would prove utterly destructive to his community of followers.

His innovative theology maintained that the Second Coming had already come, way back in AD 70. This neatly dispensed with any debate as to whether the perfect community was an illegitimate pre-emptive strike on paradise (a debate that some Jews still have with Israel, arguing that it should not be established until the Messiah arrives). Heaven, or something approaching it, was already here and available now for those with the right approach. Shameless sex, so to speak, was possible.

In those times of heightened religious passion it was perhaps inevitable that some would get carried away. At one particularly ecstatic revivalist meeting, the atmosphere of charged eroticism was so powerful that even Noyes fled. Two of the young women present could not contain themselves and during the night forced their way into one youth's bed. Later, much later, with a storm raging – in true Brontë style – they ran naked to the top of a nearby hill. By prayer and testifying, they then managed to save the village below from hellfire and destruction, so they later claimed.

Noyes himself was obviously a man with a sesquipedalian sex drive hidden under his sober suits. There could be no marriage in this heaven on earth, he preached, life was a divine feast 'at which every dish is free to every guest'. Restraint, in other words, was over, at least for the saints, and by the age of 22, Noyes recorded, he was 'inwardly perfect'.

On a 500-acre site in Vermont he gathered a small group of adherents and explained that their lives would be governed by male continence, complex marriage and mutual criticism. The latter was the easy bit: every member would regularly stand before his peers for a session of criticism. Mostly this had to deal with the effects of the second item: complex marriage. In Noyes's view no one could be married exclusively in heaven, so sexual union between any consenting couple was fine if done correctly – homosexual love does not appear to have been considered. The stipulation was that a third party had to arrange matters, thus making the liaison public knowledge. Jealousy and possessiveness were absolutely forbidden. Love affairs could happen, but exclusivity was frowned upon.

The key to the system was male continence, or *coitus reservatus* as Noyes called it. Men should have sex but no orgasm. This feat of self-control was learned with the post-menopausal women of the group who tutored the youths until they mastered the art. For the young women there was the inevitable introduction via Mr Noyes, apparently without any coercion; Noyes was handsome and charismatic. When they were in their twenties they would at last have a partner of their own age, but pregnancy was not encouraged during the community's early years.

Predictably when news of this ambitious social experiment became known, there were howls of outrage. To avert charges of fornication and adultery the group was forced to move to a new location at Oneida in New York State. Here the Edenic aspirations became clear. Noyes was identified with Moses, the journey with the Israelites moving to the Promised Land. At Oneida a large house, the Mansion, was built, looking like an English country house of the time. For the surrounding estate, the works of leading landscape authorities were consulted, Capability Brown included, and the park became a lovely arrangement of orchards, woods, gardens and lawns. If they could perfect the design, went their logic, Christ would be encouraged to come and live with them.

Inside the house, this intense interest in design led to unusual arrangements of rooms. Despite local rumours that they all slept in a big round bed, the truth was that they had a large room containing tents for couples to make love. Everything was done to facilitate social interaction and prevent cliques or schisms developing. All bedroom doors could be seen from communal sitting rooms. The country house as a paradise had come a long way from its English roots, although the façade was eminently conventional – croquet was even the favourite pastime.

Croquet, in fact, proved to be a problem – it was simply much more popular than sex. Try as he might, Noyes struggled to tempt his acolytes from the lawns to love. The new ways were alien and difficult and one member reported that sex occurred much less frequently than in the outside world because everyone was so constrained by their past and the strictures Noyes laid down. As time went by, however, things settled. The women seem to have enjoyed better sex than their sisters outside: female orgasm was probably more frequent as the men would make love for up to two hours (from behind was Noyes's suggested technique, the woman with one leg drawn up). Good sex in the right spirit, said Noyes, was a sacrament.

Unfortunately, the garden did not respond so well. The hope of self-sufficiency and profit from fruit did not materialize and the community branched out into manufacturing. Like the Shakers they had a passion for good design, but they took this a stage further, inventing all kinds of gadgets and products. The women, sick of high-heeled lace-up boots, concocted a 'Final Shoe' that looked a bit like a Chelsea boot, while one of the men came up with a very un-Edenic steel animal trap which proved a bestseller. A new technique of silver-plating also succeeded. The dedication to inventions and gadgetry not only made them financially secure but gave them useful comforts like a Turkish bath.

Noyes was keen on propagating his ideas and visitors were encouraged: 6,000 came in the summer of 1866, eating strawberries and cream and listening to the children's choir. Predictably the most pressing topic of interest was Oneida's sexual revolution, and undoubtedly that must have drawn most visitors. But the interest did not translate into converts: membership grew to a peak of about 300. By the 1870s Noyes's mission was failing as he aged.

The man's charisma, especially for women, was never in doubt, but with a decline in sexual powers, his ability to perform the function of

Alpha Male devolved upon his much less attractive son Theodore. Not only that but Theodore had returned from college with some novel ideas on procreation. If the colony was to survive, he argued, it should make lots of children, and those offspring should be as strong and capable as possible. Therefore only suitable candidates should be allowed to procreate. This was the new and revolutionary doctrine of social Darwinism.

Many of the issues had been swirling around for some time – Denis Diderot, for example, had proposed the evolution of species without any divine intervention way back in 1749[2] – but it was Darwin's *On the Origin of Species by Means of Natural Selection* in 1859 that turned what had often been empty hypothesizing into hard science. Within a few years Darwin's cousin, Francis Galton, was at the forefront, researching the inheritance of 'genius' by collating statistics from eminent men. He found, to his satisfaction at least, that they begat eminent sons – no women were ever included in his studies. (It would not be until 1883 that Galton coined the word 'eugenics' to describe his new 'science'.) Galton had travelled in Africa and his bigotry was no more than normal for a man of his class and position: 'It is seldom that we hear of a white traveller meeting with a black chief whom he feels to be the better man,' he remarked. Now this unquestioning sense of superiority appeared to be armed with scientific results (needless to say, his assumptions and methodologies were full of holes). The implication was obvious: a New Adam could be selectively bred according to the finest modern principles. Darwin's brilliant analysis of the emergence of life on earth had been poisoned.

John Noyes was impressed. Perusing a local magazine on animal breeding his eye was drawn to some homespun thought: 'A man has as good a right to be handsome as a pig, a woman as a horse, certainly.' If selective procreation worked for animals like horses, why not humans? Would inbreeding be a problem? There were several examples of successful racehorses to prove not. And humans? No, Noyes concluded, just look at the English aristocracy.

To be fair, Galton had argued that social engineering as practised by the Spartans was alien and repulsive. The system implied that some men would have to be unproductive. Noyes agreed that castration was unthinkable, but felt sure there were men around 'who love science well enough to make themselves eunuchs for the Kingdom of Heaven's sake'. Given the decadent and decayed nature of human society, he reasoned, when free love, divorce, abortion, licentiousness and scandal are all around, then 'scientific propagation' was an absolute necessity to save humanity.

Noyes was well aware of Plato's suggested breeding programme for humans in which women, 'held in common', are distributed to men in a lot-drawing contest. In Plato's system the lot contest is a fix, engineered by the guardians of the state to allow superior individuals to procreate while keeping the inferior in the dark about their exclusion.[3] To this Noyes added some Christian theology, stating that careful breeding would inevitably improve and purify the human race, generation by generation, until one day we would arrive back where we had begun: at the perfection of Adam and Eve. In this electrifying observation, Noyes had connected perfectionist dreams in religion and science, a dream of producing the Perfect Human, someone to live in paradise.

Noyes coined the term 'stirpiculture' and announced it to the colony: 'It is an attempt to create a new race by selecting a new Adam and Eve, and separating them and their progeny from all previous races.' By the late 1860s the quietly eccentric little colony had just discovered – the first to do so since the scientific revolution – the most explosive and unsettling programme for returning to Eden that had ever been devised.

Until this time, the colony had settled down to be an immodest success, but the breeding programme would change that. Initially 38 men and 53 women signed up for the task. The potential mothers agreed: 'We have no right or personal feeling in regard to child-bearing, which shall in the least degree oppose or embarrass him [Noyes] in his choice of scientific combination.'

At first Noyes decided who should procreate – he chose himself frequently – then a committee took over. Tensions soon appeared. A melancholy diary exists which documents a particular case in the community.[4] A young man named Victor Hawley had fallen madly in love with one Mary Jones, an attachment which was excessively passionate and so frowned upon. The community forbade them to be together and decided that Mary should be 'exposed' to another man's 'crisis' – Oneida-speak for impregnated. But Mary delivered a stillborn child and Victor tried again, applying to the committee for permission to have a baby with her. He was refused.

By 1876 Theodore had been installed as leader and the breeding programme was causing real antagonism. Most opportunities for breeding were being assigned to a small number of older men and the role of 'Eunuchs for Heaven' was not going down well with the inferior types. In April, Victor again asked permission and was again refused. He became ill and was censured when an illegal 'communication' – sex – was discovered to have taken place between himself and Mary. She was instructed to have a baby with Stephen Leonard, a 56-year-old elder. On 7 November Victor discovered that Mary was already pregnant, not by Leonard apparently, but by Theodore. Humiliated and broken in spirit, Victor still cared for her through the confinement. In June 1877 she gave birth to a second dead child. For Victor the enormous pressures had become intolerable and he finally left. After some deliberation, Mary decided to stay.

Living a friendless existence on the outside, Victor thought of killing himself or joining a wild expedition to a remote region. In the end, unable to settle to a new life without Mary, he dragged himself back to Oneida only to discover that Mary, after months of anguish, had left.

He tracked her down eventually, and she agreed to marry him. Even then, after all their suffering, they could not imagine life beyond Oneida and tried to return, but the previously loving community was now against them. Life would have to be on the outside.

Theirs is a small story, discovered in a lost diary and written in a dead language – Munson, an early precursor of Pitman shorthand.[5] But Victor and Mary come out of it with heroic dignity, two little people who were the first to stand fast against a new kind of tyranny, a perfectionist science that was itself a Frankenstein monster made from apocalyptic Christianity and rationalism.

The couple never returned, and it proved to be a timely separation. The home they had abandoned was now in turmoil. Nemesis for Oneida had come in the form of a self-righteous bigot called Anthony Comstock. He had formed an organization known as the New York Society for the Suppression of Vice which persuaded Congress to pass a bill in 1873 classifying all information on contraception as obscene. Soon the moral outrage was focused on Oneida, 'this Utopia of obscenity'. As pressures mounted, Noyes stopped all public pronouncements on the subjects nearest to his heart – sex and procreation – but Comstock did not relent. Then on 19 June 1879, Noyes suddenly disappeared.

There had been rumours of a new prosecution and, with the dissension in the ranks, he had had enough. Some time later he reappeared, across the border in Canada from where he instructed the community to drop the complex marriage system and the breeding programme.

Oneida was slowly wound up. The community which had begun life as a mystical Edenic idyll had worked its way through practical answers to living, but finally ended up with most members marrying their true love and settling down to a more conventional existence. Victor and Mary had five children, a tribute to the power of love, though they never prospered in the outside world. The name Oneida survived because various products and industrial processes carried on – the Final Shoe wasn't one of them, but Oneida silver-plate remains a bestseller.

The memory of their unique socio-sexual experiment in paradise gently faded. Oneida's reputation for free love and 'Bible Communism' has rather overshadowed its small-scale and short-lived attempt to rebuild Adam and Eve. A pity because Noyes had revealed the implicit Edenic assumptions wrapped inside Galton's social Darwinism. Both Oneida and eugenicists hoped for progress towards the perfect human, a being worthy of a New Jerusalem or a Kingdom of Heaven on Earth. Noyes was a clever man and saw how religion could use evolutionary theories rather than simply reject them. His message, however, was lost in the clamour of anti-Darwinist sentiment. As for the pro-Darwinists, some of them were now focusing on the question of whether natural selection could still operate in human society. If not, then here was a great opportunity for man to take responsibility for his own perfection.

18

Social Darwinism:
Eden by Eradication

When Francis Galton published *Hereditary Genius* in 1869, its reviews had been lukewarm, but by 1892 a reissue was being hailed as a classic. There was a growing fear that industrialization had disabled the process of evolution and that all the advantages bestowed on the population by the top echelons – clean water, sanitation and so on – were weakening society. In fact the least desirable elements were reproducing more rapidly than the best. The rediscovery of Gregor Mendel's pioneering work on inherited characteristics in 1900 gave an enormous boost to the eugenic cause. Perhaps the characteristics of those least desirable elements could be identified and somehow eliminated, thus improving mankind towards the perfection that evolution had promised.

There was nothing new about such fears. As far back as the Babylonian Captivity of the Jews, the prophet Baruch had lamented: 'The vigour of creation is at its end; the coming of [last] times is near.' The perception that society had become weaker, less virile and duller was a standard feature of End Time anxiety. In such dire moments it was necessary for the Chosen People to hold themselves aloof. Only then, God told the Israelites, could they be 'a peculiar treasure unto me'.[1] The difference at the end of the nineteenth century was that the apocalyptic bedrock was hidden: there appeared to be scientific evidence of 'degeneration' – and a scientific method to remaining aloof. The Chosen People had become educated white Anglo-Saxons and their path through the wilderness of miscegenation and race-decline was to be guided by scientists. The devils out there were the racial degenerates.

The climate of fear over the issue steadily intensified, bursting out in often unexpected ways. One was 'posture'. All the luxuries and soft comfortable armchairs were producing weaklings. The 'National Posture League' was begun in the United States and students were tested and found wanting. Parents worried.

The state of Indiana, the place where Robert Owen had built New Harmony, was the first to attempt to legislate for racial improvement in 1907, quickly followed by California where laws allowed the steril-ization of 'moral degenerates' and 'sexual perverts showing hereditary degeneracy'. Iowa soon added criminals, idiots, the feeble-minded, imbeciles, drunkards, drug fiends, epileptics and syphilitics to the list.[2]

In 1912 the eugenicist Henry Goddard published his findings on a disturbing case that revealed the nature of the danger to American society. His subjects were the members of an old American family that had produced many eminent men over the generations – just the kind of people society needed. Unfortunately, one of the men had allowed himself to be seduced by a sexually attractive woman from a degen-erate family. Although pretty and well-dressed, she hid what Goddard believed was a recessive gene for feeble-mindedness. Once impreg-nated by the upstanding member of society, she began a new line to the family and this branch were almost wholly tainted with the problem.

Goddard named the family the Kallikaks, a compound of Greek *kallos*, meaning beauty, and *kakos*, meaning bad. Using family trees, he showed graphically that the beautiful line produced 'normals' while the bad line managed only the 'feeble-minded'. These individuals invariably became 'paupers, criminals, prostitutes, drunkards, and examples of all forms of social pest'.

Coining another new word from the Greek, Goddard concluded that such 'morons' were 'largely responsible for these social sores'. The

moron, especially the sexually immoral female version, was the enemy
within, the slut tempting American proto-Adam to fall. Goddard's
report was widely read and hugely influential.[3]

Over in London in July of that same year 1912, the First
International Congress of Eugenics was held. Distinguished delegates
from Europe and America were met by the Lord Mayor and addressed
by Major Leonard Darwin, son of the great scientist. Allowing uncon-
trolled breeding among inferior humans, he told them, was 'weakness
and folly'. His words were loudly applauded by the audience of 750.

If something was not done quickly, it seemed, feeble-minded forni-
cators might inherit the earth. Bleecker van Wagenen, from the
American Breeders Association, spoke of 'cutting off the defective
germ-plasm in the human population'. W.C.D. and C.D. Whetham,
pure-bred authors of *Family and Nation*, whipped up the panic another
notch or two. Britishers were 'becoming darker, shorter, less able to
take in and keep an initiative, less steadfast and persistent, and possibly
more emotional'.[4]

The German contingent was the largest, providing a huge display of
their own experiments in what they referred to as *Volksgesundheit*, 'race
hygiene'.

Not everyone lost their senses, or sight of the implicit paradisical
aims. Arthur Balfour, former prime minister and aristocrat, was a man
to whom the eugenics agenda should have appealed – himself a
straight-backed proof that good breeding results in fine specimens. Yet
he was wary of claims about human perfection. Tucked away inside the
rhetoric, he realized, was the old apocalyptic myth. At the Eugenics
Congress inaugural dinner at the Hotel Cecil, he warned that anyone
could use the eugenic problem 'as a machinery for furthering his own
particular method of bringing the millennium upon earth'.

Balfour, like Noyes, had got right to the heart of the matter, but he
cannot have realized the appalling dangers of running a science on that
old rocket fuel of the apocalypse. Despite his reservations, the
Americans and Germans went home from the conference fired up

with eugenic zeal and determined to take the scientific road to perfect humans and paradise.

The film director D.W. Griffiths provided a vital rallying cry in 1915 with his explicitly racist Civil War epic, *Birth of a Nation*, the most financially successful silent movie of all time (a money-earning record unbeaten until *Snow White and the Seven Dwarfs*). A year later the race fear was whipped up again by the publication of Madison Grant's *The Passing of the Great Race*. It was clear, Grant claimed, that Old America was threatened by immigration. The 'splendid conquistadores of the New World', as Grant called them, the settler families who had crossed the Atlantic and survived the wilderness, had been proven as evolutionary successes – as evidenced by production of men like Madison Grant. (His own family had fled Scotland after the failed Jacobite rebellion of 1745.) Now their relatively low birth rate was going to ensure their defeat by what were commonly referred to as 'the little brunettes' – immigrants from the Mediterranean. Psychologists reported that the incidence of feeble-mindedness was far higher among such peoples. In 1917 Lewis Terman reported that the feeble-minded were 'responsible for at least one fourth of the commitments to state penitentiaries and reform schools, for the majority of cases of chronic and semichronic pauperism, and for much of our alcoholism, prostitution and venereal disease'.

Lots of other men with impressive seventeenth- and eighteenth-century forbears agreed with Grant's analysis. There was John Harvey Kellogg, inventor of the Race Betterment League and cornflakes; and there was Robert Yerkes, a psychologist of Dutch ancestry. In 1921 he announced that his studies of US Army personnel showed that the average American white male had an IQ barely above the level of a moron. Any chuckles among the Hispanic and Afro-American populations were quickly silenced, however, when he claimed that they were even lower, and so obviously responsible for the decline. Like most early work on intelligence, the tests were fundamentally flawed but widely accepted at the time.

A powerful campaign to control immigration then resulted in legislation. By 1924 the immigration of 'southern races' was restricted and those of 'Nordic and Teutonic' favoured. Two years later, 23 US states had sterilization laws relating to idiots and moral degenerates. In a landmark judgement in 1927, the Supreme Court heard the case of Carrie Buck, the 'feeble-minded' daughter of a white Virginian prostitute. Carrie had been raped by a relative, then when found to be pregnant, shipped off to an asylum for the crime of moral degeneracy. The child that resulted from the rape was said to be equally feeble-minded — it was six months old when tested. The asylum sought compulsory sterilization. Justice Wendell Holmes agreed, solemnly declaring: 'Three generations of imbeciles are enough.' By 1939 over 30,000 people had been sterilized on eugenic grounds.

In Germany proponents of social legislation matching the American model had been making plenty of noise but with little success. Way back in 1880 Nietzsche, influenced by Galton, had proposed 'rendering extinct' various unwanted strains, such as, 'the wretched, the deformed, the degenerate'. Man, recently promoted to Superman, was now supposed to steer his own history towards that long awaited paradise. The distinguished biologist Ernst Haeckel, founder of a new science he called ecology, had suggested eliminating the unwanted with the wonder drug morphine, the closest chemical to paradise in the scientific medical kit.

Little progress was made in Germany on this front, however, and it was in Africa that the first terrible action occurred when Lieutenant General Lothar von Trotha ordered the extermination of the Herero and Nama peoples who had rebelled against German rule. Around 75,000 died. Studying the policy was an anthropologist Dr Eugen Fischer who commended von Trotha's action and proposed the sterilization of any bastards that had resulted from sex between 'superior' Germans and the Herero, a people he regarded as animals. While in

Landsberg Prison in the 1920s Adolf Hitler read and admired Fischer's work before writing *Mein Kampf*. In 1927 Fischer was made the first director of what would become an internationally respected institute, The Kaiser Wilhelm Institute for Anthropology in Berlin. Until 1933, however, his hopes and those of other eugenicists were foiled by less hysterical elements within Germany.

When the Nazis came to power in that year, however, things changed rapidly. The first foreign book to be translated and published was Madison Grant's racist polemic, *The Passing of the Great Race,* with its reference to the 'master race'. Later that year Goddard's *The Kallikak Family* was reprinted in German. Within months of being in government came the Law for the Prevention of Hereditarily Diseased Progeny, a short time later followed by the Law against Dangerous Habitual Criminals – this statute gave power to castrate after a 'racial-biological examination'.

Hitler, however, was not going to be content with sterilizing burglars and cretins. The enemy of his Chosen People was another Chosen People. In April 1933 there was the first of a cascade of anti-Jewish laws designed to keep Germans aloof – in November 1935 marriages between Jews and Germans were forbidden.

The Nazis had begun to enforce the kind of programmes that other countries only dreamed about. Initially alcoholics, schizophrenics and the feeble-minded were sterilized, most at the behest of the various Kaiser-Wilhelm Institutes – there were other branches in Munich and Frankfurt. The director in Munich was Dr Ernst Rüdin, a Swiss-born psychiatrist who had taken over from Alois Alzheimer, the man who first identified the degenerative disease of the brain. Rüdin's protégé, Dr Otmar von Verschuer, ran the Frankfurt branch and would subsequently take over Berlin from Fischer. Verschuer was also a man dedicated to 'race hygiene' – in a 1942 publication about the 'Jewish question' he begin using the word *endgültige,* final solution. Von Verschuer's own protégé in the pre-war period was an enthusiastic racist too, Josef Mengele.

Even in the late 1930s the Kaiser-Wilhelm remained a highly respectable organization, receiving funding from the Rockefeller Foundation and James Loeb, an American-Jewish philanthropist. In 1939 one professor received the Nobel Prize for chemistry – his work on hormones would lead to the female birth control pill.

Eugenicist laws swept through Europe at that time – Denmark, Norway, Finland, Sweden, Lithuania, Estonia, Iceland, some Swiss cantons, Austria, Hungary, Italy, Greece and Spain all passed legislation. Britain was unusual in not doing so (though the empire was not immune – India had one of the first pieces of legislation influenced by social Darwinism, the Criminal Tribes Act of 1871).

In Germany in 1939, or perhaps a year earlier, the extermination of certain individuals commenced. The first victims to be gassed were probably handicapped children.

For the Nazis the perfectionist aims of eugenics were overt: it was a route to a restored Eden fit for the new blue-eyed Adams and Evas. Eric Voegelin, a university lecturer in Austria until 1938, pointed out that they had borrowed the Christian narrative myth, adopting the name Third Reich from the 'history in three eras' teachings of Joachim of Fiore. 'When God is invisible behind the world,' Voegelin wrote, 'the contents of the world will become new gods; when the symbols of transcendant religiosity are banned, new symbols develop from the inner-worldly language of science to take their place. Like the Christian ecclesia, the inner-worldly community has its apocalypse too.'[5] The Nazis were certainly expecting to inaugurate a thousand-year-long teutonic heaven, a new heretical version of humanity's most powerful myth of earthly perfection.

Voegelin went further in his analysis: secularism had not silenced the need for symbolic narratives, notably Joachim's three ages and then apocalypse, nor had it kept those narratives neatly shut away inside mainstream religions. Politics had greedily swallowed them, from the revolutionary transformations of Marxism – 'the intellectual swindler' – to the mystical anarchism of Bakunin and, closer to home, the mainstream positivism of Auguste Comte whose 'Catholicism minus Christianity'[6] had so much influenced European culture. All these secular ideologies echoed Joachim's scheme of history. Voegelin might have added Robert Owen to the list, but the point was clear: modernity itself was poisoned. As Nazi values increased their grip in Austria, Voegelin predictably lost his job and fled Austria to America where his views were greeted with little enthusiasm.

Back in Germany, now on the brink of war, recognizing 'Jewish blood' in outwardly German citizens became an art. The Devil had become a hidden enemy, eating away at society. The bright and ambitious Mengele won plaudits for devising a method of detecting race via the jaw bone. This obsession with identification was a eugenic hallmark from the beginning, when fingerprints were first studied in late nineteenth-century British India in order to identify the hereditary criminals. Clear scientific identification of the individual is a prerequisite for the orderly and precise segregation and persecution of the unwanted, those not chosen.

With war under way in Europe, Mengele fought in the Ukraine, receiving an Iron Cross for bravery, but in 1943 he moved to Auschwitz. There he was well placed to send samples back to Verschuer in Berlin. By 1945 Verschuer was worried about German defeat and how his work might be interpreted by the Russians, another race that had been slaughtered in the death camps. He had files moved west from Auschwitz, out of reach of the advancing Red Army.

With the defeat of Hitler, mankind's most unholy attempt to build paradise came to an end. Mengele fled from Auschwitz, eventually reaching South America where he died in 1979. It would be comforting to add, 'after an international manhunt', but that would be untrue. His inhuman crimes were never punished.

For the scientists who had been so much part of the international eugenics scene before the war, and so instrumental in the Nazi programme, there was no retribution. Rüdin died unpunished in 1952. Verschuer was investigated by the principal Allied war crimes prosecutor, Leo Alexander, who felt sure he was a major figure in the medical atrocities. But hard evidence was difficult to find and, despite written records showing Verschuer had known about and encouraged Mengele's activities, he was eventually fined 600 marks and released as a 'Nazi collaborator'.

Almost immediately he sought reinstatement at the Kaiser-Wilhelm, but the commission guiding its rebuilding dismissed his application, asserting that he was 'not a collaborator, but one of the most dangerous Nazi activists of the Third Reich'. Nevertheless, six years after the war ended he was appointed head of a new university genetics department in Münster – a city that had suffered apocalyptic upheavals and religious 'cleansing' way back in the 1530s when the Anabaptists had taken over. The university was Germany's third largest institute of higher education. In this Verschuer was able to arrange posts for many of his former colleagues. When he died in a car crash in 1969, his obituaries failed to mention anything of his past.

One view of the Holocaust now, in the words of Karen Armstrong, is that the Nazi Final Solution was 'a reminder of the dangers that can accrue from the death of God in human consciousness'.

Undoubtedly correct, but not the complete picture: one might also enquire of the 7,000 heretics burned alive in Béziers church; the 3,000 that Richard Lionheart slaughtered at Acre; the countless other bodies strewn over the fields of the four Crusades; the corpses left by Assassins; the thousands of Jews killed by the Inquisition in fifteenth-century Spain; the drowned and scorched Anabaptists,[7] plus all the other witches, heretics and non-conformists put to the sword, hanged, garrotted, cooked and occasionally buried alive.

Long before Nietzsche, human beings had been taking on the work of their deity and clearing away unworthy people in preparation for paradise on earth. If the secular apocalyptics have managed to amass a vaster total – Mao's account alone is said to be 70 million – it cannot hide the fact that a shared ideology of perfection achieved through a transforming Armageddon has been murdering people ever since the idea was concocted. Nevertheless, after Voegelin conservatives have gleefully been pointing the finger at Enlightenment rationality and its bastard child, modernity. Yet it was not reason that had skewed Darwin's science and created eugenics. As Hannah Arendt pointed out: 'Professor Voegelin seems to think that totalitarianism is only the other side of liberalism, positivism and pragmatism. But whether one agrees with liberalism or not ... the point is that liberals are clearly not totalitarians.'[8] What had brought about this murder was prejudice, self-interest and, most of all, the paradise myth — that great survivor of human culture that had crept into the modern world like a wolf in the lamb's clothing.

PART V

Consumer Idylls of the Twentieth and Twenty-first Centuries: Rural Retreats and Shopping Malls

Sketch of the cabin at Walden Pond by Sophia Thoreau, published as the frontispiece to her brother, Henry David Thoreau's book, *Walden; or, Life in the Woods*, 1854.

The women sitting under the sycamore tree in the village named Place of Honey knew the right man to be my guide. 'Farsheed – he's very strong.' Except when Farsheed was called, he didn't think he was the right man at all. 'The season for crossing the high passes is over,' he complained. 'The snows will come. Three youths from Isfahan died last year, heading up too late in the year and caught out by the snows the volcanic gases near See Alang crater. I won't do it. No.'

I waited under the sycamore. There was no question of going without a guide. This trail across the Iranian Elburz mountains was long and difficult, rising to over 13,000 feet. Fortunately some of the men took up my cause. After a couple of hours, there was a growing weight of opinion in the village that Farsheed had to do it. Hospitality laws dictated that someone would have to help the foreigner, despite him being from Inglestan, a country notorious for malicious duplicity, moral decay and Manchester United. 'And you gave Khomeini his beard,' added one of the women mysteriously. Despite all these crimes, I was a guest in Place of Honey and must be indulged. At midday Farsheed gave in. He would take myself and my translator to the top of the pass and show us the path to Alamut.

We set off up the valley, passing through magnificent Alpine scenery and patches of bare earth covered in white autumn crocuses. Farsheed showed us the remnants of barbed wire fences. 'The government want this to be a national park,' he said. 'They tell us that people should not live here, only the leopards and the deer. Some shepherds have been fined for grazing their ancestral grounds. We have had our shelters burned down.'

The national park, that very modern idea of an untouched and pristine Eden, had come to Iran. I could only think, with sympathy, that his way of life was doomed — it's almost always a disaster to be trapped inside someone else's paradise. I asked what might happen if he had to change his life.

'I may go to the town,' he said grimly. 'Maybe I'll be a thief — what else can I do?'

Nightfall found us at a shepherds' camp at about 6,000 feet, feeding on home-made cheese, hot milk and bread baked in the earth under the fire. I can't say I have ever tasted better food. They warned us of bad weather to come and the necessity of staying above the clouds. The route after the pass, one of them explained, was simple.

'There are two paths. The one for Alamut is longer and leads down where the new atomic power station is being built.'

My translator and I exchanged a glance which the shepherd noticed. 'Yes, that will be dangerous for you — they will assume you are spies.' He laughed. 'Of course, maybe you are spies.' We all laughed heartily.

I asked him about Hasan Sabbah, the leader of the Assassins.

'He was the Lord of Alamut,' the man explained. 'But the Mongols came and destroyed him.'

'Did he have a garden? One like paradise?'

'I never heard of that.'

'What about bin Ladin — have you heard of him?'

'The Americans gave him his beard.'

That night, we lazed by the campfire in a wooden shelter, listening to the soft breathing of the cattle. I asked the shepherds: 'What would be the best kind of life for you? What is paradise on earth?'

They looked puzzled.

'What is the perfect life? What would make life really very good for you? What do you want?'

I thought they might say: car, television, money, more sheep, even what some students on the Caspian Sea coast had said, 'Freedom.' But in fact, they said nothing. Eventually they held a whispered discussion and one was elected spokesman.

'Sorry,' he said. 'We don't understand what you mean.'

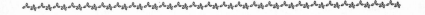

19

A Consumer Durable Eden

The distant forbears of the reactions and fears thrown up during the eugenics scare are not difficult to trace. In 1711 the English critic and playwright John Dennis had written of a 'spreading Contagion which is the greatest Corruption of Publick Manners and the greatest Extinguisher of Publick Spirit'. He was writing about the passion for 'luxury' that was rampaging through the fine shops of London. Even before that there had been isolated instances where commentators lambasted the public over their wanton squandering of wealth on sumptuous fripperies. New England's Puritan colonies passed laws in the 1630s against slashed sleeves, beaver-skin hats, ruffs, belts and hatbands. Over in England and Holland at that time, the feverish speculation in tulip bulbs drew condemnation too. Luxury, it was considered, would weaken society both physically and morally. If all that Puritan effort and work had, rather embarrassingly, produced riches and surplus, then those benefits now threatened to damage the society that had produced them.[1]

The problem was that luxuries had the habit of all too quickly becoming necessities. Tea and coffee, for example, had started as rarities and rapidly developed into standard needs. Once established as an essential, an item like an umbrella (an idea brought from China in the seventeenth century) could mark as a discomfort what was previously accepted without complaint – wet hair and clothes.[2] Year after year capitalism and free trade were creating desires that became needs. On top of that the very act of shopping and all the attendant diversions

– especially things like those entertaining French *romans* – created, in their absence, the new discomfort called boredom (the novels themselves began to mention it). For this the universal remedy was further shopping. The inevitable result was a view that we were becoming less self-reliant, less independent, less, in fact, all those qualities prized by the Puritans.

The anxiety that society was being undermined, that men and women were being dragged down into a pit of weakness, sloth and ennui, became the dark counterpoint to the Perfect Human aspirations of the Enlightenment. When this anxiety flowed into the race fears of the late nineteenth century, a man such as John Harvey Kellogg was there at the conjunction. Laziness and dependence, the products of consumer culture's addiction to novelty and luxury, were to be combatted with a healthy Puritan diet. Cornflakes, granola, soya milk, peanut butter and nut-based artificial meats were all Kellogg discoveries, all promoted with a deep conviction that diet was the key to unlock the gates of paradise. Racial enfeeblement would be defeated with improved breakfast habits and the Race Betterment League. Ironically, in the hands of his entrepreneurial brother, Will, Kellogg's cornflakes would be part of an important forward step in this debilitating consumer culture: branded products.[3]

Sylvester Graham, fire-and-brimstone preacher and dietary guru of the 1840s, introduced another brand, his Graham Cracker, the antidote to over-sumptuous food and moral infirmities. 'Millions of children,' Graham announced, would 'soon unite in one dark and mighty confluence of ignorance and immorality and crime, which will overflow the wholesome restraints of society, and sweep away the barriers of civil law, and sap the foundations of our Republican institutions'.[4] Austere wheat crackers were the answer.

In theologians and churchmen the fear of a flock that was weakened both physically and morally was very real. Giving in to the temptation of an impulse purchase or a bad food was surely a step towards spiritual ruin (and surely women, daughters of Eve, were more susceptible to the capitalist serpent). Perhaps one day religion would be swept away before this avalanche of desires that could only be assuaged by more shopping. The very ideals of perfection and bliss, rather than being taken from Scripture, would be bought in small instalments. Emile Zola was alert to such fears and spent a month in the winter of 1881 observing the life in Parisian department stores. This new form of shopping was significant, Zola realized. The department store was a microcosm of the world, a strange utopia that bore similarities to the ambitious communities of the New World set up by Charles Fourier and Robert Owen.

In Zola's *Au Bonheur des Dames* (1883) the director of the store, Mouret, is the powerful survivor in a Darwinian struggle for supremacy who sells 'dreams and yearnings' to women who are 'pale with longing' at the counters filled with 'light satins and soft silks'. In a superb climactic scene, Mouret's passion for one of his shopgirls, Denise, finally overcomes him and his wild declaration of love wins her heart, to the background noise of 'three thousand employees, turning over his royal fortune in armfuls of money'.[5]

In the United States these temples of the new paradise began to develop quickly in the 1860s as the old dry goods shops were transformed into department stores – soon known as Big Stores. By 1869 Lord and Taylor's store at 901 Broadway had a steam-driven lift and 10,000 people rode on it in the first three days of opening. Not every store could match that, but in window displays they competed to attract custom with colourful theatricality. The 1870s saw an economic downturn, but from the next decade department stores grew ever grander with nurseries, theatres, art galleries and fabulous decor. In 1896 a Chicago businessman, Henry Siegel, and a Dutch-born immigrant, Frank Cooper, went to New York and built a six-storey stone and steel giant, complete with roof-top restaurant. Anyone of any class could buy what they wanted at Siegel-Cooper's, from a humble thimble to a pet panther. A stroll through its staggering array of merchandise was like a visit to a seventeenth-century cabinet of curiosities, an endless source of diversion and delight, where time slipped by unnoticed. In fact, in many ways the department store was the new cabinet, the place where all the world came to marvel at the diversity, the ingenuity and the exotic. But with purchase in mind.

Window displays became ever more fantastic, and entry led to a world of glamour, luxury and perpetual pleasure. At the opening of Marshall Field's in Chicago in 1902, the department store hit a new high: flowers decked every counter, the music of six orchestras filled the air, and it was all lit with superb modern lighting. Like explorers setting foot in a new world, those who came struggled for words, and found that only the language of paradise would do.[6]

At Macy's in Manhattan they were quite clear about their Edenic objectives: all kinds of rare tropical fruit and vegetables were sold 'irrespective of season', foreshadowing the situation a century later when every supermarket aspires to an Eternal Spring in the fruit and veg department. The copywriting whizz and publishing maverick, Elbert Hubbard, who came from a staunchly Protestant background, made the connection absolutely plain: 'When I want to hear really good sermons nowadays, we attend a weekly lunch of the ad club, and listen to a man who deals in ways and means and is intent upon bringing about paradise, here and now.' At Tiffany's on New York's Union Square, they built the new store on top of a Puritan church. 'Real jewels will be sold there instead of bogus ones,' remarked one diarist waspishly. The earthly paradise was on order, and due for delivery any day.[7]

The mantra for these new consumer paradise-seekers was 'Work hard, play hard.' During office hours the ethical standards were for sober restraint and dedication to honest toil, in the manner of the first Puritan settlers tending their livestock and crops. Once out of the building, however, the fatted calf could be sacrificed in a splendid splurge of wasteful self-indulgence and hedonism. Paradise-seeking was shifting fundamentally: the old belief in hard toil was still there, but now salvation and paradise came in the consumption of the fruits of that labour.[8]

As if to reinforce this, America was swept by a fashion for the Oriental, a potent symbol for slothfully silky pleasures ever since Galland's *Arabian Nights* in the early eighteenth century. Islam had long since ceased to be a military threat, while grabbing Jerusalem for Christendom appeared to be a long-dead historical period without any relevance to the United States. This American vision of the Orient, and by association Islam, was about lolling around on tasselled divans, languorously drawing on Turkish cigarettes while gazing at shamelessly sexual odalisques doing a dance called the hoochy-coochy. (The latter was supposedly invented by showman Sol Bloom who had to come up with a musical accompaniment for the belly-dancing troupe at the World's Colombian Exposition in Chicago in 1893.) As a vision it was curiously similar to popular notions of what constituted Islamic heaven, with its limitless resources in wine, women and winsome youths, if not tobacco and honky-tonk piano-playing.

Louis Comfort Tiffany, inheritor of the jewellery business, lived out this fantasy more than most, swanning around in full rajah regalia at parties and designing gorgeous saracenic ceramics and glass. Like other aficionados of the cult, his experience of the Orient was rather limited: his month in Cairo had been spent in bed with a fever. Perhaps it was that dreamlike quality that he valued, filling his apartment and later his mansion with sumptuous eastern finery. Alma and Gustav Mahler, visiting him in 1908, found their host high on hashish in gorgeous rooms inhabited by 'beautiful women wearing strange shimmering dresses'. 'It was like a dream,' wrote Alma, 'the Thousand and One Nights in New York.'[9]

Popular novelists loved this orientalist fantasy, tirelessly transporting heroines east where they indulged in wild freedom and close encounters with exotic men. *The Garden of Allah* by Robert Hichens, a huge bestseller in the United States, has the heroine kissed by a desert campfire whereupon 'her nature galloped like an Arab horse across the sands towards the sun'. The novel was reworked twice as a stage play, three times by Hollywood (the last time with Marlene Dietrich), and several times as a theme for spectacular department store promotions. It also spawned a spin-off bonanza in everything from table lamps to candy boxes.[10]

For the department stores orientalism was just another fashion to promote sales. By this time they already had a good many other tricks to cultivate impulse shopping – particularly among women – and many of the finer subtleties of selling were understood. Although the economy of these vast consumer paradises crashed after the First World War, the trends started would continue later in the twentieth century with the development of the mall.[11]

In 1928 President Herbert Hoover observed that Americans had become 'happiness machines', a comment that seemed to announce the arrival of a full-blown consumer society. Others had noticed the changes: *True Story Magazine* ran full-page ads declaring the arrival of the 'economic millennium', brought on by easy credit, shorter working hours and higher wages.[12]

That same year the possible manipulation of those happiness machines was proposed by Sigmund Freud's nephew, Edward Bernays, whose book *Propaganda* (1928) would be a favourite for Josef Goebbels. Born in Vienna in 1891, Bernays emigrated as a child to New York where his first job was promoting Broadway shows. The power of the media in influencing, even controlling, public opinion fascinated Bernays, but it was not until 1915 that the scale of the possibilities were revealed when the movie *Birth of a Nation* caused an upsurge in recruitment to the Ku Klux Klan. This ability of the mass media to evoke powerful emotional responses was noted and during the First World War, when the US government set out to sway public opinion towards intervention, Bernays was part of the successful team.

Bernays had read his uncle's work on human psychology and after the war he sought to apply it to the market place. If behaviour was influenced, even controlled, by underlying stereotypes and irrational emotional factors, Bernays reasoned, then a salesman might manipulate

those factors in order to influence purchases. 'The conscious and intelligent manipulation of the organized habits and opinions of the masses is
an important element in democratic society,' he wrote. 'Those who
manipulate this unseen mechanism of society constitute an invisible
government which is the true ruling power of our country.' There was
something of Plato's *Republic* about this, but instead of Guardians
pulling the strings, the puppetmasters were public relations wizards
employed by large corporations. Bernays had realized that unspoken
yearnings in this life could be used to sell products. All that was
required was to find a way to connect the product with the emotion.

In fact the trend in advertising for some years had been to reduce
the level of information and increase the appeals to emotions. Nor was
sales hyperbole anything new: think of James Graham and his 'celestial
bed'. But Bernays brought a fresh psychological rigour to the art and
an almost preternatural level of cunning.

In 1928 Bernays was running campaigns for the tobacco industry,
trying to encourage more women to smoke. Noting that several states
made it illegal for women to light up in public, Bernays planted stories
in the press that equated cigarettes with 'torches for freedom'.
Suddenly smoking had become a civil rights issue. Not content with
this, Bernays also managed to promote the idea that cigarettes were
dieting aids. Sure enough female smoking rates began to rise and
Bernays could congratulate himself for not actually issuing a single
advertisement during the entire campaign. This was manipulation on a
different plane altogether, manipulation that he termed, 'engineering
of consent'.

Advertisers and marketing gurus were quick to see the genius in
Bernays' work. They also realized that yearnings for perfection and
paradise were some of the best allies they could hope for. Years before
the political philosopher Eric Voegelin began to work out how
paradise-seeking behaviour had snuck into secularism, the people
selling merchandise had grasped the fact and were turning it to profit.
Appeals to Golden Age nostalgia, rural arcadian bliss or the Perfect

Body could sell almost any product, no matter how mundane the article or dismal its industrial origins. Hook up to paradise standards in relationships, health, sex, children, work, beauty, fitness and intelligence, and units could be shifted.

Emotional branding, as it came to be known, would be so successful that almost every major product that goes on sale today gets some help in sales with this engineering of consent. With large consumer purchases, particularly cars, the advertisements are wholly built around emotional responses to various forms of perfection, be they sexual attractiveness, masculinity, power, freedom. The anticipation of purchasing the car, then finally actual purchase, releases a small dose of pleasure. The buyer, all too briefly, becomes the person he or she wants to be, a temporary salvation in a plastic paradise.[13] Marx recognized this as 'commodity fetishism'. In this scenario consumption has become the opium of the people, and the human need for salvation, the paradise beyond, is sold back to us as products. The engineers of consent are our puppetmasters with government merely their henchman.

In fact, consumers can and do find ways to either sidestep or defeat this kind of manipulation. In 2005 it was reported, for example, that sales of fruit and vegetables in supermarkets in Britain were falling, replaced by farmers' markets and small-scale organic producers. Despite every attempt of the major supermarkets to tap into our shared mythology of Eternal Spring and perfection, the consumer had chosen an alternative. This new behaviour may be steeped in paradise imagery too – hopes for purity in diet and dreams of a Golden Age of bucolic bliss – but on this occasion the paradise-seeking works in our favour. We can taste the difference.

20

'Wilderness is Paradise Enow'

Almost as soon as department stores hit their stride in the late nineteenth century, novelists and commentators began to spot that shopping was strangely akin to a new religion and these commercial cathedrals were a kind of paradise. But there was another, very different, face to paradise at that time, also in the United States.

The world's first national park had been started in 1870, when, according to legend, a group of white men sitting around a campfire in Wyoming agreed that the incredible landscape around them should become a national park, a place without private ownership and where everyone could come to experience nature. The area was Yellowstone and the 2 million acres eventually subscribed to the park would become the world's first such preserved natural wilderness, a sort of Edenic lung, 'a virtual manifestation of God's original design for America', as academic Mark David Spence puts it.[1] This manifestation had much in common with the original Persian ideal of a *paradeiza*, an enclosed hunting ground reserved for the king that was fantastically abundant in plant and animal life – except that in this version no one was allowed to hunt. (In what was one of the more surreal anachronisms of history, some Native Americans from the Bannock tribe, angry at the loss of ancestral hunting grounds, harassed early tourists in the park and were hunted down by the US Army. In keeping with their Eden mythology, the park's founders had decided the area was 'untouched', but in fact mankind had been using it for thousands of years.)

With the official closing of the frontier in 1890 had come the real-
ization that the limitless availability of land was over and what remained
of the true wilderness might one day be reduced to national parks. These
broad areas of remote, supposedly uninhabited territory were rather like
the medieval concept of the Garden of Eden – faraway, magical, pristine
– except this time day trips were permissible. In the words of the 1964
Wilderness Act, 'where man himself is a visitor who does not remain'.[2]

In the mid-eighteenth century, the wilderness as paradise had been
proposed by Jean-Jacques Rousseau, who argued that man's fall dated
from the moment someone enclosed a parcel of land and declared,
'This is mine.' Furthermore, claimed Rousseau, out there in the
wilderness 'inequality is hardly felt'. Despite this appeal to primitive
democracy, positive attitudes to wilderness were not shared by many
in America. In 1831 Alexis de Tocqueville had seen scant interest in the
new ideas of wilderness.[3] But there were a few pioneers – botanists,
painters, gentlemen-at-leisure – whose attitudes to nature began to
carry weight, building a new mood that the wilderness was a source of
American pride, the prize to be compared with all the man-made
wonders of Europe.[4]

Ralph Waldo Emerson, the radical philospher, was one such pioneer.
In 1844 he purchased a small plot of land around Walden Pond in
Concord, Massachusetts, then encouraged his friend Henry David
Thoreau to retreat there the following year in order to write.
Thoreau's move was in a great tradition stretching back to Pliny the
Younger, Virgil and Epicurus. But it was American and it was different.
Unlike Sir William Temple whose simple rural bliss of the 1690s
included an estate and Jonathan Swift as secretary, Thoreau had few
privileges. The cabin was just 10 feet by 15, and his only financial
requirements were satisfied with 27 cents a week. At that frugal rate,
he calculated, he could earn enough for one year in six weeks. This was
no English or Roman lord retiring to his estates; when Thoreau wrote
about growing beans, he was, like any self-respecting and self-reliant
Puritan, reporting what he had done himself.

Thoreau's vision was of a life that did not wholly reject civilization, yet would learn from the wilderness. His account of the two years, two months and two days he lived in the cabin made the name Walden a synonym for a certain kind of personal paradise. 'In the Wilderness,' Thoreau once said, 'is the preservation of the world.'

By the end of the ninteenth century in the United States, the preservation of the world was looking like a much needed counterbalance to the artificial paradise of the department store and consumer society. Increasing numbers of Americans had no conception of life such as Thoreau had lived. They worked for faceless bureaucratic corporations in climate-controlled offices, their diet insulated from seasons and their lives numbed by boredom whose sole alleviation was shopping. Many suffered from 'over-pressure' and 'neurasthenia', one of those lost diseases that identify an age and a cultural crisis. 'We have lost the capacity for separate selfhood,' grumbled *Atlantic Monthly* in 1909.

The wilderness on the other hand was pure and virginal and uncomplicated. Not surprisingly it attracted advocates who felt the anxiety of consumerization most deeply. Madison Grant, who had bemoaned the decline of the white man in his *The Passing of the Great Race*, was also an early environmental activist. In 1895 he and several other eminent men, including Theodore Roosevelt, formed the New York Zoological Society. Grant believed that human character was formed by the landscape, and therefore America was a land for heroes – white 'Nordic' ones. He used his position and influence to promote wildlife and land conservation, founding both the American Bison Society and the Save-the-Redwoods League. The most notable success for American environmentalists at this time was Glacier National Park in Montana, formally created in 1910 on what had been land of the Blackfeet tribe.

These pristine parks were scarcely compatible with America's other emerging paradise, the shoppers' Wonderland, which came with an ugly industrial hinterland of factories and installations, all greedily ripping resources from the land. There was a growing feeling in some quarters that this monstrous new environment was a version of hell, a feeling given powerful focus in novels such as Upton Sinclair's, *The Jungle* (1906). In August 1913 as the United States hurtled headlong into mass consumerism at the expense of its own environment, a young man named Joseph Knowles pulled off a public relations stunt that somehow encapsulated all the madness and contradictions of America's two incompatible paradise dreams.

Having summoned journalists from the *Boston Post* to the edge of a forest in Maine, Knowles smoked a last cigarette, then removed all of his clothes. He was, he announced, going to live as Adam had done. With a final wave, he turned and disappeared into the trees, taking nothing with him, as Oscar Wilde might have said, but his genius.

Some weeks later a message arrived at the *Post* headquarters. It was written on a length of birchbark in charcoal and told that Knowles had managed to build a fire – by rubbing two sticks together – and had survived the first few days on a diet of wild berries. Other newspapers picked up the story and readers waited eagerly for the next missive from the primeval regions. When it came, it informed them that the new Adam was doing well, having killed partridge and deer. He was no longer naked but clad in bark cloth and skins. More instalments followed and the excitement spread: papers as far away as Kansas were demanding syndicated press releases from Eden. The primitivist urge to retreat from consumerism into nature, taken to its extreme, had become a commodity in itself. And the vast industrial machine that brought entertainment and distraction to American homes had discovered that anything could be sold, even an apparent rejection of its own values.⁵

Knowles's next missive told how he had dug a pit and trapped a bear. He now wore a fur coat against the chill of oncoming fall. Adam was a hit in paradise. On 4 October 1913 Knowles emerged from Eden to a tumultuous welcome. Dressed in his bearskin, he paraded through Boston to a gathering of 20,000 people. Observers noted how he mounted the rostrum with the leap of a tiger, before addressing the rally. Afterwards came gala dinners, a meeting with the governor of

Massachusetts and a flurry of press stories, including a spoiler in the
Post's rival, the *Boston American*, revealing that Knowles had spent the
entire time in a luxury cabin.

It didn't matter. None of the 300,000 people who bought Knowles's
book, *Alone in the Wilderness*, wanted to believe it was a hoax. He had
proved that American wilderness was still an Eden and that Americans
remained hairy-chested pioneers, not lily-livered pushovers that
haunted department stores. 'My God is in the Wilderness,' he wrote.
'The great open book of nature is my religion. My church is the church
of the forest.'

Knowles repeated the stunt on the West Coast, this time backed by
the *San Francisco Examiner*. On 20 June 1914, he plunged, 'naked as a
snake, into the untamed, cougar-infested wilds of the Siskiyou
Mountains of Oregon'. Newspapers all down the coast syndicated the
story, but it didn't quite capture the public imagination this second
time. After one further foray, this time with an Eve, Knowles retired to
a remote log cabin in Washington State where he died in obscurity in
October 1942.

The paradise of the American Eden has remained a powerful ideal,
however, and become an important global export, delivering its
promise of natural perfection all over the world. As happened with
the Native Americans in Yellowstone, that vision of perfection has
often entailed ejecting local people.[6] For the myth to be preserved,
man can only be an observer, a fallen outsider looking back at what he
has lost.

The worldwide dissemination of the American Eden in the national
park has been far outstripped by the spread of the other side of
paradise in consumerism. The supermarket and the mall are increasingly the places where the world does its shopping. This consumer
culture has spread like a bush fire in the last twenty years. With satellite
television, countries that were off the atlas as far as global capital was

concerned are now junior partners, not yet allowed to the feast, but able to watch. The world's largest malls are no longer in America at all; they are dwarfed by giants in China. Elsewhere Singapore, Hong Kong, Dubai and Australia are well ahead but other countries are making ground. Thirty miles from the Khyber Pass in the Pakistani city of Peshawar, a large mall is being built just a few hundred yards from the old bazaar. Shopping patterns all over the world are being altered and the trend appears to be unstoppable, sucking more and more populations into a global mass market economy.

The dangers to the environment are obvious to most of us. Extend American and West European patterns of consumption and wastage to the rest of the planet and the results will be ugly, no doubt threatening those tiny slivers of Eden that we have set aside to remind us of what we have lost. (Many countries that are plunging into the consumerism feast have not even taken that essential side-dish of American Eden.) Globalization is usually taken to mean a market force that is drawing consumers and producers into a single world economy. It is presented as a side effect of capital's endless need to locate the cheapest resources, producers and means of distribution, then connect with consumers, preferably wealthy ones. But there has been another globalization occurring, one of ideals, as the paradise-seeking behaviour that grew from the European Enlightenment is promoted and spread. Now it has thrown its plastic paradise into the laps of peoples unprepared for its nature either by their history or by their economics. For Islam this is proving a particularly tough test. The end of the Ottoman empire was like a scene in a Persian *paradeiza*, Western powers cutting up the bacon and carting it away. Islam lost its global power and has never regained it, despite oil. With this larger insult to pride came poverty, ignorance, oppression and uncertainty in many Muslim lands, and they have led, inevitably, to apocalyptic hope and movements like those of bin Ladin and others. Since his election in 2005, the President of Iran, Mahmoud Ahmadinejad, has put his own belief in the return of the Messiah, the

Shi'ites' 'hidden Imam', at the centre of his public pronouncements. This faith in a saviour who will 'emerge and establish justice in the world'[7] is no doubt also held by those Western leaders with firm Christian beliefs.

Following Columbus's discovery of the New World it appeared that the titanic struggle between Christianity and Islam for the Holy Land had been circumvented. Early Americans (Mormons, for example) frequently identified their own land with the Promised Land of Canaan. In Jerusalem the pressure was off. But now there are no more new worlds to sail away to and the paradise-seekers with bombs strapped to their chests have destroyed forever any orientalist daydreams. It is easy to see how some might construe that we are back in medieval times with a resumption of ancient enmity: Islam facing off against Christianity. On the eve of 2000, extremist Christians even attempted to reach Jerusalem where they hoped to foment fighting between Jews and Muslims that would precipitate a Second Coming. But there is a vital difference to this latest struggle, and the apocalyptic agenda of religious folk should not blind us to it. The real source of Islamic anxiety is not the Bible or missionaries, but the godless faith of consumerism, and, as such, more and more Muslims are becoming prey to the same anxiety that has been troubling Western societies.

In the late 1920s when Herbert Hoover and others were recognizing that people had become 'happiness machines', D.H. Lawrence was writing that the connection between money and paradise-seeking was a cancer destroying us. Every time a person tries to buy a bit of paradise, Lawrence argued, they are actually spiritually bought out themselves. And once we start, we cannot stop. But the old Sunday School boy did not counsel a return to the former tyrannies of church, mosque and synagogue – the temples where the paradise quest all began. He didn't see the need for that kind of defeat. He'd reached a point where he was back at the start, with Pythagoras and the harmony of the spheres and a pagan relationship with nature. 'What we want is to destroy our false, inorganic connections, especially those related to money, and re-establish the living organic connections, with the cosmos, the sun and earth, with mankind and nation and family. Start with the sun, and the rest will slowly, slowly happen.'[8]

Lawrence was writing before the full horrors of the Nazi and Stalinist paradise had happened, but he warned against those who would lead others to any kind of perfection. Almost a century later we can see that the list of such people is longer than he could have possibly expected. In Khomeini's Iran thousands were shot to purify the nation ready for Islamic perfection. At Jonestown in Guyana the Reverend Jim Jones, who had been brought up as a Disciple of Christ, led his flock into death. Bin Ladin and his cohorts clearly hope for an apocalypse of their own making. Those types of fanatic are obvious, they announce themselves. But there are others, more subtle and less violent, in the places where democracy and multinational corporations rule, shepherding us further into an anaemic consumer heaven where self-reliance and individual independence are stifled.

It is men like Lawrence, Thoreau, Hartlib, Omar Khayyam and Pythagoras who come out of the vast story of human paradise-seeking with credit. They managed to look for the good life without ever linking progress to hate, or to the noxious notions of Chosen People and Armageddon. For the most part paradise-seeking for the individual – be it like Thoreau in a woodland cabin, or Omar Khayyam in mathematics and poetry – is a creative and beneficial act. Those great men were intellectually independent and self-reliant, but also tolerant and wise. They help us stand tall and believe in the possibility of transcending our own imperfections, and those of others, which is about as close as we will ever get to that elusive state called paradise. In an age when religious hope is resurgent and faith in scientific knowledge at a low,[9] it is certainly time to question our headlong rush towards that mythical, and unreachable, destination.

Epilogue

In an Iranian shrine to an Islamic saint, I sat cross-legged and watched men and women coming in to kiss the tomb and pray. A middle-aged man with a ponytail sat down and explained who the saint was and what he had done. Everywhere there were reminders of martyrdom and death. When the people prayed, they pressed their foreheads to small tablets of baked earth from Karbala, last resting place of Hussein, the Shi'ite hero and martyr. Others invoked Ali, son-in-law of the Prophet Muhammad and martyr. Some had tears in their eyes, as though these heroes had expired yesterday, not 1,300 years ago.

'Are *jihad* and death the finest goal?' I asked Abbas, the ponytailed mystic.

He was rocking himself gently. 'You mean like those 9/11 hijackers?'

I nodded.

'The real meaning of *jihad* is internal,' he said. 'Fighting evil inside yourself.'

'What about the rewards – paradise with the dark-eyed damsels, the perpetual virgins?'

He smiled indulgently. 'That is a simple level of understanding. Go up a level – you see paradise is inside yourself.'

The ancient Greeks separated their levels by dividing writing into two categories: *mythos* was reserved for things like the tales of the gods. Although such stories might contain lies and distortions, there was also a higher truth about human nature and existence. *Logos* on the other hand related to external realities and verifiable facts. Confuse the two and you are in serious trouble, wandering around in a South American estuary looking for the Garden of Eden, or waiting at the Pearly Gates expecting paradise to contain anything so mundane as pretty nymphettes. In paradise everything is endlessly renewed: each action is blissful, eternally recapturing that experience of the first time.

The room was filling with people. Men taking up places, cross-legged around the tomb.

'Do you have to be a Muslim to achieve paradise?'

'You have to be good.'

'Are we talking about paradise in this life?'

A circle had formed and I had unwittingly become part of it.

'I fought in the Iraq War for eight years on the front and was wounded ten times. After that experience I no longer cared if I lived or died, but I did learn to believe that paradise is possible here and now.'

We watched the men take their places. Abbas looked through a notebook, reminding himself of something.

'You know of Jalal al-Din Rumi?' he asked. I nodded, remembering sitting in the square at Balkh. 'There is a story he tells of a merchant.' He turned a page, reading, then looked up. 'This merchant had a beautiful parrot in a cage. When the merchant went to India he asked the parrot what he would like. "Just ask the Indian parrots if it is right that I am in prison and they are in rose gardens," said the bird. "And ask them what is the remedy." So the merchant went away and during his journey he came across a flock of parrots in India and passed on the message. Immediately one bird stopped singing and dropped down dead – the dismayed merchant thought that he must have somehow killed a relative of his own beloved parrot.'

Abbas smiled, he had told this tale many times, but still enjoyed it. 'Arriving back home the merchant sorrowfully related what had happened in India to his own parrot, and to his horror that bird now stopped singing and dropped down dead too. The merchant was

inconsolable, he rushed round and round the room crying, "O beautiful and sweet-singing parrot, what happened to you? What sorrow!
My sweet-sounding bird! Oh what misery!"

'Then he opened the cage and, taking the body, threw it out the
window. At that moment, the parrot spread its wings and rose like the
sun, flying into a nearby tree.'

Abbas closed the notebook and got up, stretching his legs. 'We can
talk more later, now please – join us.' He took his place in a circle that
was forming around the tomb of the saint, and the men, realizing he
had invited me to stay, made a space.

The men began chanting and Abbas suddenly began to sing, a
wonderful deep baritone voice filling up the space. Above us a
thousand mirrored tiles in the dome shattered the light of a single
candle, then fell on the circle of men around the solitary tomb. Abbas
was cross-legged like the rest of us but rocking so vigorously that his
forehead touched the ground, then went right back to face the dome. I
started thinking of my father and his own spiritual quest – what he'd
make of this experience. He would have appreciated the sense of
community, I imagine. Self-reliant people usually do, as their path is
generally a recipe for solitude. When I was 14, he had suffered
expulsion from Christadelphian paradise, rejected for pushing a relax-
ation of rules on youth culture – a disco in fact. The urge to exclude is
never far from religious life: paradise is enclosed of course. Then, quite
suddenly, he was diagnosed with cancer and died at the age of 48,
before any new spiritual direction could be found.

At that moment my reverie was disturbed by Abbas's mobile phone.
He put his hand in his pocket and switched it off, never missing a beat,
but not before I recognized the ringtone – theme to the television
series and Hollywood movie, *Mission Impossible*.

After an hour the gathering finished with a handshake passed around
the circle, joining everyone, then we went out into the courtyard to eat
rice pudding and drink tea. Someone handed me a photocopied
banknote with the face of Imam Ali on it, a kind of credit note for the

spiritual effort I'd expended. Later, out in the street, I found myself walking along with one of the men who had been in the circle. He spoke English well and I asked which brotherhood of Sufis he belonged to. He shrugged. 'I don't want to be labelled or put in any one camp.'

He delved into his bag and pulled out a battered notebook. It was his collection of poems and sayings, noted down in faint pencil. 'There's something Ibn 'Arabi said ...' He searched through, found the quotation and translated it for me: 'The man of wisdom will never allow himself to be caught up in any one form or belief, because he is wise unto himself.'

Notes

Introduction (pp. xi–xv)

1 A highly tentative but commonly given date. The first definite
   evidence of the Pentateuch, the first five books of the Bible, is in the
   time of the prophet Ezra, c. 400 BC, though the discovery of a book,
   probably Deuteronomy, in the Temple of Jerusalem in 621 BC
   suggests more ancient origins. References in Genesis to the
   Philistines, a people who did not reach the coasts of Canaan until
   the late twelfth century BC, put a limit on how far back it might go,
   though of course it may have been written, and re-written, over a
   long period by several authors.
2 Dilmun is now thought to have been a real place – Bahrein.
3 Tablet I translated by Maureen Gallery Kovacs, Stanford
   University.
4 Diogenes 412–323 BC. Since he lived in a barrel, 'like a dog', the
   Greeks derived their word cynic from the word for dog-like.
5 Lawrence to Frederick Carter, 10 October 1929. Vol. 7, *Collected
   Letters*, CUP, 1993.

PART I   Origins: 800 BC–AD 1000

1 The precise eschatology of millenarianism varies, but the original
   idea was that Christ would rule for a thousand years before Satan
   was finally destroyed and a permanent paradise established.

Chapter 1   Pythagoras and Harmony (pp. 8–14)

1   Bertrand Russell rather playfully placed abstention from beans at
     the top of his list of Pythagorean rules of living in *A History of
     Western Philosophy*, chapter 3.

2   Some academics now believe the gardens may have been in
     Nineveh, another of Cyrus's cities, but the king was undoubtedly a
     great builder of gardens.

3   I use the word paradise even though Pythagoras would not have
     known it. The Greek's own touchstones would certainly have
     included the relevant passages of Homer, such as the idyllic
     descriptions of the Gardens of Alcinous, here in Alexander Pope's
     translation:

          Four acres was the allotted space of ground,
          Fenced with a green enclosure all around.
          Tall thriving trees confess'd the fruitful mould:
          The reddening apple ripens here to gold.

4   There are still faint echoes of the belief in healing music around the
     world. The French musicologist Jean During has proposed that the
     Pythagorean healing tradition survives in the Sufi trance music of
     Baluchistan, once an outpost of the Persian empire. The instrument
     used is a violin, but nothing that Stradivarious might recognize,
     much more like some fetishistic totem with a dense skull-like body
     pockmarked with curious spigots and keys. The sound is equally
     unusual: a droning, edgy keening that scratches the line between
     music and shamanism, some might say between pleasure and pain
     too. The Baluchi Sufis use various tunes to create trances and
     everyone is thought to be susceptible to at least one melody. Jean
     During has traced the history of this sound back to thirteenth-
     century texts that describe healing certain ailments, and this
     tradition, he believes, was inherited from the Pythagoreans.

5   Western ideals of female beauty are globalizing rapidly, a trend
     revealed in local variations in plastic surgery. Iranian women

favour nasal surgery, Chinese women have eyelid enhancement and leg-lengthening, while in Fiji liposuction is favoured. Television is the main carrier of the ideals. In Fiji television was introduced in 1995 and three years later the previously unrecorded condition of bulimia was afflicting 11.9 per cent of teenage girls.

Chapter 2   Apocalypse and Eden (pp. 15–26)

1   This is now the Temple Mount where the Dome of the Rock mosque stands.

2   Isaiah thus ensured his central place in Jewish history. Modern Israel's Shrine of the Book Museum in West Jerusalem makes the earliest copy of Isaiah, dated to 100 BC, the totemic centrepoint of a vast hallowed chamber. See 2 Kings 18 and 19 for the Biblical version of these events. The quotation is 2 Kings 19:6–7.

3   The word Armageddon comes from this period of history. When the Jews were comprehensively defeated in battle at Megiddo in Galilee, the town's name was spliced with the Hebrew for hill, *har*, to create a term for final destruction.

4   Although produced long after the Jewish captivity when Christianity was well under way (the haloes and angels look positively Byzantine) the central imagery was ancient.

5   He had come to Persia in 401 BC with Cyrus the Younger, pretender to the throne of his brother Artaxerxes II. Xenophon uses the word in Greek as *paradeisos*, describing walled parks that were the epitome of luxury, fecundity and fertility. He also gave us an enduring image of Cyrus working in his own garden, not at all the behaviour one might expect of a despot. The idea of the garden as an idyllic sanctuary where all are equal is an early one.

6   Apocalypse is Greek meaning to uncover, hence 'revelation', but in a secular world has come to be the term for an extreme and violent end to everything, hence *Apocalypse Now*. There doesn't seem to be

much idea of a restoration of paradise in that and the correct theological term – apocatastasis – has fallen into disuse.

7 The orthodox opinion over the centuries has usually been that all will die in Armageddon, a chosen few to be resurrected. The eighteenth-century politician John Asgill was expelled from Parliament for suggesting that some would survive throughout the whole miserable episode and go directly to heaven. cf. *Flesh in the Age of Reason*, Roy Porter, p. 97.

8 As for the number of the beast, it is usually explained by adding the numerical values of the Greek letters that make up Nero's full name, Neron Caesar, to give 666. The variation given by some manuscripts, 616, is the value for Nero Caesar. Revelation 13:18: 'Here is wisdom. Let him that hath understanding count the number of the beast: for it is the number of a man; and his number is Six hundred threescore and six.' See A. Yarbro Collins, 'The Book of Revelation' in *The Encyclopedia of Apocalypticism*, Vol. I.

9 See Revelation 21 for the full description.

10 Quoted in *Heretics: The Other Side of Early Christianity* by Gerd Lüdemann.

11 There were doubts, too, about the identity of John. Was he the same man as the Apostle? It barely seemed credible considering the very different style of the Gospel. Linguistic experts then and now agree: the Gospel shows a writer fully at home in elegant Greek prose, while Revelation on the other hand is often inaccurate and, in the words of Dionysus, uses 'barbarous idioms'. Eusebius, Bishop of Caesarea 315–340, named this second John, 'Presbyter', a possible origin of the old Prester John myth. See Bruce Metzger's excellent *The Canon of the New Testament* for a discussion of the controversies.

12 For example, Justin the Martyr in c. AD 150 and Hippolytus.

13 From John Julius Norwich's *A Short History of Byzantium*. Chrysostom was eventually exiled to Bithynia.

14 The *Encyclopedia Judaica* points out that in Hebrew the root word is ambiguous: *'adamah* would be soil or ground, hence *'adam* could

imply 'earthling' or simply 'human'. In the oral tradition of the Jews, the *Haggada*, there is a story of Adam being hermaphrodite, a being composed of two sides, an original she-male. This actually makes the myth much more satisfactory since it is with the split into duality – Adam and Eve – that self-awareness, and consequently shame, arises.

15 Augustinian values had not quite won the day – it would take until the Council of Trent in 1562 for an unequivocal statement: 'If anyone denies that it is better and more godly to abide in virginity or celibacy than to marry, he shall be excommunicated.' This was enough to convince many Catholic priests to jump ship and join Luther's followers.

Chapter 3   Muhammad and the Perfect Man (pp. 27–35)

1 This first chapter, sura, to be 'sent' is not the first in the Qur'an, it is the ninety-sixth. In fact, the earlier and more poetic revelations are at the end of the Qur'an, something that can deter the curious non-believer because the first verses tend to be more practical, even mundane.

2 The Qur'an does not describe the creature, it was the twelfth-century geographer al-Balkhi who said it was like the stone creatures guarding Assyrian palaces. Neither does the Qur'an mention Jerusalem, but Islamic tradition claims it. Abraham reputedly went to sacrifice his son on the Rock, the symbolic moment when monotheism began. When I sat in the cave I tried very hard to feel some spiritual resonance, but it was difficult as a lady was cleaning the carpet with a vacuum cleaner.

3 From his introduction to *The Sufis* by Idries Shah. The word 'vulgar' says more about Graves than Islam.

4 See Al-Khatir's account of the visit in the *Journal of the Royal Asiatic Society*, 1897. The ninth-century historian al-Ya'qubi described Mesopotamia as the navel of the earth and Baghdad its centre.

5   In fact the word algebra itself comes from the title of Al-Khwarizmi's famous treatise *Kitab al-jabr w'al-muqabala* (The Book of Completion and Comparison – *al-jabr* has various meanings, including bone-setting, but all have the connotation of force). Al-Khwarizmi's name was itself mangled in the mouths of Europeans, emerging via algorizm as algorithm, an arithmetical process. This innovative mathematician's use of Indian numerals was also ground-breaking and reflected the growing breadth of Islamic culture, bringing Indian and Persian influences together with Greek.

6   Born in 1165 and raised in Seville, then part of the Islamic kingdom of Andalus, Ibn 'Arabi showed an early interest in spiritual matters, claiming to have received visions as a youth from Moses, Jesus and Muhammad. He went on to travel across the Islamic world and died in Damascus in 1240, leaving a massive catalogue of writings and a tomb that is still a pilgrimage site. This tolerant and wise man was widely read in the Islam world as Sufism achieved greater prominence in the thirteenth century.

7   The message of Al-Ghazali (1058–1111) in his *Mishkat al-Anwar*, the Niche of Lights.

PART II   Hastening the Apocalypse: 1000–1500

1   A few months later, on a Samos beach, I would have the chance to muse on the strange congruity between total nudity and total covering – both being attempts to remove sexual attraction from social relationships, to return modern Eves to some pre-Fall state. Sudden immersion in either state can be shocking. In Aden in Yemen, after the Communists were replaced by conservative Islam in 1994, I sat in a living room with a large hole in the wall – caused by an RPG – and heard the wife of the family wail against the sudden restrictions. Utopian socialism had freed her, given her a job, money, clothes, friends. Now she was a prisoner in a veil.

A few months later I heard she had abandoned her husband and gone to Africa.

2   This is E.H. Whinfield's translation from 1881.

Chapter 4   Martyrs, Messiahs and Assassins (pp. 45–52)

1   He was already a puppet, the position of caliph having been hijacked by other bodyguards a century before.

2   The details in my account of Nizam's assassination come from the fourteenth-century historian Rashid al-Din who had access to Isma'ili documents.

3   The tale of the three schoolboys was repeated by Edward Fitzgerald whose translation (or rather reworking) of Khayyam introduced the poet to a Western audience in the nineteenth century. According to Ali Dashti, the story comes from *Rouzat as-Safa*, a fifteenth-century book by Mir Khand.

4   Pope Urban II hatched the idea after a visit to Constantinople in late 1094. The crusaders took Jerusalem on 15 July 1099 and promptly murdered every non-Christian inside – to purify the Holy City.

5   He might have been all but forgotten if not for Edward Fitzgerald whose translations were certainly imaginative. Some scholars have even disputed whether Khayyam was the original author, but the consensus now appears to be that Khayyam did write many of the verses and was both a great poet and mathematician.

6   When the sixth Imam died there was a dispute over the succession. The Isma'ilis chose the grandson of the sixth Imam, but when he died in 795, they declared he was 'hidden', waiting to return as saviour. Mainstream Shi'ism believes the hidden Imam to be the twelfth Muhammad who died in 874. For these reasons most Shi'ites are sometimes referred to as 'Twelvers' while Isma'ilis are 'Seveners'.

7   Kamal al-Din of Aleppo quoted in Lewis, *The Assassins*, p. 111.

Chapter 5 Crusaders and Last Days (pp. 53–66)

1 Joachim's analysis of history was always curiously botanical, his choice of numbers curiously similar to that of *The Hitchhiker's Guide to the Galaxy* in which the meaning of everything is also 42.

2 It was at that meeting that the Old Man reportedly laid on an impressive demonstration of his *fida'in* loyalty: commanding a foot soldier to leap from the fortress walls. The man immediately obeyed and was dashed to pieces on the rocks below. Unfortunately, the expert on Nizari history, Dr Farhad Daftary, regards it as highly unlikely that this incident ever took place. Richard's involvement with the Assassins was widely accepted at the time, but one Muslim source, the historian Ibn al-Athir, claimed that it was Saladin who had contracted the assassination. See Saladin and Richard the Lionhearted: selected annals from al-Umari edited by Eva Lundquist (1996). Al-Umari makes no mention of Richard's connections with the Assassins, blaming Conrad's murder on a dispute over booty with the Old Man of the Mountains.

3 From Persia the belief had travelled into Bulgaria where the heretics were called the Bogomils, a group so hated and abused that their name entered the English language as 'bugger'. Cathar comes from the same Greek root as catharsis.

4 Signs of that fire are still visible in the ruins at Alamut. The various quotations from Juvayni come from *The Assassins* by Bernard Lewis, and *The Assassin Legends* by Farhad Daftary.

5 The view of the custodian of restoration, Abbas Shamshedi, when I visited in October 2004.

6 Raphael began work in 1508, using Plato and Aristotle as his central figures. Pythagoras appears in the foreground, reading a chalkboard on which can be seen a diagram of his theories on musical harmony. Ibn Rushd, Averroes, is behind him.

7 Procopius who wrote the scandalous exposé had much more to say. 'And certain slaves whose special task it was would sprinkle

grains of barley over her private parts; and geese trained for the purpose would pick them off one by one with their beaks and swallow them.' This was during her career as an 'actress' – before her ennoblement.

Chapter 6   Christopher Columbus Discovers Eden (pp. 67–78)

1   This was the moment when Europeans finally hit the American mainland, if you exclude some lost Roman sailors who reputedly left a hoard of coins on a Venezuelan beach.
2   In the Middle Ages the first two were usually thought to be the Nile and the Ganges. The King James Version refers to the Tigris as Hiddekel. The name Gihon is preserved in the freshwater spring that lies just below the ancient walls of Jerusalem.
3   The Church and poverty had had a tricky relationship. St Francis of Assissi started a movement based on extreme poverty, but within a century of his death in 1226 the Inquisition was burning Franciscans over the matter.
4   In Seville Cathedral, in a chamber off the Court of Oranges, a few fragments of Columbus's library survive, among them a heavily annotated 1477 edition of *Imago Mundi* by Pierre d'Ailly (1350–1420). This vast description of the cosmos was written around 1410 when d'Ailly was the Bishop of Cambrai. It elicited a barrage of marginal comments by the navigator, 898 in all. Maps included in the work placed the Garden of Eden in temperate southern latitudes and raised it above 'the lower air'. Columbus also shows particular interest in d'Ailly's assertion that the earth is round – a theory first proposed by Aristarchos of Samos. A second book read and annotated by Columbus, the *Historia Rerum Ubique Gestarum* by Aeneas Silvius Piccolomini, later Pope Pius II (1405–64), suggests Eden is located closer to the equator, the heat tempered perhaps by height. The top of a mountain was a favourite location; Dante put it there in his *Divine Comedy*. The thirteenth-

century French chronicler of the Crusades, Jean de Joinville, favoured Ethiopia because, he claimed, nets cast in the Egyptian Nile would catch those paradisical substances, spices and rhubarb.

5 The figure is commonly quoted but there is disagreement: it varies from 40,000 up to 200,000.

6 When some of the *conversos* later fled from Portugal to Amsterdam, they quickly reinstated their original religion, rather confirming the Inquisition's fears.

7 Richard Kagan in *1492: Art in the Age of Exploration*, Yale, 1991, edited by J. Levenson.

8 In this vision God also made several pointed remarks about Columbus's detractors at the Spanish court and went on to insist that he had assigned the Indies and their riches for the navigator alone – a thoughtful touch by the supreme deity.

9 *The Four Voyages of Christopher Columbus*, ed. J.M. Cohen, pp. 303–4.

10 This has been thrown into doubt recently with suggestions that the bones in Seville are of Columbus's son, Diego.

11 Sir Walter Raleigh, who had overseen Barlowe and Amadas's voyage to North Carolina, was not impressed by the claims of the tropics to be paradise. Yes, they had 'perpetuall Spring and Summer', but against that were the 'dangerous diseases, the multitude of venimous beasts and wormes'. Vespucci was quick to mention the women: 'they showed a great desire to have carnal knowledge of us Christians.' And also referred to Brazil as the Garden of Eden, but his version owes more to Dante than Genesis. See *Amerigo and the New World*, German Arciniegas (1955). The belief in an actual Garden of Eden continues with some American Churches who have realized that Creation and original sin – both aspects of the garden myth – are necessary to make Jesus's self-sacrifice meaningful. Hence despite the overwhelming evidence of evolution, they persist in describing it as a 'theory'.

PART III   New Edens in an Old World: Sixteenth and Seventeenth
Centuries

Chapter 7   New Routes to Paradise: Relics and Indulgences
(pp. 84–91)

1   See *Christianity* by Bamber Gascoigne, an entertaining, and deli-
    ciously irreverent, introduction to the religion.
2   There is a chapel on the site, deep in the bowels of the Church of
    the Holy Sepulchre.
3   Three centuries after the Reformation, the Jehovah's Witnesses
    would set the figure at 144,000 – all reserved for members of their
    congregation. The figure comes, inevitably, from the book of
    Revelation and had been used by many other groups before. When
    the Church faithful exceeded that number, it was realized, provi-
    dentially, that there would be some standing room too: the elect
    would rule with Christ, but others would be allowed in to be
    ruled.
4   Quoted in Peter Stanford's *Heaven*, p. 210.

Chapter 8   The Collectors (pp. 92–106)

1   Potatoes 1590, sunflowers 1568 and lilacs 1565. The oldest plant
    in the garden now is a palm dating back to 1585. In 1786 Goethe
    examined the tree and used it in his essay *The Metamorphosis of
    Plants*, an early evolutionary theory.
2   The Renaissance had seen the rise of the *wunderkammer*, the
    collection of wonders, a princely possession that had more to do
    with status. It was later that the collection took on its universalist
    aspirations. Cf *The Origins of Museums: Cabinets of Curiosities in 16th
    and 17th century Europe*, Impey and Macgregor (1985). The
    collecting phenomenon does not appear to have been partisan:
    both Protestants and Catholics indulged in it.

3 Genesis 1:29 and 2:19 respectively. The idea of a man's dominion comes in 1:28.

4 Contrast this with Ibn Sina's microcosm inside the Perfect Man: all the discoveries and exploration had given Western paradise-seeking a new outward orientation.

5 Quoted in *The Origins of Museums*, from the *Gesta Grayorum* 1595.

6 See *English Factories in India 1630–33* by W. Foster.

7 Holbein's 'Ambassadors' in London's National Gallery features just such an anamorphic image – a skull that appears as a long smudge.

8 In 1638 a live dodo was shown in London, a rather sorry display witnessed by one Dr L'estrange. It may have been this specimen that Tradescant acquired after its premature death.

9 See R.F. Ovenell, 'The Tradescant Dodo', *Archives of Natural History*, Vol. 19, no. 2.

10 Mundy and Weddell sailed east together in 1636 but the latter never made it home again, disappearing with his ship, the *Dragon*, in 1639. Mundy was more fortunate, returning in December 1638, only to set off around the Baltic for eight years. Compiling his copious journals as an old man, he reckoned on having completed $100,833\frac{5}{8}$ miles. He died in Penryn, Cornwall in 1677.

11 Unfortunately the plane trees that once shaded the Kabul garden where Babur is buried are now dead and guards warned me about land mines when I visited in 2004. The garden, however, is undergoing restoration, despite controversy over whether to keep the Soviet swimming pool.

Chapter 9   The English Eden (pp. 107–19)

1 In 1578 Elizabeth was already complaining of the foul 'taste and smoke of sea-coles', but a generation later things were much worse and in 1661 it was so bad that all the orchards in London ceased to bear fruit.

2   Luther, *Lectures*, p. 102, quoted in Jean Delumeau's *History of Paradise*. The prophet Muhammad, of course, also condemned the monastic life, though for rather different reasons.
3   Charles Butler, *The Feminine Monarchy or the History of Bees* (1609). He was vicar of Wotton St Lawrence in Hampshire.
4   Now Elblag in eastern Poland. Hartlib's family were of Lithuanian origin but had settled there after persecution of Protestants by the Jesuits.
5   Goropius reasoned that Eden's language must have been simple, therefore with short words, a feature of old Flemish. The name Eve, for example, was eu-vat, meaning 'barrel from which people originated'. Since this word was actually longer than Eve it is perhaps unsurprising that Goropius's widely read theories were often derided. See *Origines Antwerpianae* (1569).
6   Prynne's primary objection was to female actors at a time, 1633, when Queen Henrietta Maria was appearing in a masque. Surprisingly he became a loyal servant to Charles II after the Restoration.

Chapter 10   The Separatists Head for America (pp. 120–23)

1   In England she acted in a Ben Jonson masque and later died in Gravesend.
2   From his *The Art of Travel*.

Chapter 11   The Birth of Science (pp. 124–36)

1   The comparison comes from D. McCullough's excellent book, *Reformation*.
2   And they had a long reach. In north-east Madagascar there is a village called Rantabe (Ranters Bay), a name given by seventeenth-century pirates after the radical Civil War sect, the Ranters.
3   See *Alexander Pope* by Maynard Mack.
4   And some gentry took up the challenge: see *Gentlemen and Players* by Timothy Mowl (2000).

5 Quoted from Milton's 'The Ready and Easy Way to Establish a Free Commonwealth' in *Britain in Revolution* by Austin Woolrych (2002).

6 The chance discovery of lost Royal Society documents in 2006 has shown that it was Oldenburg who was responsible for one of science's longest-running controversies: the argument between Christiaan Huygens and Oldenburg's successor Robert Hooke over the invention of an accurate timepiece. In 1675 Huygens announced that he had built a corrected watch using tiny springs, a statement that incensed Hooke who claimed to have done the same five years earlier. The recovered documents prove that Hooke was right: he had announced the invention at the Royal Society in 1670, but Oldenburg failed to transfer the record from the draft minutes to the final copy.

7 The best source for the story of both John Tradescants is Prudence Leith Ross's biography to which I am much indebted.

Chapter 12   The Decline and Fall of Witchcraft (pp. 137–41)

1 Spinoza was not an atheist at all, but a deist. However, the abuse stuck.

2 See *Radical Enlightenment* by Jonathan Israel (2001), p. 400. Israel's excellent book also covers the story of Leenhof.

3 Religious sects proved much cannier than atheists in adopting the terms of abuse: Quakers, Puritans, Shakers and many more all started as pejoratives.

4 A popular heresy that the Christadelphians would adopt in the nineteenth century.

5 For example, Charles Own, *The Scene of Delusions Open'd in an Historical Account of Prophetick Impostures...* (1712), an exposure of the malpractices and abuses of so-called prophets.

6 Robin Barnes in *Images of Hope and Despair: Western Apocalypticism 1500–1800*, in *The Encyclopedia of Apocalypticism* (2000).

Chapter 13   Selling the American Eden (pp. 142–48)

1 John Locke, *Two Treatises*, II.49.
2 Quoted in Paul Johnson's *A History of the American People*, p. 30.
3 Thomas Morton, *New English Canaan* (1637).
4 Quoted in *Reinventing Eden* by Carolyn Merchant (2003).
5 A survey of private gardens in London conducted after the Restoration found 22 out of 24 had glass houses.
6 Mentioned by Sir Hugh Platt in his book *Garden of Eden* (1654).
7 Charles Howard was governor of Jamaica until 1677 and owned St Lucia. The Lascelles of Harewood had Barbadian plantations.
8 Pineapple-passion reached its height in 1761 when a house was built in the shape of a 40-ft-tall fruit at Dunsmore in Scotland – it is now a holiday home.
9 The dinner took place at Londesborough in East Yorkshire where the ruined old walled garden and hothouses remain. See *The Letters of David Garrick*, 20 July 1750, edited by D.M. Little and G.M. Kahrl (1963). Garrick complained: 'I eat so much here…every button of my Waistcoat is this moment cocked.'
10 Quoted in *I Have Spoken*, a compilation of Native American speeches edited by V.I. Armstrong (1971).

PART IV   The Modern Paradise: 1700–1945

Chapter 14   The Comforts of the New Earthly Paradise (pp. 154–60)

1 A. Bartlett Giamatti in a 1974 review quoted in *Paradise Preserved* by Max Schulz (1985).
2 Sophie von la Roche in 1786, quoted in *A History of Shopping* by Doris Davis, 1966.
3 197,000 yards of wallpaper were sold in 1713, but 2,100,000 in 1785. See Porter, *English Society in the 18th century*. The breeding of horses and dogs was very popular. English thoroughbreds are supposedly descended from three eighteenth-century stallions: the

Darley Arab, the Byerly Turk and the Godolphin Arab. Gervase Markham, author of the self-help books of the early seventeenth century, was the expert and his *Compleat Jockey* was reprinted more than 20 times.

4 The furious pace of commerce might be judged in the coins exchanging hands: they were getting smaller – silver shillings that had been circulating since the late seventeenth century were worn down to around three-quarters of their correct size by the time of George III. Shopkeepers would occasionally pile them on to scales and demand the shortfall be made up.

5 Hence Henry Fielding's definition of a nobody: 'All the people in Great Britain except about 1,200.'

6 From his *Essays*. Temple's heart is buried under the sundial in his garden – the house is now the Constance Spry School of Flower Arranging.

7 Roy Porter, *Flesh in the Age of Reason*, p. 280.

8 Quoted in *Flesh in the Age of Reason*.

9 It was translated into English in 1741. The sofa was then an exciting development in furniture brought from the Orient. The origin of the word is obscure, but is probably Arabic's *suffah* – bench or ledge. The sofa itself came to be something of literary device, a handy euphemism for licentiousness, a space on which normal rules might be bent, a tradition upheld in Britain by television sit-coms.

10 His copy, now in Paris, remains the oldest in existence, though there are earlier references. Records of a Jewish bookseller in Cairo in the twelfth century show the loan of a book called *The Thousand and One Nights*. The Arab historian al-Masudi's *Meadows of Gold*, written in the first half of the tenth century, also mentions *Alf Layla* – a Thousand Nights.

11 Plate IV.

12 Left unfinished when he died in 1722, it was published in 1730 in French, then in English the following year.

Chapter 15   Creating the New Adam (pp. 161–69)

1   Franklin was very much an idealist, but no charlatan. When he
     invented a superior type of stove in the winter of 1740–1, he
     declined to take out a patent, saying that since he had enjoyed
     'great Advantage from the Inventions of Others, we should be glad
     of an Opportunity to serve others by an Invention of ours'.
2   From *The Prelude*, Book X, 1805.
3   The words of Alexis de Tocqueville quoted in *Earthly Powers* by
     Michael Burleigh.
4   Revelation 7:4: 'And I heard the number of them which were
     sealed: and there were sealed an hundred and forty and four
     thousand of all the tribes of the children of Israel.' The number
     came from 12 tribes × 12,000. Hence the Jehovah's Witnesses'
     belief in 144,000 places for believers in the paradise on earth to
     come.
5   Her successor was George Turner, who announced that total
     destruction would soon kill everyone in Britain, except his
     followers who would divide the spoils. After a spell in York
     asylum where he found time to plan his New Jerusalem – 50
     square miles enclosed by solid gold walls – he was let out and
     resumed his work with a demand for 15,050 wives. He died
     short of his target in 1821. His successor, a hunchbacked wool-
     comber called John Wroe, started out celibate and a tad obsessed
     with personal hygiene, even having himself publicly circumcised
     in Ashton-under-Lyne (a town he believed would be the New
     Jerusalem). By 1830, having established a following and built a
     sanctuary in the town, the heavily bearded Wroe was ready to
     make an announcement: he required seven virgins for himself.
     This relatively modest request was met with outrage and Wroe
     was asked to leave Ashton, taking his 'Christian Israelites' with
     him. Many emigrated and became Mormons. The Southcottians
     still exist as the Panacea Society who have possession of

Southcott's famous sealed box containing her prophecies, only to be opened when the Messiah appears. They are based in Bedford which they confidently believe to be the site of the original Garden of Eden.

6 See Richard Holmes' *Shelley: The Pursuit* (1974), chapter 9 for an account of this period in the poet's life.

7 Written while with Byron in Ravenna in 1821 and quoted in Max Schulz's *Paradise Preserved* (1985).

8 Schulz, p. 99. For example, Byron's Toobonai Island in 'The Island', the 'green isle' in Shelley's 'Lines written among the Euganean Hills' and others.

9 The others were Plutarch's *Lives*, Goethe's *Sorrows of Young Werther*, and Volney's *Ruins: a Survey of the Revolutions of Empire.*

10 See Richard Holmes' *Shelley*, p. 334.

Chapter 16   Robert Owen and the Godless Millennium (pp. 170–82)

1 In a house now demolished and replaced with the HSBC.

2 Quoted from *The Life of Robert Owen by Himself* (1857).

3 Quoted from E. Royle's *Robert Owen and the Commencement of the Millennium* (1998), p. 15.

4 From a lecture he gave to cotton manufacturers in Glasgow in January 1815.

5 The Pentridge Revolutionaries were hanged and drawn that November.

6 Between 1793 and 1820, 3 million acres of land were enclosed by Act of Parliament.

7 He was the first to use the word socialism in print. The *Dictionary of National Biography* has an excellent summary of his life and work.

8 *Robert Owen and the Owenites in Britain and America* by J.F.C. Harrison (1969), p. 100.

9 The first gold strike was in January 1848 in the Sacramento Valley but the Rush came a year later. In the first decade a staggering $550

million was extracted, and for many that cemented forever the connection between a Promised Land and America.

10 No one apart from Smith ever saw them. The weird symbols he copied from the plates and later translated into the Book of Mormon were seen by an independent witness at the time and described as a transparent hoax. The plates were spirited away by an angel.

11 *The Selected Works of Robert Owen* (1993), Vol. 4, p. 316.

12 The Shakers were supposed to walk in straight lines, turning at right angles. They started up stairs with the right foot. They cut their food in squares. They lay straight in bed on their backs 'in the fear of God' and their clothes were hand-made to fit each individual. Millennial Laws proscribed all kinds of immoral behaviour, including curses such as 'Good Heavens!' But they did have a chance to break free in their ceremonies when brethren would speak in tongues and dance wildly. Charles Dickens visited in June 1842 and was unimpressed: 'I recognise the worst among the enemies of Heaven and Earth, who turn the water at the marriage feasts of this poor world, not into wine, but gall.'

13 Quoted in *A History of the American People* by Paul Johnson (1997), p. 323.

Chapter 17   Religious America Tries to Build a New Adam
(pp. 183–91)

1 See *Special Love / Special Sex – An Oneida Community Diary*, edited by R.S. Fogarty (1994).

2 In *Lettre sur les aveugles*.

3 Plato, *The Republic*, Part 6, Book 5.

4 See R.S. Fogarty, *op. cit.*

5 Academic R.S. Fogarty was lucky to find a last 'speaker' of this lost language who transcribed it for him.

Chapter 18   Social Darwinism: Eden by Eradication (pp. 192–201)

1   The idea of separation in order to be Chosen recurs throughout
    the Old and New Testaments. The first appearance is this one in
    Exodus 19:5. It is echoed at the other end of the Bible in I Peter
    2:9: 'But ye are a chosen generation, a royal priesthood, an holy
    nation, a peculiar people.' It was a favourite verse for the Puritan
    émigrés.
2   See *American Eugenics* by Nancy Ordover (2003) and *The Racial
    State: Germany 1933–45* by Burleigh and Wippermann (1991).
3   It was later shown that scientists had vastly underestimated
    cultural factors, invalidating Goddard's methods and results. To
    Goddard's credit he later withdrew his conclusions and strenu-
    ously tried to make amends, but by then, the late 1920s, it was too
    late. More intelligent women, it was feared, were far less likely
    than morons to be satisfied with the role of mother – a fear that has
    not disappeared. A report in Britain in 2005 claimed that a 16
    point rise in a woman's IQ diminished her chances of marriage by
    40 per cent. Though people are more likely to draw cultural
    conclusions than racial or genetic ones, the alarmist message of
    fear remains.
4   Their address and others are reprinted in *The History of Hereditarian
    Thought*, ed. Charles Rosenberg (1984), p. 246 for this quotation.
5   Voegelin, *The Political Religions* (1938), p. 51.
6   The definition is T.H. Huxley's. Comte had identified the reli-
    gious need in secular society and tried to close the gap with his
    positivism.
7   The Anabaptists suffered terribly; an estimated 2,500 died in the
    Netherlands alone. As for the Jews in fifteenth-century Spain, around
    13,000 were murdered in the first 12 years of the Inquisition.
8   Quoted in *The Banality of Evil: Hannah Arendt and the Final Solution*
    by Bernard J. Bergen (1998).

PART V   Consumer Idylls of the Twentieth and Twenty-first Centuries:
Rural Retreats and Shopping Malls

Chapter 19   A Consumer Durable Eden (pp. 208–15)

1   Hence Simon Schama's title for his book about the Dutch Republic of
the seventeenth and eighteenth centuries, *The Embarrassment of Riches.*
2   See *Consumerism in History* by Peter Stearns for this example and
many other fascinating insights.
3   A committed Seventh Day Adventist for most of his life, Kellogg
believed in vegetarianism, prolonged mastication, eight glasses of
water per day, lots of fresh air and plenty of exercise.
4   Graham aroused passionate responses: on two occasions he was
physically attacked by butchers for denouncing meat as sexually
arousing. For Kellogg and Graham see *American National Biography*,
OUP (1999).
5   The Bon Marché store is often cited as the first French department
store in 1852, though there are earlier claims.
6   See *Land of Desire* by William Leach (1993) and *New York 1900* by
Robert Stern (1983).
7   Advertising agencies appeared in the 1880s in the US, way before
they did in Europe. The man who did more than most to lure
Protestant America towards shameless consumption met his end in
1915 when he sank with the *Lusitania.* The diarist who commented
on Tiffany's was George Templeton Strong, writing in May 1868.
8   The word 'splurge' appeared in the US at this time. The consumer
cycle of work and waste does seem to hark back to pagan rites: I
think of the Aztecs sacrificing people to make sure that the sun
rose.
9   Quoted in *Alma Mahler or the Art of Being Loved* by Françoise
Giroud (1991). The orientalist fantasy was shared by Frederic
Edwin Church, an artist of the renowned Hudson River School.
From 1870 until his death 30 years later he worked on Olana, his

orientalized mansion where Saracenic arches and Turkish carpets were combined with views of the Catskills, 'A perfect Eden of picturesque beauty,' gushed one visitor. For Tiffany see *The Oriental Obsession: Islamic Inspiration in British and American Art and Architecture 1500–1920* by John Sweetman, CUP (1988).

10 See *Noble Dreams, Wicked Pleasures: Orientalism in America, 1870–1930*, ed. Holly Edwards (2000).

11 The West Edmonton Mall in Canada contains 11 department stores within its 5.2 million square feet of heaven, along with 800 other shopping outlets, a 360-room hotel, an ice rink, and recreations of Bourbon Street in New Orleans and the boulevards of nineteenth-century Paris. Shoppers can also visit one of 20 movie theatres, or sit and admire the Siberian tiger, the penguins and the robotic submarines. In a final touch that brings a sense of historical completion to the entire cornucopia, the lake boasts a full-size replica of Christopher Columbus's ship, the *Santa Maria*.

Reviewing what this fantastic display might add up to, Margaret Crawford wrote: 'This implausible, seemingly random, collection of images has been assembled with an explicit purpose: to support the mall's claim to contain the entire world within its walls.' The cabinet, the universe in one place, God's creation under our thumb – the Mall has illustrious forbears and perhaps no peers, except a few of the world's larger museums. For shoppers this kind of crass perfection obviously worked: West Edmonton was soon generating annual profits of over $3,000 per square metre – double that of other malls.

12 Lizabeth Cole in *Consumer Society in American History*, ed. L.B. Glickman (1999).

13 See *Culture of Consumption* by R. Wightman Fox (1983). The most emotionally charged of brands can become the focus for new communities – like a fetish object in pagan times. I once saw a field full of people camping and beside each tent was the quintessential British car, the Mini. If this is a religion, then splits should emerge

before long – old-style Mini and new could be the Sunni and Shi'ite of the Owners' Club.

Chapter 20 'Wilderness is Paradise Enow' (pp. 216–23)

1   See Mark David Spence, *Dispossessing the Wilderness* (1999).
2   See *Wilderness and the American Mind*, Roderick Nash (1981).
3   See de Tocqueville, *Democracy in America*, Vol. 2, p. 74.
4   See Nash, *op. cit.*
5   In a sense Knowles had invented the format for the reality television show long before TV was invented itself. Almost a century later the medium has learned to love this paradise-seeking countercurrent. Survival on tropical islands, back-to-basics for celebrities on farms, or even just a chef choosing to live hand-to-mouth in the country, they have all been tried.
6   At Girnar in the Indian state of Gujarat villagers were removed from the park where Asia's only population of wild lions lived. The lions promptly left too: they had been living on the people's cattle. Similar stories emerge from Africa where the contrast between inside and outside the perimeter fence can be stark: shacks and scrubby wasteland on one side, abundant greenery and well-fed animals on the other.
7   Quoted in the *Guardian*, 21 February 2006.
8   *Apocalypse and the Writings on Revelation*, D.H. Lawrence, CUP (1980), p. 149.
9   Around 45 per cent of Americans are said to believe in a literal Creation and an earth of around 6–9,000 years in age. Wherever America goes, of course, Britain is sure to follow.

Selected Bibliography

PART I: Origins: 800 BC–AD 1000

Armstrong, K., *Muhammad: a Biography of the Prophet*, HarperCollins, 1992

Armstrong, K., *A History of Jerusalem*, HarperCollins, 1996

Beasley-Murray, G.R. (ed.), *The Book of Revelation*, Marshall, 1974

Boyce, M., *The History of Zoroastrianism*, Brill, 1989

Eaton, C. Le Gai, *Islam and the Destiny of Man*, London, 1994

Esposito, J. (ed.), *The Oxford History of Islam*, Oxford University Press, 1999

Ferguson, E. (ed.), *Encyclopedia of Early Christianity*, Garland, 1997

Finkelstein, I. and Silberman, N.A., *The Bible Unearthed*, Free Press, New York, 2001

Gascoigne, B., *The Christians*, Constable & Robinson, 2003

Hillenbrand, R., *Islamic Art and Architecture*, Thames & Hudson, 1999

Hourani, A., *A History of the Arab Peoples*, Faber & Faber, 1991

Jonstone, J., *A History of Wonderful Things in Nature*, London, 1657

Lüdemann, G., *Heretics: the Other Side of Early Christianity*, Westminster John Knox Press, 1996

Luxenberg, C., *Die Syro-Aramäische Lesart des Koran: Ein Beitrag zur Entschlüsselung der Koransprache*, 2003

McGinn, B. (ed.), *The Encyclopedia of Apocalypticism*, Continuum Publishing Group, 1998

Metzger, B., *The Canon of the New Testament*, Clarendon Press, 1997

Norwich, J.J., *A Short History of Byzantium*, Penguin, 1997

Rogerson, B., *The Prophet Muhammad: a Biography*, Little, Brown, 2003

Russell, B., *A History of Western Philosophy*, Routledge, 1996

Stewart, I., *Nature's Numbers*, Basic Books, 1995

Walzer, R., *Al-Farabi on the Perfect State*, Oxford University Press, 1985

PART II: Hastening the Apocalypse: 1000–1500

Arateh, A.R., *Rumi: The Persian, The Sufi*, London, 1965

Bakhtiar, L., *Sufi Expression and the Mystic Quest*, 1976

Cohen, J.M. (ed.), *The Four Voyages of Christopher Columbus*, Penguin, 1969

Columbus, C., *The Book of Prophecies*, University of California, reprint 1997

Daftary, F., *The Assassin Legends: Myths of the Isma'ilis*, I.B. Tauris, 1995

Dashti, A., *In Search of Omar Khayyam*, Columbia University Press, 1971

Fernandez-Arnesto, F., *Columbus*, Duckworth, 1992

Flint, V., *The Imaginative Landscape of Christopher Columbus*, Princeton University Press, 1992

Grabar, O., *The Great Mosques of Isfahan*, New York, 1990

Levenson, J., *1492: Art in the Age of Exploration*, Yale, 1991

Lewis, B., *The Assassins*, Weidenfeld & Nicolson, 1967

Lundquist, E. (ed.), *Saladin and Richard the Lionheart: Selected Annals from al-Umari*, 1966

Malouf, A., *The Crusades Through Arab Eyes*, London, 1994

Morison, S. (ed.), *Journals and Other Documents on the Life and Voyages of Christopher Columbus*, Limited Editions Club, 1963

Reeves, M., *Joachim of Fiore and the Prophetic Future*, Sutton Publishing, 1976

Runciman, S., *A History of the Crusades*, London, 1991

Shah, I., *The Sufis*, Anchor paperback, 1971

PART III: New Edens in an Old World: Sixteenth and Seventeenth Centuries

Allan, M., *The Tradescants: Their Plants, Gardens and Museums*, Gresham, 1964

Austen, R., *The Spiritual Use of an Orchard*, 1647

Bacon, F., *Essays*, Everyman edition, 1906

Boas, G., *Essays on Primitivism and Related Ideas in the Middle Ages*, Baltimore, 1948

Bynum, W.F. and Porter, R., *Living and Dying in London*, London, 1991

Davies, J.C., *Utopia and the Ideal Society: a study of utopian writing, 1516–1700*, Cambridge University Press, 1981

Faber, R., *The Brave Courtier: Sir William Temple*, London, 1983

Greengrass, M., *Samuel Hartlib and the Universal Reformation*, Cambridge University Press, 1994

Hartlib Archive, Sheffield University CD Rom

Hunter, M., Clericuzio, A. and Principe, L. (eds), *The Correspondence of Robert Boyle*, 6 vols, London, 2001

Impey, M., *The Origins of Museums: Cabinets of Curiosities in 16th and 17th Century Europe*, Oxford University Press, 1985

Jardine, L. and Stewart, A., *Hostage to Fortune: the Troubled Life of Francis Bacon 1561–1626*, Victor Gollancz, 1998

Leith-Ross, P., *The John Tradescants*, Peter Owen Publishing, 1984

Markham, G., *The English Husbandman*, London, 1613

Mowl, T., *Gentlemen and Players: Gardeners of the English Landscape*, Sutton Publishing, 2000

Mundy, P., *The Travels of Peter Mundy*, Vol. III, Hakluyt Society, 1919

Nash, A., *Living in Lambeth 1086–1914*, Lambeth Borough Council Public Relations Committee, 1950

Nicolson, A., *Power and Glory: Jacobean England and the Making of the King James Bible*, HarperCollins, 2003

Plat, Sir H., *The Garden of Eden*, 1654

Porter, R., *London: A Social History*, London, 1994

Quest-Ritson, C., *The English Garden: a Social History*, London, 2001

Turnbull, G.H., *Hartlib, Dury and Comenius*, Liverpool, 1947

Webster, C., *The Great Instauration: Science, Medicine and Reform 1626–1660*, London, 1975

Webster, C., *Utopian Planning and the Puritan Revolution*, Oxford University Press, 1979

Wheelock, A., *A Collectors Cabinet*, Washington, 1998

PART IV: The Modern Paradise: 1700–1945

Armstrong, V.I., *I Have Spoken* (a compilation of Native American records), Sage Books, 1971

Batey, M., *Alexander Pope: the Poet and the Landscape*, Barn Elms Publishing, 1999

Beadman, D., *The Origins and Aims of Two Christian Movements: The Disciples of Christ and the Christadelphians*, 1972 dissertation, University of Leicester

Brown, D., *Bury My Heart at Wounded Knee*, London, 1971

Burleigh, M. and Wippermann, W., *The Racial State: Germany 1933–45*, Cambridge University Press, 1991

Davis, D., *A History of Shopping*, London, 1966

Diderot, D., trans. Hawkes, S., *The Indiscreet Jewels*, Marsilio Publishers, 1993

Dunn, R., *Slaves and Sugar*, 1972

Fogarty, R.S., *Special Love / Special Sex: An Oneida Community Diary*, Syracuse University Press, 1994

Gilham, N.W., *A Life of Sir Francis Galton*, Oxford University Press, 2001

Goddard, H.H., *The Kallikak Family: a Study in the Heredity of Feeble-Mindedness*, New Jersey, 1913

Gragg, L., *Englishmen Transplanted: the English Colonization of Barbados 1627–1660*, Oxford University Press, 2003

Harrison, J.F.C., *The Second Coming: Popular Millenarianism 1780–1850*, Rutgers University Press, 1979

Hayden, D., *Seven American Utopias*, Massachusetts Institute of Technology Press, 1976

Henrey, B., *No Ordinary Gardener: Thomas Knowlton 1691–1781*, British Museum, 1986

Holloway, M., *Heavens on Earth: Utopian Communities in America 1680–1880*, New York, 1966

Israel, J., *Radical Enlightenment*, Oxford University Press, 2001

Johnson, P., *History of the American People*, Weidenfeld & Nicolson, 1997

Klaw, S., *Without Sin: The Life and Death of the Oneida Community*, New York, 1993

Locke, J., *Two Treatises of Government*, 1690

MacCulloch, D., *Reformation: Europe's House Divided 1490–1700*, London, 2003

Mack, M., *Alexander Pope, a Life*, New York, 1985

Merchant, C., *Reinventing Eden*, London, 2003

Miller, P., *Errand into the Wilderness*, Harvard University Press, 1956

Morton, T., *New English Canaan*, 1637

Nash, R., *Wilderness and the American Mind*, Yale University Press, 1981

Neave, D., *Londesborough: History of an East Yorkshire Estate Village*, 1977

Ordover, N., *American Eugenics*, University of Minnesota Press, 2003

Owen, R., *Early Writings*, 1815

Owen, R., *The Selected Works*, 1993

Parker, R., *A Yankee Saint: J.H. Noyes and the Oneida Community*, 1935

Pollard, S. and Salt, J. (ed.), *Robert Owen: Prophet of the Poor*, Associated University Press, 1971

Porter, R., *English Society in the 18th Century*, London, revised edition 1991

Royle, E., *Robert Owen and the Commencement of the Millennium*, Manchester University Press, 1998

Spence, M.D., *Dispossessing the Wilderness*, Oxford University Press, 1999

Temple, W., 'Upon the Gardens of Epicurus', in *Essays*, 1685

Turner, J., 'Ralph Austen, an Oxford Horticulturalist of the 17th Century', *Journal of the Garden History Society*, Vol. 6, no. 2, 1978

Verney, F., *Memoirs of the Verney Family during the Civil War*, 1892

Voegelin, E., *Collected Works*, University of Missouri Press, 2002

Wagner, P., *Eros Revived: Eroticism and the Enlightenment in Europe and America*, David & Charles, 1988

Woods, M. and Warren, A., *Glass Houses*, Aurum Press, 1988

PART V: Consumer Idylls of the Twentieth and Twenty-first Centuries: Rural Retreats and Shopping Malls

Belk, R. W., *Collecting in a Consumer Society*, London, 1995

Bowlby, R., *Carried Away*, Columbia University Press, 2001

Lawrence, D.H., *Apocalypse*, Albatross Library, 1934

Leach, W., *Land of Desire*, Vintage, 1993

Sorkin, M. (ed.), *Variations on a Theme Park*, Hill & Wang, 1992

Stearns, P., *Consumerism in World History*, London, 2001

Stern, R., *New York 1900: Metropolitan Architecture and Urbanism 1890–1915*, New York, 1983

Wightman Fox, R. (ed.), *The Culture of Consumption: Critical Essays in American History 1880–1980*, New York, 1983

Zukin, S., *Point of Purchase: How Shopping Changed American Culture*, New York, 2004

Index

260 INDEX

Arcadia   xii, 5, 24, 70, 156
Arendt, Hannah   201
Aristotle   31
the Ark (Lambeth)   97, 98–102, 104, 107, 114, 117, 126–7, 130–1, 133–5, 136
Armageddon   xiii, xiv, 5, 47, 59, 65, 66, 95, 181, 201, 223
Armstrong, Karen   200
Arrani, Bu Tahir   45–6
asceticism   25
Ashmole, Elias   96, 126–7, 130–1, 133–5
Ashmolean Museum   90, 135
ashrams   10
the Assassins   46, 48–50, 51, 56, 57, 60, 61, 120, 166–7
Assyrians   15–16
astronomy   10, 47, 60, 132
Athanasius   21
atheism   137–8, 139–40, 165
Aubrey, John   135, 146
Augustine, St   22, 24–6, 29, 32, 35, 58, 88
Auschwitz   199
Austen, Ralph   111, 117, 127
Australia   221
Austria   199
Avesta (holy book)   41
Avicenna see Ibn Sina

Babel, Tower of   117
Babur, Emperor   xv
Babylon/Babylonians   xii, 8–10, 16–17, 192
Bacon, Francis   94–5, 106, 111–12, 113–14, 146
Baghdad   30–1, 32, 45, 61
Bakunin, Mikhail   198

Balfour, Arthur   194
Balkh   30, 39, 41, 42, 226
Banks, Joseph   157–8
Bannock tribe   216
Barbaro, Daniele   92
Barlowe, Arthur   77
Barlowe, Thomas   97–8
Barnes, Robin   141
Baruch, Book of   16, 192
Bayt al-Hikma (House of Wisdom)   30
Beaufort, Mary, Duchess of   146
Becanus, Johannes Goropius   116
bees   111
Bekker, Balthasar   138–9
Bermuda   144–5
Bernays, Edward   213–14
Besant, Walter   96
Beza, Theodore   88–9
Béziers   59, 200
Bibles, Revelation missing from   20
bin Ladin, Osama   30, 206, 221, 223
Birth of a Nation (film)   195, 213
Blackfeet tribe   218
Bloom, Sol   212
Bobadilla   72
Boccaccio, Giovanni   85
bonfire of the vanities   65–6
Boniface, Pope   84
Book of Life   19
Book of Prophecies (Columbus)   74–5
Boston   123, 144, 219
Boston Post   219
botanical gardens   92–3, 95, 99, 135
Botton, Alain de   123
Bougainville, Louis de   158
Boulainvilliers, Henri de   160
Boyle, Robert   128–9, 132, 138